Juliana Vasiljevic was herself a victim of domestic abuse that spanned a period of three decades, a subsequent survivor and now a warrior in the war against violence and abuse in all its forms. She is a retired Jungian based, Soul Centred Psychotherapist, whose wholistic practices were based on the premise that "The body remembers." As a consequence of her own personal journey with abuse and her training and experience as a psychotherapist, she gained a deep insight into the anatomy of human behaviour and how one's upbringing combined with personal internal and external experiences in life impact on the development of the human psyche.

This book is dedicated in memory of my mother Sylvia, a woman who is the embodiment of resilience and strength.

Juliana Vasiljevic

KINGDOM OF WOLVES

AUSTIN MACAULEY PUBLISHERS™

LONDON * CAMBRIDGE * NEW YORK * SHARJAH

A CIP catalogue record for this title is available from the British Library.

ISBN 9781398478909 (Paperback)
ISBN 9781398478923 (ePub e-book)
ISBN 9781398478916 (Audiobook)

www.austinmacauley.com

First Published 2022
Austin Macauley Publishers Ltd®
1 Canada Square
Canary Wharf
London
E14 5AA

To my children Sara and Eddie, you are my inspiration.

To my soul-sister Sonia, you have my eternal gratitude and love for your unwavering belief in me, and for all the nights you dedicated to support seeing my book come to fruition.

To my sister Mariana, brother-in-law Rosco and my sisters in arms Marie, Karen, and Anna, I thank you deeply for your ever-present optimism and encouragement.

A special and most profound thank you to Dr Kaalii Cargill and Andrew Cargill, who without their valuable, life altering training this book could not have come into existence.

To Mary Coughlan, you will always hold a special place in my heart, thank you for taking me under your wing and sharing your unconditional love and acceptance, you brought me back to myself.

Table of Contents

Juliana Vasiljevic

A guide and a handbook that provides a unique insight into the emotional, psychological, and behavioural profiles of predators, abusers, bullies, their victims, and the forces that draw them to each other.

All acts of abuse emotional, psychological, and physical in all its forms are a crime and a violation and the responsibility rests solely with the perpetrator.

Message from Author

Kingdom of Wolves came into being after a long battle with self-doubt, fear of failure and fear of exposure and is a culmination of my own personal journey with domestic abuse which spanned a period of three decades. Looking back, I came to the conclusion that there were three critical realisations that had taken place, each acting as a catalyst to propel me on my journey towards freedom, reclamation, and wholeness. The first realisation was pivotal, setting everything into motion, I realised that I needed to accept that we (myself and my children) were never going to be rescued and that I had to find the courage to fight for our liberation. I had to become my own hero, there was never going to be "divine intervention," wishing, hoping, and praying for something to happen to change our circumstances was futile and idealistic. "It" came down to two choices: stay, suffer, and hope for the best, or fight to be free to live the life that myself and my children deserve.

The second realisation was that as much as I needed to understand our abuser and the motivations that drove his actions, I also had to understand and take responsibility for my own actions and decisions, and part of that entailed taking a journey inward. It was through extensive research into the behavioural psychology of both victims and abusers that I gained integral, life-altering knowledge about myself, my abuser, and our maladaptive relationship. It soon became apparent to me that the more I learned the more empowered I became, shifting the seat of psychological and emotional power from my abuser back to me. By exploring both of our psychological histories and their influences on our present-day decisions and behaviours, I was able gain a clearer perspective of the nature of our individual and relationship dysfunction. This in turn gave me the vital emotional space I needed to think more clearly, act more rationally and become detached enough from the drama to formulate a plan of action and safe exit strategy.

The third and most important realisation was that in order to truly be free from "The Wolf" (my ex-husband and abuser) I had to become "The Wolf." I learned as much as possible about how his mind functioned, what drove him psychologically, emotionally, and biologically, what were his motivations (needs and desires) and what were his goals (gratifications). Through embodying "the wolf," I could view life through his eyes and comprehend his world, his illusions, delusions, capacities, and limitations, but more importantly, I acquired valuable knowledge as to what he believed he wanted, needed, or gained from our marital relationship and from me personally. By inhabiting his world (psyche), I gained a powerful insight into how he functioned, giving myself precious tactical information that helped to formulate my ultimate and most successful strategy, then I went to war.

This book is based on the training and experience I received as a Soul Centred Psychotherapist, my personal experience as a victim, and my vehement belief that knowledge is the most powerful weapon in the war against violence and abuse. My goal is to dispel any myths and misconceptions that surround victims and abusers, empower past and present victims of abuse, and prevent potential victims from becoming future victims. I hope to achieve this by providing a comprehensive outline of the psychological and emotional profiles of both the victim and the abuser and the powerful underlying currents that draw them to each other. I believe that it is essential to understand both the world that the predator/abuser/bully inhabits and the world that the victim inhabits if we are to get a complete picture of the issues surrounding abusive and violent behaviour. The collective intention of *Kingdom of Wolves* is to help reduce the incidence of abuse and prevent offenders from flourishing in our current societal conditions.

Introduction

I truly believe that knowledge is power and I hope through this book to provide a clear and comprehensive profile of the behavioural patterns of the predator/abuser/bully and that of the victim. One of my most important objectives is to empower potential victims with the knowledge to recognise abusers and abusive behaviour, and for existing victims to make more informed decisions concerning the abusive situation or relationship they have found themselves in. For a victim to exit an abusive relationship/situation, it is vital that they be able to evaluate the level of danger the perpetrator of the abuse is capable of committing before making plans for themselves and their loved one/s to exit in the safest way possible. By arming victims and potential victims with an understanding of the fundamental elements that drive the thoughts, emotions and behaviours of both victims and abusers alike, it is possible to prevent or decrease the incidence of abuse.

Understanding the psyche of the abuser is as equally important as understanding the psyche of the victim, it is essential to know how both their worlds operate in order to protect society and reduce crimes of this nature. By delving into the mind of the predator/abuser/bully, we can gain an understanding of the motivations behind their behaviour i.e., what drives them, how they select their victims, the type of background they come from, their psychological framework, their emotional body, who they target and why, and most importantly what draws the perpetrator to a particular victim. By delving into the mind of the victim, we can gain a better understanding of their vulnerabilities and the motivations that drive their behaviours by exploring the victim's psychological framework, emotional body, the type of background they come from, why they were targeted and what puts them in the sights of a predator.

Before we begin our foray into the world of the predator, abuser, bully, and victim, I feel it is essential that we acknowledge that all human beings possess a personal history that is exclusive to each individual. We are all made uniquely different by our anatomical and physiological make-up, socio-economic circumstances, level of education, cognitive development, sociological influences (environmental, cultural, and religious) and our psychological and emotional level of development. To fully comprehend or understand how we came to be who we are today it is necessary to go back through our personal history and analyse the significant experiences and direct influences that shaped our character, personality, belief system and how we interact with others and the world at large, to create a blueprint of our earlier and present-day life. This blueprint may be referred to as "Our Map," a chart that reflects our individuality and gives us a clearer understanding of what drives our emotions, decisions, and actions.

Please note: For the purposes of this book, I often refer to the predator/abuser/bully using the one single general term "abuser." However, at times, I found it was necessary to use each distinctive term.

The Body Remembers

Understanding the Human Condition

"Our mind is not separate from our physical being"
Every second of our life is recorded and stored in the memory bank of our mind and our body.

From conception onwards, our memories are made up of a series of experiences that we undergo as we live and grow. These memories are stored waiting for us to draw on when needed, however, often, our memories can also come forward unexpectedly when not consciously called for but rather triggered by a subsequent experience. With every experience that we undergo, physical, psychological, and emotional, combined with the way in which we respond to that experience, is unconsciously being recorded by our mind and our body in a uniquely particular way. In other words, every happening in our life whether it is seemingly insignificant or largely significant will encode itself into our memories not only through the usual assumed channel "our mind," but also simultaneously and just as meaningfully through our physical form "our body" (including our organs and our senses). Our experiences and the way in which we responded to those experiences form a series of memories that can influence how we respond to future similar experiences and more importantly how we interact with others and the world at large. Please note, that memories and how they are encoded into our system are distinct to every individual.

Our Map

Every human being is on an individual and unique journey starting from conception and ending at death. On this journey, every one of us is consciously and unconsciously creating a physical, psychological, and emotional map of this journey which is specific to each individual alone. This map is created by many influencing factors, our genetic make-up, our ancestral background, the type of parenting we received from birth to adulthood (how we were parented and by whom), our environment (what were our social, economic, and physical living conditions) and most importantly, our individual physical, emotional and psychological experiences throughout life. The impact of our internal experience of our upbringing, combined with our environmental and personal experiences and how we interpret, respond to, and metabolise them are the main factors which determine and form our unique and individual character structure, the ego-ideal we hold of our-selves and our personal belief system. This belief system consists of three parts, our beliefs about our-selves, our beliefs about others and our beliefs about how the world operates. Our character structure, defence system, beliefs, life experiences and our psychological, emotional, and physiological make-up are all contributing factors which influence every emotional response, cognitive decision, and every action that we take. From the moment we are conceived through to adulthood and beyond, our every experience will continue to shape us. All these factors together create a unique footprint that forms our individual blueprint (map) of our past, and influences if not determines our future.

Predators/Abusers/Bullies

"We are all fragmented and divided, and knowing or not we are all searching for our souls"
Carl Gustav Jung

Profiling the Abuser

All perpetrators of abuse share a distinctive set of characteristics which are the main contributing factors that govern their actions and set them apart from others in society while at the same time ironically helping them to blend in. Abusers are possessed with a driving force to satisfy their self-serving and egotistical needs and will use any means at their disposal to achieve their goals both personally and professionally. Attaining their goals and fulfilling their needs will always be at the expense of a victim, and may include using varying degrees of emotional, psychological, and physical abuse perpetrated without shame, guilt, or remorse.

Every abuser is unique, in that they all have a different combination of psychological and emotional pathologies, capacities, coping mechanisms, intelligence levels and life experiences. These are the significant factors that determine the behavioural pattern of the abuser, the seriousness and type of crime they commit and their capacity for rehabilitation. These variables need to be taken into consideration when assessing, understanding, and dealing with perpetrators. Every abuser has a back story that is unique to them that separates them from other each other however, their fundamental needs, desires, character traits and how they operate is undeniably similar.

Their level of "success" and by "success," I mean how long they can operate for, going undetected and unpunished, is dependent on each individual's level of intellectual, social, emotional, and psychological intelligence. The "clever predator" has honed their skills over a time learning to use charming yet manipulative proficiency to attain his or her personal and professional goals and achievements. They are able to exercise restraint when necessary and know how to gain acceptance and trust from an intended victim, with the aim of exploiting their vulnerabilities.

They can for the most part go about their lives in a normal and unassuming fashion to create a persona that would allow them to assimilate into society without drawing unwanted attention to themselves, their hidden agendas, and their dark natures. They have learned very early on that in order to maintain their carefully constructed façades, there are times when they will have to restrain their baser violent and abusive urges to avoid exposure.

The abusers who lack restraint are usually at the mercy of their volatile emotions and most likely lack the aptitude needed to cover their tracks and avoid detection. They are prone to act in an outwardly abusive manner without regard to exposure, therefore making themselves easily identifiable. These abusers have a limited emotional range and an inadequate capacity to manage unpredictable and/or overwhelming feelings, who consequently are predisposed to resorting to frustration, anger, or rage as a first or perhaps only response. This often results in spontaneous and unrestrained acts of violence and abuse against a victim without immediate concern for the possible repercussions. These perpetrators are more likely to act out publicly and are not concerned with exposing themselves to witnesses, nor are they expecting any interference from witnesses. In cases of domestic abuse that often occurs in the privacy of the abuser's home, they assume that they are untouchable and usually act without moderation or control. For some, their abusive behaviour may be fuelled by a substance addiction such as alcohol and/or licit or illicit drugs, which enhances the inability to control their baser emotions and often increases the level of violence.

Understanding the Level of the Abusers Pathology

When assessing the pathology of the abuser, it would be helpful to take into consideration which two of the following "four categories" they fit into. Firstly, whether they are in the category of the "conscious" or "unconscious" abuser and secondly whether they are in the category of the "high-functioning" or "low-functioning" abuser.

The "Conscious or Unconscious" Abuser

The unconscious abuser is someone who is "not" consciously aware of his/her motives for their actions. To clarify, this is not to suggest that the "unconscious abuser" is not aware of their actions and the consequences of their actions but that they are not aware of the underlying propellants (impulses) for their actions. The unconscious abuser is generally at the mercy of his or her emotional, physiological, and psychological states of being, often acting impulsively and without premeditation. They seek immediate self-gratification intent of fulfilling their self-serving and narcissistic needs, without remorse, guilt, or shame. In other words, they do not as a rule analyse or think about their actions before making them, they act from a more primal (infantile) level of need which indicates they possess an emotional and psychological immaturity. The unconscious predator has a tendency for random acts of violence and abuse and does not follow any particular pattern. They quite often do not possess the capacity or the desire to reflect upon their actions prior to or after they are undertaken.

The conscious abuser is someone who is consciously aware of his/her motives for their actions, who also operates from emotional, psychological and physiological states of being. However, it is with some level of maturity or mastery over their volatile emotions and therefore performed with varied levels of premeditation, who are consciously seeking to gratify their self-serving needs and desires. They possess the capacity to analyse and think about their actions before making them, in other words they take calculated steps to attain an objective. They possess the ability to reflect upon their behaviours prior to and after they are undertaken, using rationalisations to justify their egotistic motivations, and who also act without remorse, guilt or shame. They have the capacity to premeditate and plan activities to ensure that their emotional, psychological, and physical needs are met, however this does not in any way exclude the conscious abuser from the capacity to act impulsively.

Please note: A "conscious abuser" was most certainly an "unconscious abuser" during the early period of their life prior to evolving into a more calculating and scheming cognizant abuser.

When we establish which one of the above categories the abuser fits into, whether they are a "conscious or unconscious abuser", we must now determine their capabilities and their limitations with the following two categories.

Is the Abuser in the "High Functioning or Low Functioning" Category

A high-functioning abuser is someone who may possess most, if not all the following characteristics, enabling them to appear non-threatening, allowing them to integrate into their environment without attracting significant negative attention.

- They may hold a level of academic intelligence ranging from above average to highly intelligent, providing them with the means to be employed in a position of influence, power, or authority. They can be self-employed or employed in any general field requiring a middle to high level of education.
- They can range from average to being highly successful personally, professionally and/or financially and may hold a low or high profile in society.
- They can maintain an unassuming or harmless façade, blending into their environment being careful not to draw unwanted attention to themselves.
- They may have a substance abuse issue or addiction (including gambling or sexual), however are reasonably adept at hiding it.
- They will possess enough social and emotional intelligence to be able to charm, disarm and manipulate potential victims.
- They feel superior, omnipotent and think they are smarter than everyone.
- They can integrate well into society using their academic and social intelligence with the purpose of shielding their baser instincts and ill-intent towards others as they know that it is essential to maintain a socially conventional demeanour to be accepted by others.
- They have a need to be accepted by their peers, other family members and society in general (stemming from deep-seeded insecurities and

narcissistic traits) so they are clever enough to hide their intent and behaviour to maintain a façade of respectability.

- They are prone to suffer from substance abuse, addiction, anxiety, depression, psychosis and eating, personality and behavioural disorders.

A low-functioning abuser is someone who may possess some or all the following characteristics hindering their ability to integrate successfully into society and making it difficult to hide their ill-intent and true nature:

- They will have a low to average academic intelligence level, which means he/she will be unemployed or employed in a low to mid-range type of employment.
- They have limited, little or no emotional and/or social intelligence, making it difficult for them to maintain friendships, integrate socially with others and hinders their ability to hide their negative intentions.
- They will not be overly concerned with hiding their behaviour, as he/she feels omnipotent and/or superior to others, believing themselves to be more intelligent, cunning, or crafty.
- They are not preoccupied with maintaining façades or being accepted by others.
- They are not capable of hiding their true character behind a façade of respectability.
- They are unable to modulate or control their baser emotions particularly their frustration, anger, rage, jealousy, or envy, and are prone to suffer from substance abuse, addiction anxiety, depression, psychosis, or a personality, eating or behavioural disorders.

Character Structure

Character Structure is one of the most important defining factors that underpins all human behaviour and is one of the keys that provides us with insight into the motivations that inform the actions of all human beings. According to Wilhelm Reich, who is considered the Western originator of the science of "Body Mind Psychotherapy," he believes that every human being has a combination of character types, each with subtypes, as no person is one character type. We are a blend of all of them at some level, but typically one or two of them pre-dominate and reveal our primary bodily, emotional, and psychological personality defences towards life. Through his analysis and exploration, he proposed that there exists, five key types of individual personality groups that develop from our early patterns of relating to, and attaching to others. He postulates that problematic, interrupted, or traumatic experiences can be "wired" into the brain and the body, becoming repeated patterns of behaviour in adulthood. It is therefore necessary to understand the traits of character types in order to gain an insight into the driving forces of both abusers and victims.

Our overall character structure is the sum of many parts and is unique to each of us individually, it can be described as a series of traits developed over time that define our character, determine our behaviour, influence our actions, and reflect our qualities or lack thereof. They are made visible through our personalities and revealed in how we interact with others and the world at large. Our character is formed throughout our lives evolving from conception onwards and is influenced by our experience in the womb, our birth, the way in which we were parented, our life experiences, the conditions of our environment and how we responded both internally and externally to that environment. It is the driving force behind all the decisions we make and sets the stage for the life we live and how we live it.

The quality of our life is determined by these character traits, they can be limiting or liberating depending on whether they are tempered by balance. There can be positive and negative aspects to all the character traits we possess. For example, a particular defining character trait might be that an individual is "self-sacrificing." In other words, they always without fail place other people's needs before their own. There are times when putting others needs before our own is necessary, as a healthy level of helping others is psychologically and emotionally rewarding for both. However, always placing others needs above our own is detrimental to our wellbeing and can be psychologically, emotionally, and possibly physically overwhelming, exhausting and ultimately harmful to one's wellbeing.

When you are self-sacrificing, you are often also a "people pleaser" and "overly compliant" as your need to please others to gain approval and feel valued is achieved vicariously at best, however it comes at the expense of your own real needs being met in a healthy fashion. Being "self-sacrificing" would have formed from an earlier dysfunctional life experience and is a negative psychological method in which to receive much needed positive emotional and psychological fulfilment.

Character Structure and the Abuser

Thankfully, most society consists of human beings who possess character structures that are significantly adaptive, these individuals have developed healthy levels of empathy towards other human beings allowing them to integrate with others in society and providing them with a capacity to temper their baser instincts. They also have reasonable enough social, emotional, and cognitive intelligence, respect for others and their possessions and the capacity to care for and/or love others. A perpetrator of violence and abuse has a character structure formed in much the same way as everyone else. However, for them, there were prevailing negative psychological, emotional, physical, and environmental experiences and conditions which were extremely adverse and sometimes irreparably damaging, creating maladaptive beliefs, behaviours, and personality disorders. This dysfunction would have likely formed during the abuser's early childhood and/or adolescent developmental years as a result of:

- Insufficient psychological, emotional, and physical care from their biological parents or guardians (in other words poor or non-existent parenting).
- Bearing witness to and/or being the victim of a parent/caretaker with substance abuse or addiction related issues and has suffered neglect and abuse as a result.
- Grew up witnessing, and/or had been a victim of emotional, psychological, verbal, sexual or physical abuse themselves (or any combination of the aforementioned).
- Under parenting – Lived in a neglectful environment (squalid living conditions) and/or with neglectful and uncaring parents/caregivers.
- Over parenting – controlling, manipulative and coercive parenting from self-serving, narcissistic parents/caregivers.

Some abusers who exhibit pathological behaviours (excluding those with an obvious clinically diagnosed mental illness) possess a character structure which may have developed over time, although not necessarily because of early childhood and/or teenage neglect and abuse. They exhibit anti-social and abusive behaviours that have emerged later in life as a possible result of either adverse physical, emotional, and psychological experiences and conditions (including economic hardship) or as a direct result of the influence of substance abuse and/or addiction.

A Perpetrator of Violence and Abuse Can Come from a Seemingly "Normal" Background

Any combination of negative influencing factors will impact the forming of the abuser's character structure however, they do not necessarily have to have come from the extreme conditions mentioned earlier. On the contrary, abusers may have come from a relatively healthy and nurturing environment, with ostensibly caring parents or guardians and with the absence of obvious, notable physical, emotional or psychological abuse. Yet, despite their relatively "normal" upbringing, they have become predators, abusers, and bullies, making them more difficult to recognise and harder for society to understand and accept, particularly those who commit heinous crimes. These abusive behaviours may have emerged as a direct result of alcohol and/or substance abuse, or the abuser may have been possessed of a latent "psychosis" which was sitting dormant and activated later in their life. It may also be a result of the impact of a single or a combination of personal negative life experiences that affected their emotional, physical, and psychological wellbeing in a fundamentally detrimental manner.

Most parents no matter their religious denomination, race, culture, social status, or educational level will tell you that they want their children to have the best life possible, usually easier, or better than their own. Unfortunately, for some parents despite their best intentions for their children, have inadvertently laid the foundations for their child to become a future predator, abuser and/or bully. A parent/caregiver can only provide parenting based on their own level of social, emotional, psychological, and cognitive level of knowledge and understanding. This is combined with strongly held beliefs and influenced by their own past experiences and upbringing.

Some parents are harsh disciplinarians who have uncompromising expectations of their children, a reflection of their own harsh and disciplined background. Other parents project unfulfilled desires onto that of their child expecting them to either follow in their footsteps or exceed "their" achievements. Some parents have unrealistic expectations of their children, thinking that by setting high and more than likely unattainable goals and/or standards that they will motivate their children to strive to achieve it.

This type of parenting will always have a harmful and extremely negative impact, impeding the healthy development of a child's psychological and emotional wellbeing. These children may have grown up in seemingly healthy environments where they were physically safe, well cared and provided for, however they unfortunately have also simultaneously undergone possible irrevocable emotional and psychological injury. There are many parents/caregivers who abuse their power by engaging in manipulative controlling and coercive behaviours to achieve their own selfish and narcissistic ends. Remember, many crimes are committed under the guise of "love" whether intentional or unintentional, and are performed by individuals both male and female with immature, underdeveloped and maladaptive psychological and emotional functioning.

The Effects of Negative and Adverse Parenting

There are many ways in which negative and adverse parenting is perpetrated, some parents exploit their children's vulnerabilities (varying in style and intensity) over time as the child grows from infancy to young adulthood. They may engage in a range of physical, emotional, and psychological manipulative, controlling and coercive behaviours to display either their approval or disapproval to their child. They may include any or all the following behavioural tactics:

- Showing approval through undue "positive reinforcement" in the form of praise, gratuities (gifts or monetary rewards), excessive adulation, public recognition (telling friends, family and/or others of their child's achievements) and/or engaging in "absorbed attention." Then contradicting the "positive reinforcement" whereby the parent shows extreme disapproval through "negative reinforcement" in the form of the silent treatment, nagging, sulking, crying, playing the victim and emotional blackmail i.e., withdrawal of affection and/or attention, or guilting the child.

- They may engage in "intermittent or partial reinforcement" which causes constant anxiety and confusion in the child. It can work in two ways, if used as "negative reinforcement" then the purpose is to create a climate of fear and doubt in the child, if used as "positive reinforcement" then the purpose is to encourage the child to persist.

- They may use isolation as a "control tactic" such as, keeping the child/children isolated from other children in society under the pre-text of "home schooling," or through intentional geographical isolation, or simply by preventing them from socialising after school hours (weekdays and weekends).

  Please note: Home schooling is not as rule a pretext for isolating children on purpose, for some families it is in fact essential, particularly for those in rural and remote farming and agricultural communities, due to illness and in rare situations when it became mandatory i.e., world-wide pandemic.

- Mind-games in the form of lying, disinformation (deception or distortion of the facts), confusing, trivialising, brainwashing and denial of the child's reality (gaslighting) are used by parents to manipulate and intimidate their children into compliance. This undermines the confidence and self-esteem of the child, inhibiting healthy adaptive emotional and psychological development. This type of parenting is a deliberate act that destabilises and confuses the child so that the parent/caregiver can gain or maintain control.

These types of parenting methods are clearly abusive and are likely to be irreparably damaging to the developing "psyche" of the child/teenager/young adult. Unnecessary and undue pressure is placed on the child creating a climate of insecurity, fear, constant anxiety, and stress, whilst at the same time fostering an unhealthy co-dependence with the parent that ensures they maintain their power and control over the child, now and in the future. The consistent giving and withdrawing of affection and attention is confusing and destabilising to an evolving psyche and will inevitably cause negative "attachment disorders."

Attachment disorders are a psychiatric illness that can develop in young children resulting in problems that hinder healthy emotional attachment to others. The symptoms are that they have difficulty forming emotional bonds to others, suffer anxiety, mood swings and depression, are likely to respond with intense agitation, anger, or rage in changes to routine or if they have perceived loss of personal control, they are likely to engage in high-risk behaviours and may be prone to substance abuse and/or addiction.

Every child will innately seek to gain the love, approval, and acceptance from those they look up to and love expecting these fundamental emotions to be mirrored back to them regardless of their achievements or failures. If love and acceptance are only reciprocated when the child has met the parents' conditions or expectations and when that child fails to do so, then it is the child who will inevitably develop a negative sense of self. Perpetual feelings of failure will be experienced by a child who is not equipped emotionally, psychologically and/or physically to accomplish the goals set out by the unrealistic and demanding parent. This will inevitably engender deep-seated feelings of shame, guilt, inadequacy, unworthiness, low self-esteem, failure as well as provoke emotions such as anger and rage. This type of on-going torment and/or despair will ultimately lead to depression, substance abuse, addiction, eating, anxiety and behavioural disorders, psychosis or in the worst-case scenario suicide.

There are many of us who suffer from some level of negative self-image or low self-esteem, this does not consequently equate to a person becoming a perpetrator of abuse. Having negative emotions that are directed inward towards ourselves are personally damaging and limiting in varying degrees in our own lives. For the abuser, the opposite is true; these negative emotions were detrimental to the degree that they resulted in the development of a psychosis or a negative behavioural pattern that dominates their psyche, which is not only inwardly malignant, but is also outwardly destructive and is expressed by harming others.

Now we understand that a significant number of the psychological issues experienced in adulthood have likely stemmed from inadequate or inappropriate parenting and care in one's early developmental years. However, there is another particularly distinct and insidious but subtle type of dysfunction that can arise from one's early childhood/adolescent growing years that must be acknowledged.

This dysfunction is considered notable in that it causes the psyche to develop an over-inflated ego-identity, a sense of entitlement, unrealistic expectations of oneself and others, an inability to accept or cope with disappointment or failure and engenders feelings of omnipotence. It is the result of parents or caretakers who have placed all their hopes and dreams onto one or more of their offspring creating an amplification of varied levels of narcissistic development in the chosen child. If focused attention is centred on a particular member of a parents/caregiver's offspring, then that child may commonly be referred to as the "Golden Child" who may be female or male in gender. Golden child syndrome can develop not because a child is ignored or maltreated, but because the child is loved with an unhealthy over-intensity, they are praised for capacities or attributes that they do not possess and are made to feel as if they are special and/or destined for personal or professional greatness.

This type of parenting will inevitably be setting the child up for future psychological and emotional suffering when they fail to hold up to overly ambitious and exacting aspirations and goals. The child may develop substance abuse issues, addiction, risk taking behaviours, delusions of grandeur depression, anxiety, paranoia, rage, excessive shame and/or guilt, stemming from their attempts to avoid feelings of failure. Failing to meet one's own personal or parental unrealistic and perhaps lofty expectations can have severe detrimental repercussions on the normal development of a child's or adolescent's emotional and psychological wellbeing. We know that experiencing healthy levels of shame and guilt is necessary to regulate behaviour however, for those who experience high and consistent levels of these disempowering emotions will without doubt develop some type of negative behavioural pattern, disorder, or psychosis, resulting in antisocial and/or criminal behaviour and the development of superiority and/or grandiosity complexes.

The need to avoid experiencing emotions such as remorse, shame and/or guilt by the "psyche" is instinctual in human beings. However, for some, who experience debilitating levels of these unwanted emotions can lead to the onset of maladaptive behaviours that encourage a complete evasion of these feelings. Negative avoidant psychological and emotional responses can come into being as a result, starting at one end of the spectrum as a mild but detrimental response or advancing to the other end of the spectrum becoming an extremely adverse maladaptive response.

For example:

a) At the mild end – "telling lies" – at the maladaptive end – evolving into "sociopathic lying."

b) At the mild end – "blaming others" – at the maladaptive end – evolving into "a complete avoidance of taking responsibility for their actions."

c) At the mild end – "avoiding feeling vulnerable" – at the maladaptive end – evolving into "a need to control, dominate and/or subjugate others."

There are several distinct combined character traits that can be attributed to the character structure of most predators, abusers and bullies which can help to identify them, separating them from others in our society. These character traits accompanied by their schemas (strongly held beliefs) and their core behavioural defences and how they come about, need to be explored and understood so that we can get a clearer picture of the origins of abuser. We must also understand, what drives their behaviour and what their cognitive, psychological, and emotional distortions, capacities and limitations are. With my research, I have concluded that the "psychopathic character structure" also referred to as the "charming and manipulative character structure" is the most commonly shared structure among predators, abusers and bullies. I believe there are several critical components to this structure that greatly influence the abuser's thoughts, actions, emotions, and beliefs.

Please note; you will find that I will often refer to the "psychopathic character structure" as the "narcissistic character structure" as I believe that narcissistic wounding is at the core of this structure, influencing every emotion, thought and action and underpinning the belief system of whomever is afflicted with this structure.

The Psychopathic Structure is based on the feeling of being "special" and is referred to as an "aggressive or controlling" pattern of behaviour. It likely started to develop around the age of three, usually by self-serving, narcissistic parents/caregivers, sometimes by other family members or later by teachers. All of whom have to some degree denied or manipulated the child's curiosity, their play, and their natural impulses.

This child may have experienced shaming or belittling when they needed help, were required to achieve unattainable and unreasonable goals and/or expected to hold to unrelentingly high standards, while having their true feelings, needs and wants ignored or unacknowledged. When the child failed to meet the parent's needs, they were made to feel a deep sense of shame and inadequacy which triggered the development of avoidant defensive measures to counteract these debilitating emotions and the accompanying wound of betrayal. This may have led to the unconscious belief that they are alone and that the world is a hostile place in which only the strongest, fittest, and most cunning survive.

Having had their vulnerabilities exploited from a young age, they have learned to protect themselves and take back their personal power by becoming master manipulators. As adults, they may appear to be intelligent, charming, affable, gregarious, or pleasant, however this will be masking their true underlying character that is ruthless, demanding, dominating, and controlling. They lack real empathy for others and are unable to form authentic connections or lasting social, workplace or intimate relationships as they will ultimately betray or use them in their quest to have their own needs fulfilled.

Psychopathic/Narcissistic Character Structure

Narcissism is described essentially as the erotic gratification derived from the admiration of one's own physical and mental attributes, it is a normal condition at the infantile level of our personality development, however, needs to be outgrown as we develop humility and empathy. Let us consider narcissism on a spectrum, if we look at the healthy end of the spectrum, narcissism might be thought of as someone seeing themselves as being a bit special or talented, giving them a necessary sense of confidence to accept challenges, reach goals and become high achievers. At the unhealthy and problematic end of the narcissistic spectrum is someone who exhibits arrogance, grandiosity, entitlement, superiority, disdain, omnipotence, is unempathetic and does not feel remorse, guilt, or shame.

The narcissist has a personality disorder which is very different from someone who is just vain or self-absorbed. Someone who is simply vain or self-absorbed may appear to be narcissistic; however, they are still capable of sustaining healthy relationships and are able to co-exist with others harmoniously. Whereas a true narcissist will have difficulty sustaining a healthy relationship and will come into conflict with others as their narcissistic drives are extreme.

Predators/abusers/bullies all display narcissistic traits in varying degrees, these narcissistic traits tend to dominate their psyche, informing their decision-making processes. Narcissists believe they are smarter, more important and a cut above their peers and all those they associate with. Every action they take is centred primarily on getting their own needs met first and foremost, everyone else is secondary. Their desires take priority above all others in life, even those whom they claim to love, however the inability to express empathy, remorse, guilt, or shame makes sustaining healthy relationships difficult if not impossible.

The narcissist has a sense of superiority and entitlement believing that they are special and that the rules that govern others do not apply to them, giving them an air of arrogance and condescension.

Appearances mean everything to the narcissist, they need to feel that they are respected, adored, loved, exalted, important, special, or accomplished and they cannot cope with falling from grace in the eyes of others whom they like or respect. If they feel that their image is being tarnished or perceive an offence of any kind, they are likely to respond with disproportionate retaliation often resorting to spite, vindictiveness, malice, anger, or rage as their fall-back response. Narcissists never take responsibility for their own erroneous actions as they believe that they are never wrong and so are quick to blame others, they also tend to hold a grudge and may seek revenge.

Remember the narcissist is grandiose, in other words, they have an unrealistic sense of superiority and view themselves as better than other people, they have an inflated self-image, can appear excessively self-important, are often opinionated and cocky, and may hold others in contempt. They see themselves as a good person regardless of their abusive behaviour as their ego does not allow them to think otherwise. They may appear to be affable, helpful, caring, thoughtful and generous, however do not fooled their good behaviour is motivated by the need to either further a hidden personal agenda or to create or enhance a fake and perhaps benevolent persona.

Please note: Having elements of this "structure" does not make a person a "psychopath." A psychopath is someone who displays signs of possessing an "antisocial personality disorder" and who engages in violent, abusive, and criminal behaviour without remorse for their actions or empathy towards others.

Psychopathic/Narcissistic Abusers Will Shame and Blame

We have already established that narcissists are unable to cope with feelings of failure, remorse, embarrassment, shame, or guilt, and so, if for any reason those emotions are triggered then the abuser will engage in any number of offensive and defensive behaviours to avoid them. According to Christine Hammond, MS, LMHC, (author of the "The Exhausted Woman"), "There is nothing worse for the narcissist than having someone point out even the slightest fault, however ironically, they have no problem openly doing it to others." "This method of casting shame allows them to feel superior while minimising any impact the other person might have on them; it serves as a way of discounting any future comments the victim could use to embarrass them."

The psychopathic, narcissistic abuser will always find a way to rationalise and justify their shortcomings, failures, and abusive behaviours. This is accomplished by diminishing their involvement, distancing themselves from their actions and/or deflecting taking responsibility by blaming others or extenuating circumstances. They are expert manipulators, often controlling their victims with a range of tactics, including building a connection with positive reinforcement such as praise, flattery, ingratiation, love bombing, gifts, and attention. Before the victim realises that this is all part of the superficial charm of the narcissist, they may have entered some type of committed relationship, putting themselves exactly where the narcissist wants them and it is then that they begin to show signs of their abusive, controlling, and bullying behaviours.

The narcissist is now likely to engage in contradictory and confusing abusive manoeuvres that keeps the victim in a state of angst, self-doubt and feeling insecure about the relationship. For example, where the narcissist was once attentive to their partner, they now become inattentive, positive reinforcement turns to negative reinforcement or intermittent and partial reinforcement. The abuser now feels confident to practice any number of abusive tactics that are common among all abusers who exercise control over their victim, using a range of coercive behaviours in the form of physical, emotional, and psychological abuse such as nagging, silent treatment, emotional blackmail, shaming, blaming, verbal threats and derogatory remarks, physical and psychological intimidation or violence and sexual abuse.

The psychopathic/narcissistic abuser needs to have people in their life in order to have others to cast blame onto when needed, this can occur in any or all areas of their life, whether it is their social, workplace, family and/or intimate partner relationships. They will avoid at all costs the discomfort that comes with emotions such as guilt, shame and/or remorse by projecting these unresolved feelings onto those closest to them. By blaming others for any real or perceived mistakes or failures they themselves have made, the abuser absolves themselves of culpability. They use shaming tactics not only as a method of avoidance of personal accountability, but also as a method of sustaining feeling superior, grandiose, smarter than and/or dominant over others.

The "shame and blame" tactics may include behaviours such as, belittling, ignoring, criticising, demeaning, discrediting, slandering, vilifying, and humiliating their intimate partners, their children, other family members, social or workplace peers, business associates and their competition.

Psychopathic/Narcissistic Abusers and Their Friendships

For the psychopathic/narcissistic abuser, friendships are usually one-sided, emotionally, and psychologically they are programmed to take from others and so they never really give in their friendships. Friendships are used as a yardstick for comparative and competitive reasons; they need to measure their success and worthiness against their peers. If they believe these peers may be doing better than they are whether it is personal or professional, it will invariably trigger their competitive side. Remember the narcissist truly believes they are smarter, stronger, faster, better looking, wittier etc., than those that surround them and they like to think of themselves as uniquely superior to their peers in every way.

They are very clever at hiding their true feelings behind carefully crafted façades which varies with each individual's degree of competence, and may consist of traits such as, being charming, affable, shy, and unassuming or confident, gregarious, witty and humorous. They may come across as a person who it would be enjoyable to be around in a social capacity particularly those narcissists who have honed their charming/manipulative skills. In fact, those that are more practiced do tend to draw people to themselves; however, they can only really connect on a superficial level and are incapable entering into a mutually rewarding relationship that requires give and take on both sides.

There are distinct psychological and emotional limitations and behaviours present when one is in a relationship with a psychopath/narcissist: Firstly, they are unlikely to be available emotionally in a deep or meaningful way for a friend at a time when the friend really needs them. For example, a friend who is going through a tough emotional time perhaps they have lost a loved one, the narcissist will show up in a perfunctory manner as required, showing the modicum of respect and sincerity and that will be the limit of their emotional capacity. The narcissist's inability to experience true empathy towards another is not present, however they are usually smart enough to know that to maintain a friendship they will need to pretend they care.

Secondly, the psychopathic/narcissist is likely to be unreliable, remember the narcissist's first priority is themselves and all others are secondary including their intimate partner and/or children. If they find a request from a friend is too difficult, taxing or they are simply not in the mood to help, they will most assuredly not. When "the chips are down" so to speak, you can never rely on the psychopathic friend to be a genuine support, however conversely if they need you, they will expect you to be there for them pronto. Narcissists expect absolute loyalty and immediate rapt attention when needed from those closest to them. After all, in the eyes of the narcissist, they believe themselves to be the best friend to their peers.

Thirdly, you can count on the psychopath/narcissist to be extremely competitive with his/her peers, they are driven by the need to feel they are, and can do, better than those that surround them. They may be overtly competitive, in other words they will openly express their competitive nature either verbally using sarcasm, humour, mocking, taunting, scoffing and being generally disparaging or physically, by being challenging, antagonistic or outright combative. Or they may be covert with their competitiveness using underhanded tactics, by appearing to have your back and be your best friend, however, all the while they are plotting and planning to undermine or perhaps betray you, their envy and jealousy well hidden. Narcissists are not to be underestimated they can be cunning, calculating, devious, opportunist, scheming, deceitful, ruthless, and unscrupulous when they deem it necessary.

Psychopathic/Narcissistic Abusers, in the Workplace

Psychopathic/narcissists in the arenas of career, business and the workplace in general will show their true colours in obvious and not so obvious practices. As mentioned earlier they can engage in overt or covert conspiratorial and scheming competitive behaviours, using subterfuge to attain their goals and they are not particularly concerned with who they burn along the way. When it comes to the narcissist's career, business and workplace objectives and ambitions they can be extremely driven and ruthless, easily compromising ethics, standards, and principles if necessary. They may lie, cheat, slander, perjure and backstab to undermine whoever they deem to be the competition or is standing in the way of their desired objective.

They are also competitive in the extreme and can be cold, calculating, and crafty whether they are vying for a promotion, business expansion or a job contract. They are known to misuse positions of power and will exercise controlling and manipulative tactics to ensure they remain in that seat of power. They have no problem throwing a peer, work colleague or competitor "under the bus" when necessary, this always seems to shock their peers because they simply do not expect their friendship to be abused and their loyalty unrewarded by those whom they trusted to look out for them.

Successful psychopathic/narcissistic businessmen/women who have achieved financial and/or career success who may also hold an influential position of power invariably feel exalted, superior, and grandiose. They often abuse positions of power by mistreating and exploiting employees, clients, and those less fortunate than themselves. They have a flexible moral compass that allows them to bend the rules to their advantage at the expense of a victim, believing themselves to be untouchable. These types of abusers may appear to be happy and content with their successes and/or achievements however, this is far from true, as underneath the façade they are usually found to be extremely psychologically and emotionally troubled. The abuser never feels satisfied for very long as they are addicted to the hyperarousal (adrenalin) that accompanies acquisitions, business projects or workplace accomplishments. They never experience real contentment or sense of achievement as they possess an immature psychological and emotional developmental deficiency that reflects their true underlying feelings of self-doubt, insecurity, and inferiority. They are programmed to experience only momentary or short/term satisfaction or satiation, always seeking endeavours that provide instant gratification, some of whom may also possess the "god complex" which is a disorder characterised by an inflated sense of self-importance, entitlement, and a deep need for admiration from others.

However, there are also many career-orientated, general workplace and/or business narcissists who have set themselves unrealistic and unattainable goals and ambitions believing themselves to be better than they actually are. When they fail to reach these lofty goals and ambitions, are unable to accept much less cope with the disappointment and disillusionment that accompanies failure. As a result, they may develop mild to severe depression and/or eating, behavioural and anxiety-based disorders, which can lead to substance abuse and addiction (including gambling and sexual addictions).

Failure to achieve their goals may also trigger retributive and vengeful actions from the narcissistic abuser towards the person, persons, or organisation they believe are responsible for their misfortune and adversity or stands in the way of their advancement or success. Or alternately, the abuser may redirect unresolved disappointment, disillusionment, anger, or rage towards those closest to them in the form of family and domestic abuse.

Psychopathic/Narcissistic Abusers, their Sexuality and Sexual Narcissism

Sex has four main purposes for the psychopathic/narcissistic abuser all of which are performed without any concern for their intimate partner (victim). They are driven to either satiate a physical (biological need), use sex as an outlet for unresolved disappointment, anger, rage, shame, or guilt, use sex as another area in their lives in which they can aggrandise themselves (I am a great lover etc.) and they may use sex as way to express their need to feel powerful, dominant and in control or all the aforementioned.

Sexual narcissism occurs when one partner has a grandiose view of their sexual prowess, and uses this aggrandized self to manipulate their partner emotionally and physically in and out of the bedroom. The sexual narcissist is a person who lacks the ability to share real intimacy with a partner, and will more than likely exploit the partner both sexually and emotionally, using coercion to get what they want, and this includes sex. They have a hard time swallowing disappointment, so if a victim expresses sexual or emotional dissatisfaction to their abusive partner then the victim will have to contend with swift retaliation from this partner with either or both overt and passive aggressive reprisal.

If the narcissists sexual ego-identity feels threatened in any way, in other words if they experience a real or perceived slight to their over-inflated prowess, they will want to turn the tables onto the victim. They can be spiteful, vengeful and/or resentful and may either retaliate immediately or plan and wait for an opportune and more advantageous time to strike back. These types of perpetrators may respond with malicious, demeaning, and belittling taunts, intimidating and/or threatening behaviour or with outright aggression or rage. The aim is to make the victim feel undeserving and unworthy, using tactics that shame, frighten, manipulate and/or undermine a victim's self-esteem.

The sexual narcissist needs to always maintain control and the perception of superiority over a victim, they will engage in an unrelenting campaign to undermine a victim's self-confidence and cause them to doubt their desirability and acceptability. The victim in turn may feel used and betrayed and/or become dissatisfied with their appearance, developing a negative sexual identity. By putting their victim in a constant state of psychological and emotional distress and conflict, they are better able to control, dominate and manipulate, whilst simultaneously having their sexual needs satisfied. Sexual narcissism is perpetrated by adulterous, promiscuous, and opportunistic males or females who possess self-serving, elastic, and underdeveloped consciences driven by a deep need to self-gratify.

Psychopathic/Narcissistic Abusers and Intimacy

Psychopathic/narcissistic abusers use sex to reassure themselves that they are good lovers, pretend that sex is for the partner when it is for their gratification only. They may use a partner's sexual past against them, it may be dissected (torn apart) or thrown in the partners face during or after the relationship has ended. However, the abuser revels in telling a partner all about their own sexual past and that he or she (the victim) may never measure up to the abuser's past lovers. The abuser may instigate sex but then at the last minute, change their mind, usually for manipulative purposes, not caring if the partner is upset or wounded psychologically or emotionally by their abusive actions.

They may even enjoy hurting an intimate partner, by exploiting their vulnerabilities with either private or public humiliation by making fun of, shaming, or belittling a partner's sexuality or physicality (body). They are highly likely to push their intimate partner's sexual boundaries by coercing them into engaging in deviant, exhibitionistic, public and/or risky sexual activity that the partner is not comfortable with, or has expressed a resistance to. Due to the narcissists' lack of empathy, they have a hard time understanding or feeling others discomfort or pain which results in intimate and sexual limits being crossed at the victim's expense. Everything about a psychopathic/narcissist is fabricated, they resist showing their true feelings and emotions and are likely to have a deep-rooted fear of intimacy (closeness and affection) cultivated since early childhood.

They are characteristically selfish and manipulative and are not typically capable of expressing real sentiment or empathy towards others. This is reflected in all personal relationships including family, friends, workplace peers, intimate partners, or children. They are not willing to show, much less give their true selves to another person, this makes expressing physical affection least on their list. The narcissist may perform the bare minimum of affection towards others for only three reasons, to sustain an existing relationship, to entice a potential victim, or for manipulative reasons to advance a personal agenda.

They avoid engaging in simple acts of affection such as handholding, hugging or a kiss on the cheek if they can help it, as they struggle with real connection to others. In fact, they will find the intimate act of kissing challenging, if not very difficult to perform as it requires a level of familiarity and trust that they will never allow themselves to experience. Intimate kissing for a narcissist is only a means to an end; it is mechanical or aggressive and usually kept to a minimum in their relationships.

True intimacy in relationships is usually characterised by acceptance, openness, and vulnerability everything the psychopathic/narcissist is incapable of giving to another human being. Sexual relationships for this type of abuser are simply a means through which they can experience satiating their fundamental needs and desires. Which includes the need to, satisfy their own physical sexual desire, nurture their sense of superiority, exert their dominance and control over another to feel powerful, aggrandise themselves (I am a great lover etc.) and lastly, they need to use sex as an outlet to express any unresolved feelings such as anger, rage, shame, or guilt.

The abuser will never place anyone before themselves and their needs, they have no qualms using and abusing a victim, however violent sexual offenders will also de-humanise victims, making them an object. According to Albert Bandura, renowned psychologist, and author of "social learning theory," the perpetrators prime motivations stem from their need to express either or all of the following, domination, power, revenge and rage through aggression and violence and not from a desire for sexual gratification.

Psychopathic/Narcissistic Abusers and Intimate Partner Sexual Abuse

As we have established, sex is not about connection for the narcissistic sexual abuser, rarely is emotion involved, it is an opportunity for them to focus on fulfilling their baser needs and desires first and foremost. They do not respect boundaries and will use bullying, intimidation, manipulation, coercion (force) to get these needs met, consequently they are likely to pressure a partner into participating in sexual activities that the partner (victim) is not ready for, or comfortable with. The abuser is only concerned with his/her own gratification and is usually neglectful after sex, leaving a partner feeling emotionally and/or sexually unfulfilled, or as if they have been taken advantage of. The psychopathic/narcissistic sexual abuser is linked to high levels of infidelity, family, and domestic abuse, sexual assault, and paedophilia, (this is particularly true of male sexual narcissists).

Sexual abuse in an intimate relationship is usually a result of the abusers need for control, domination, sexual satiation and in some cases sexual addiction. The abuser may start the relationship off being romantic, caring, considerate, showering a victim with attention and adoration however, before long they are likely to devolve into their selfish, self-centred, and narcissistic ways. The abuser's true colours will begin to emerge as soon as they believe that they have their victim firmly ensnared in a relationship, asserting their controlling, dominating and adverse intentions. They will expect the victim to cater to their every whim and will treat the victim as their property, an object they now own.

If the abuser perceives a real or imagined threat to the control, they have established in "their" relationship, they will likely respond with psychological abuse (blame games), neglect and emotional, verbal and/or physical abuse. If an intimate partner (victim) disagrees with the abuser's sexual preferences, then the victim may be openly criticised for their differing sexual desires or subjected to a campaign of coercion until they concede to the abusers demands. Victims often become the target of debasing insults and humiliation and at the same time, they may be accused of being either "prudish" or "uptight" or the opposite "whore" or "lecher" whatever the case may be. The narcissistic sexual abuser believes they are entitled to, or owed sex by a partner and are not concerned with whether a partner is willing or not.

If a victim shows reluctance to perform sex, the abuser will most definitely engage in coercive and manipulative strategies such as harassing, tormenting, humiliating and/or shaming their victim to achieve their ends. Some victims will submit to unwanted sexual acts that may have breached their sexual boundaries out of fear because they were either threatened with violence, subjected to humiliation, or threatened with infidelity and/or abandonment. This type of abuser is known for being heartless and relentless with their sexual desires and will put pressure on a victim to provide sex, regardless of a victim's physical or emotional condition.

The perpetrator may demand that a victim have sex at any time that suits them, to either have the victim reaffirm their loyalty to the abuser, or simply because the abuser wants sex. For some abusers, the behaviour can escalate to include psychologically, emotionally, and physically harmful degrading, sadistic and/or violent sex being forced on their victim. These abusers have no boundaries and see a victim's semi-compliance as a green light to do as they please irrespective of the victim's wellbeing or consent.

A narcissistic abuser can also withhold sex as a means of manipulating their partner and maintaining their sense of entitlement and control over the relationship. Just as forcing a partner into sex is damaging, withholding sex as a form of manipulation and control over a partner is just as damaging. Sexual narcissists confuse their victims by alternating between conflicting and opposite emotions, they may act completely disinterested and treat a victim with disdain or act intensely jealous and possessive at other times.

Psychopathic/Narcissistic Abusers and Infidelity

Infidelity/adultery is not a crime punishable by law in the most countries around the world (there are of course some exceptions to that rule), however for many societies, cultures, and religions it is considered a crime against morality and is most definitely an act of abuse. It is an abuse committed by both men and women, and even though there are a growing number of female narcissistic sexual abusers in this area of abuse, males still dominate in the numbers stakes in committing acts of infidelity. On the surface, it appears as if the act of infidelity is simply about sexual fulfilment or lack there-of, and to a small degree for the narcissistic abuser this is true.

However, the truth is that infidelity is a by-product of the narcissists dysfunctional psychological need to feel in control, powerful, youthful, and attractive, and at the same time allowing them to exercise their sense of entitlement. Other obvious traits that are easily recognisable is a failure to accept accountability for their actions, they will habitually blame others (usually their sexual counterpart) or extenuating circumstances for their infidelity to justify and rationalise their wrongful behaviour. The psychopathic/narcissist's sense of entitlement and the need to feel youthful and attractive to others is directly linked to their sexual identity which they express through sexual activity.

As a result, they may seek more than one partner at a time (preferably someone younger than themselves) but not exclusively, to continuously prove to themselves that they are in fact youthful, attractive, and powerful. This can lead to repeated acts of infidelity, through either a series of "one-night stands" or affairs and can lead to sexual addiction. For some, the act of infidelity is accompanied by the experience of an adrenalin rush similar to that of an addict, as the fear of getting caught and the excitement of the secrecy acts as a "high" so to speak. These narcissists are often referred to as "serial daters" or "serial adulterers" who lack the ability to commit to a significant other or to engage in an emotionally and sexually mature and mutually rewarding relationship.

If for any reason the virility of the male narcissist is threatened in any way, whether through illness or as a result of erectile dysfunction than this can be experienced as catastrophic to their emotional and psychological stability, in other words they feel as if their world has come to an end. This can cause them to react in either of two ways they may become depressed and/or suicidal or the opposite can occur and they become enraged and/or vengeful towards their sexual counterparts. Remember the psychopathic/narcissist will always blame others for their real or perceived shortcomings and any problems they are having.

It will come as no surprise then that it is possible for the sexuality of a narcissistic abuser to be linked to, and influenced by what is commonly known as the "Peter Pan syndrome" and/or the "Madonna–whore syndrome" also known as the "Virgin–whore complex." Even though the psychiatric community in general does not formally recognise these concepts as medical disorders, many psychologists, psychotherapists, and some psychiatrists find the symptoms of these concepts useful to refer to.

After much investigation, I have concluded that the narcissistic abuser's sexual psyche regardless of gender is wholly or partially impaired by either or both these syndromes. However, for male abusers whether they are showing signs of being afflicted with symptoms of "Peter Pan syndrome" or not, they will very likely be afflicted with the "Madonna–whore syndrome." Both these syndromes present a particular set of traits that reflect maladaptive emotional and psychological development that determines the abuser's sexual identity and influences the abuser's sexual behaviours.

Psychopathic/Narcissistic Abusers and the "Peter Pan" Syndrome

Both male and female narcissistic abusers can be afflicted with what is termed as the "Peter Pan syndrome," and even though there is a growing number of females afflicted with this syndrome, it is more commonly known to be experienced by males. This term refers to an adult male or female whose emotional and sexual maturity is trapped in "Never-Never Land" (early to late adolescence) a time when their sexuality was emerging and their sexual identity was developing. For both females and males, this sexual emergence is usually accompanied by feelings of omnipotence and youthful entitlement which is a normal and healthy part of teenage development, however it needs to be out-grown as the teenager matures into adulthood, this does not happen for someone with "Peter Pan syndrome." Those who are afflicted with this syndrome have likely sustained an arrested development in this area of their life, entering adulthood with an emotional and psychological immaturity attached to their sexual identity. "Peter Panners" have trouble committing to relationships with longevity in mind and those that do enter a committed relationship are highly prone to committing multiple infidelities. They have a predilection to participate in promiscuous and even dangerous sexual activities outside of their primary relationship and may also participate in high-risk non-sexual behaviours as a result of their immature and omnipotent attitude.

Male "Peter Panners" tend to link their masculinity to their virility (sexual prowess), whereas female "Peter Panners" tend to link their femininity to their desirability (sexual appeal). Both, however, express and fulfil their needs through sexual activity. In other words, they believe that having more than one sexual partner or even multiple sexual partners reinforces their youthfulness, keeps their insecurities at bay, gives them a sense of power and/or control and ultimately builds and/or feeds the ego-ideal they hold of themselves.

The "Wendy Syndrome"
"Wendy" (the victim) is a possible female counterpart to the male "Peter Pan" (the abuser)

There also exists a "Wendy syndrome" which refers to a female who essentially becomes a mother figure to her male counter-part in an intimate relationship. This can and does often occur without the female realising that she has slipped into this role, as it is gradual, and plays into a woman's natural maternal instinct to nurture and take care of others. "Wendy's" role in a relationship is easily identifiable and most certainly heavily imbalanced as she will find herself burdened with making the majority of the decisions in the relationship by taking on the "lions share" of the responsibility for things such as child rearing, household cleaning, family holiday and social events planning, and managing household finances. She will more often minimise or excuse a partner's bad behaviour, treating them more like an errant child than an adult partner. In this type of relationship, the female "Wendy" will often feel emotionally, psychologically, and physically exhausted from having to act as parent to both her children and her partner. She may experience feelings of loneliness, neglect, and abandonment in her relationship, as her "Peter Pan" counterpart is incapable of reciprocating to her the same level of support, he demands and is receiving from her (The Peter Pan & Wendy theories initially developed by Dr, Dan Kiley).

Psychopathic/Narcissistic Abusers and the "Madonna–Whore Syndrome"

Sigmund Freud (founder of psychoanalysis) developed the "Madonna–whore" theory to explain men's anxiety towards women's sexuality, suggesting that men cast women into either of two categories to ease the uncomfortable dichotomy (split) between fear and desire. His theory implies that a troubled male psyche cannot consider that both opposing idealisations can exist in the same woman and therefore he relegates all women to one of two categories without exception. One being the "Madonna" (mother figure) who is someone that he admires and respects, someone who represents maternal goodness, acceptance, forgiveness, and purity. The other is the "whore" who is someone he is attracted to but disrespects who represents desirability, sensuality, and impurity.

With this syndrome, "Love" is associated with the "Madonna" and her virgin-like qualities such as piety, wholesomeness, reverence and is non-sexual in nature, whereas intimacy is associated with the stereo-typical "whore" and her whore-like qualities such as being sordid, shameful, and sinful, and is sexual in nature. This cause's healthy relational sex to be suppressed and redirected towards the secrecy and perversion found in pornography and sexual deviancy where the concept of the "whore" is paradoxically, outwardly despised but inwardly craved. This is the cause of many intimate relationship issues, especially when the male in the relationship projects the position of the Madonna "good girl" onto his partner and then seeks the whore "bad girl" in the form of an infidelity in order to fulfil what he considers his baser, sexual needs/desires.

When it comes to a relationship where the "Madonna–whore syndrome" is present, there is a predictable pattern of behaviour by the sexual narcissist. He will only choose a primary partner (Madonna) that he thinks is a "good girl" hopefully a virgin if not, he would prefer her to have minimal to no sexual and/or relationship experience. He believes that the less experience she has the less threat he will have to his sexual performance, in other words he could set the "sexual bar" low, thinking she will be satisfied and not want more for herself. He also believes that the "good girl" will behave in a chaste and sexually undemanding manner and will be less likely to commit an infidelity or have an affair.

In the early stages of the relationship, sexual relations appear to be "normal" and by this, I mean that they both share a reasonably mutually satisfying intimate relationship. Once the relationship has established itself in the form of some type of commitment, perhaps even marriage the same level of intimacy they shared in the early stages of their relationship may continue for a short while or it may peter out. For some, the intimacy may have become seldom at best, or non-existent at worst, particularly when children enter their relationship. This is because the male counterpart in the relationship cannot accept the duality of his partner being both the caretaker (mother figure) of his children and being his sexual partner the bad girl (whore) too. This self-defeating belief system (Madonna–whore) can have an adverse physical effect on the abusers overall sexual performance whereby he may experience for example, a low sexual libido and/or impotence.

Which can result with the abuser becoming inwardly depressed and outwardly rageful and accusatory towards their primary intimate partner and/or all women in general. As is typical of the narcissistic abuser he will engage in verbal, emotional, psychological and/or physical abuse towards his intimate partner/s, with the intent to blame, shame and humiliate and thereby maintain the belief that it is the partners (victim's) fault.

Abusers afflicted with this syndrome will have idealised the "Madonna" or "mother figure," regarding her with a kind of reverence, for him she represents someone who possess only positive benevolent motherly traits such as caring, nurturing, understanding and is all-forgiving, even though in reality that may not have been their actual personal experience of their own mother/caregiver growing up. At the extreme end of the scale, some abusers with this affliction have projected exalted, archetypal "Madonna type" associations such as piety, modesty, and purity onto their chosen intimate partner, expecting absolute fealty (unquestionable loyalty), fidelity, faithfulness, and constancy despite their abusive actions. For them, all other women fall into the category of "whore" and are not worthy of the respect, esteem and high regard which is bestowed upon the chosen few of his intimate acquaintance. This is reserved for very few women in his life perhaps a daughter, sister, mother, grandmother or chosen intimate partner.

However, when the chosen intimate partner of the abuser, who is the object of his "Madonna" projection fails to live up to his lofty and unrealistic expectations, she will be become the target of his disdain, mistrust, and abuse. Sexual predators such as stalkers, flashers, rapists, serial rapists, and serial killers of women may have elements of, or be completely afflicted by this syndrome; however, it is also combined with other personality and behavioural disorders and/or psychosis. These criminals believe that the victim is not only deserving of abuse and mistreatment, but that she should also expect it.

This belief system is misogynistic in nature and has a powerful influence over the abuser's behaviour towards women, particularly for a female that does not meet their "Madonna" criteria. All other women fall into the only other category available in the abuser's psyche, this being the category of "whore," giving the abuser permission to objectify a victim and therefore treat her with the contempt, disrespect, and debasement that he believes she deserves. If you are not a "good girl" (Madonna), then you are a "bad girl" (whore) and prey to unwanted sexual advances from the abuser.

The abuser's narcissistic nature will always prevail and therefore he will blame and may even resent his victim believing she is inciting him to commit his abusive actions towards her. He will use rationalisations to justify his actions and absolve himself of accountability and thereby free himself from feeling the guilt, shame and/or remorse that is normally associated with harmful behaviour. Many of these types of criminals are known to target prostitutes in particular seeing them as easy prey, as the nature of their profession makes them more vulnerable and more easily accessible. "They" think of these women as objects (not human) to do with as they please, treating them with deeply held contempt and disdain.

The basis of the "Madonna–whore syndrome" stems from the abuser's inability to psychologically reconcile his morality represented by the "Madonna" with his immorality represented by the "whore." He unconsciously redirects his own inner self-loathing and "rage against the self" to an outward projection of "rage against other" in the form of resentment and punishment towards his female victim. In other words, he is confused by and struggles with unresolved emotion and an immature sexuality that leave him feeling as if he is at the mercy of his sexual desires and not in control of them. When this happens, his psychological and emotional defences become activated as he has perceived a loss of personal power, which also equates to a loss of control for the abuser. The perception that the seat of power has shifted from him to his victim is something that cannot be tolerated by the abuser and triggers his need to assert or re-assert his dominance over his victim.

Those afflicted with the "Madonna/whore syndrome" may engage in behaviours that are aimed at degrading, demeaning, and dehumanising women, reminding "them" of their "inferiority" to ensure they maintain their subservience, while the abuser simultaneously fortifies his believed supremacy and feelings of grandiosity. A man who slut-shames, insults, and debases women does so with the intent to suppress her natural sexuality and prohibit her from expressing her need for equal sexual satisfaction. He fears rejection, blames women for his own sexual inadequacies and is terrified that his sexual performance may be deemed poor or inadequate. By relegating women to two opposing categories either the "Madonna" or the "whore," he feels as if he is regulating her sexuality, providing him with the illusion of feeling powerful and appeasing his need to be dominant and in control.

When in fact the opposite is true, the need to dominate and control stems from his fear of his own sexual needs, he equates his need for sex as a loss of his personal power. If he perceives a threat to his position of power, whether it is real or perceived, it is likely to trigger over-compensatory defensive behaviour from the abuser in the form of emotionally, psychologically, and physically abusive actions to restore the balance of power in his favour.

"Narcissism reflects the core obstacle to real authenticity, wholeness and personal satisfaction." A. H. Almaas

The Origins of Narcissism in Psychology

Many psychoanalytical papers have been written on the subject of narcissism by reputed psychologists, essayists and physicians since the mid to late eighteenth century onwards. However, the following two psychoanalysts were among the first who pioneered studies and published papers devoted to the exclusivity of narcissism and the negative impact of narcissistic wounding on one's sexuality and personality. Both Havelock Ellis (sexologist – 1898) and Sigmund Freud (neurologist – 1914) had linked narcissism to excessive vanity, grandiosity, a need for admiration, an inability to empathise, and is responsible for creating personality disorders. The myth of "Narcissus" gave rise to the term "narcissism", a fixation upon oneself, one's physical appearance and one's public perception. There are several versions of the myth; the following is the classic version by "Ovid" found in book three of his Metamorphoses.

This Is the Myth of "Echo and Narcissus"

When Liriope gave birth to the handsome child Narcissus, she consulted the "seer" (psychic) Tiresias; he predicted that the boy would live a long life if he never discovered himself. One day, Narcissus was walking in the woods when Echo (an Oread mountain nymph) saw him, fell deeply in love, and followed him. Narcissus sensed he was being followed and shouted, "Who's there?" Echo repeated "Who's there?" She eventually revealed her identity and attempted to embrace him. Narcissus stepped away and told her to leave him alone. She was heartbroken and spent the rest of her life in lonely glens until nothing but an echo sound remained of her. Nemesis (the goddess of revenge), noticed this behaviour after learning the story and decided to punish Narcissus. Once in the summer, he was getting thirsty after hunting, and the goddess lured him to a pool where he leaned upon the water and saw himself in the bloom of his youth. Narcissus did not realise it was merely his own reflection and fell deeply in love with it, as if it were somebody else. Unable to leave the allure of his image, he finally realised that his love could not be reciprocated and he melted away from the fire of passion burning inside him, eventually turning into a gold and white flower (daisy).

Charming/Manipulative
A Defining Trait of the
Psychopathic/Narcissistic
Character Structure

To be charming and manipulative is to use "charm" to gain the confidence and/or trust of an intended victim with the sole purpose to exploit a victim for personal and/or professional gain. Being charming and manipulative can go hand in hand with being narcissistic, the abuser uses their considerable charm to manipulate intimate partners, family, friends, co-workers, business associates and even strangers. It is an automatic fall-back response that has served them well in the past, a skill that is honed throughout their life that was likely embraced at an early age. This type of abuser (male or female) can be extremely persuasive, using their wit, humour and "supposed" affable nature to appear harmless and to disarm and deceive potential victims, making identifying them more difficult. Please note; the perpetrators who possess this trait, will be more commonly found among those who are in the "higher functioning category" of abuser (refer to higher functioning p14).

Most often an abuser has learned the skill of being charming and manipulative early on in childhood, the first experience being through their relationship with their predominant caregiver or parent who is likely themselves to be a parent or caregiver afflicted with a narcissistic disposition or disorder. Typically, this type of parent/caregiver is exclusively close to the child they think of as special, having high hopes for the child's future and a tendency to project attributes onto them that are non-existent or unrealistic. The parent/caregiver and the child form a conditional and unhealthy relationship from the start which quite often results in creating a dysfunctional symbiosis between the two and can leave the parent/caregiver feeling threatened as the child begins to grow in independence.

The development of the psyche of a charming/manipulative abuser begins in infancy with one or more of the child's parents/caregivers believing that their child is profoundly exceptional, asserting that they are uncommonly beautiful, intelligent and/or talented, and are set for a special destiny. They hold high hopes for the future of the chosen child and have both consciously and unconsciously placed this burden upon the child's shoulders. The child may become the favourite of the parent/caregiver and may be referred to as the "golden girl" or "golden boy." This "golden child" has big shoes to fill, usually that of the parent/caregiver and even though much is expected of them, they may also be given much leeway where their behaviour is concerned.

This golden child can do no wrong and so any negative, harmful, or anti-social behaviour they commit is either ignored, excused, or minimised by the parent/caregiver, this is particularly true of a mother with her son or a father with his daughter. There also exists the parent/caregiver who may have their own unfulfilled personal or professional dreams projected onto a son or daughter, grooming them from a very young age, hoping to fulfil these dreams vicariously through the child's successes.

However, in the long run and over time, the "golden child" is inevitably destined for "moments of breakdown;" this happens when the hopes invested in them fail to be realised and the golden future they anticipated never materialises. These parents/caregivers do not cope well when their child fails to meet the expectation's they have set out for them, experiencing the child's failures as if they were their own. When this occurs, the parent/caregiver can be extremely punishing and may withdraw love and affection from the child.

During early childhood and adolescence, any withdrawal of love and affection may be experienced as devastating to a child/adolescent and their fragile developing ego-self. As a result, when they are faced with the threat of the occurrence of a real or perceived failure and the prospect of losing the parent/caregivers affection and love, it may trigger the advent of specific negative behavioural defences. The child cannot cope with a personal failure or a fall from grace in the eyes of his/her parents or those they look up to, learning very early on to avoid the conflict associated with disappointing others. One way in which they achieve this is to avoid taking responsibility for any real or imagined failures or any wrong-doing on their part.

They have learned to become adept at distorting the truth, minimising their accountability, distancing themselves from their negative actions, telling outright lies or pointing the finger. This child grows into adulthood navigating their lives with these maladaptive, avoidant, and dysfunctional defensive behaviours. They have now become expert at using their considerable charm and appeal to manipulate people and situations to their advantage. Their egotistic nature leads them to believe that they are smarter than everyone that they associate with or encounter. It is therefore not uncommon for some abusers to be afflicted with a narcissistic disorder in the form of "delusions of grandeur" wherein they possess an exaggerated or an over-inflated view of themselves, their attributes, and their future. They believe themselves not only to be superior in their sexual prowess, power, influence, talent, or smarts, but that they are also unique and/or destined for greatness.

Schemas and the Abuser

Our behaviours are motivated by our defences and our defences are underpinned by our core beliefs also referred to as schemas, they can be either positive (adaptive) or negative (maladaptive) in their constitution. A schema is defined as strongly held belief about oneself, others, and the world at large, and is responsible for informing our thoughts, emotions, and actions. We all possess some elements of various schemas in our personalities; however, they are considered to become dysfunctional when they dominate our thoughts, emotions, and actions with an adverse and/or limiting effect on our life. They are most often formed in early childhood or adolescence but not exclusively, one can form a schema from events subsequent to one's early youth.

Either way, maladaptive schemas are a result of negative and harmful experiences, environments, and relationships, usually influenced by those responsible for one's care, rearing or education, and may include other family members, teachers, other students, or one's social peers. Schemas once formed are rigid in their nature and therefore resistant to change; they ultimately become self-perpetuating and grow stronger the longer they are left unaddressed, particularly if left unchallenged as one enters adulthood. When a schema is maladaptive in nature, the negative beliefs dominate the psyche influencing every decision that is made and determining the nature and quality of intimate, social, workplace and community relationships.

Please remember that often we are not aware of our schemas, they usually remain underlying influences that drive our thoughts, emotions, and actions without conscious participation. Following, you will find a list of the possible negative schemas associated with those individuals afflicted with the psychopathic/narcissistic/charming/manipulative character structure, they may possess several or all these schemas (core beliefs).

The Schemas Associated with the Psychopathic/Narcissistic, Charming/Manipulative Character Structure

"Defectiveness and Shame" Schema

Those that are afflicted with this schema harbour deep-seated feelings of defectiveness, unworthiness and shame believing themselves inherently "bad" and fundamentally flawed. They possess a heightened sensitivity to criticism and blame, and suffer from insecurity and self-consciousness. If the thoughts and feelings associated with inadequacy such as shame or guilt are triggered, the abuser will employ powerful negative avoidance, deflective and compensatory defences to counter the debilitating affect. The abuser will have a propensity to overreact when this schema is activated, he/she cannot bear the emotions associated with this schema and therefore their defensive response may be disproportionate when one or more of these emotions are triggered. They may respond with physical, psychological, emotional, or verbal abuse as a retaliatory reaction, or they may minimise their accountability for actions taken, by deflecting or redirecting the blame.

"Failure" Schema

This schema is closely linked to the defectiveness and shame schema both sharing the same deep-seated feeling of defectiveness and inadequacy, except with this schema there is also an innate belief that one is a failure and inferior in comparison to others. This schema may manifest itself through behaviours that include perfectionistic and/or self-defeating practices and endeavours. It may be reflected as a relentless driving of oneself, expecting those who they work with such as their employees or work colleagues or those who they live and socialise with such as their friends, family and/or intimate partner to attain or reflect the same impossibly high standards they expect. Those afflicted with this schema tend to be hyper-critical of themselves and others and can become dismissive or rejecting of anyone who does not meet their standards or holds up to their ideals. The underlying feeling of being fundamentally flawed often leads to a strong sense of shame which cannot be accepted or tolerated by the abuser and may result in triggering avoidance, retaliatory or compensatory defensive action.

"Abandonment and Instability" Schema

Those who are afflicted with this schema, may have come from a family where at least one parent was physically and/or emotionally absent or neglectful (through divorce, mental or physical illness, death, or addiction), or the parent/parents were abusive and/or rejecting towards their offspring. This resulted in creating feelings of abandonment, insecurity, instability, fear, and mistrust in the child sending the message that life is precarious. This schema is based on the expectation that one will soon lose a significant other with whom they have formed a deep emotional attachment and is centred on the core fear of being abandoned or rejected. They possess an obsession or preoccupation with their personal relationships that can generate above average levels of insecurity, anxiety, and mistrust particularly if they experience a real or imagined threat to the constancy of their relationship. To avoid or compensate for their feelings of insecurity and anxiety an abuser can become needy, clingy, possessive, jealous and/or over-controlling, angry or rageful.

"Mistrust or Abuse" Schema

Those who are afflicted with this schema harbour an excessive mistrust for other people and the world in general. This schema developed in early childhood and/or adolescence as result of dysfunctional and abusive parents, who were either abusive themselves towards the child/adolescent or failed to protect the child/adolescent from abuse. Those who possess this schema have a general distrust of everyone, they have a persistent fear or anxiety that they are going to be taken advantage of by others, are cynical and doubting of others' intentions and expect others to hurt or cheat them. They often think in terms of attacking first, and can be vengeful or retaliatory in nature; this inevitably causes instability and volatility in friendships and intimate relationships. Abusers with this schema tend to compensate for their insecurities and mistrust by being over-controlling and manipulative with their intimate partners, family, co-workers, business associates or business partners.

"Insufficient Self-Control/Self Discipline" Schema

Those afflicted with this schema possess an inability to tolerate any frustration in the pursuit of their goals, as well as a limited capacity to regulate their impulses and feelings. This schema likely developed during early childhood and/or adolescence by inadequate parental guidance and disciplinary action and/or poor parental modelling of self-control. As adults, the need to self-gratify cannot be managed and will ultimately lead to the onset of addictive, abusive and possibly criminal behaviours in order to have one's immediate or long-term goals and desires fulfilled. An abuser with this schema lacks the ability to restrain his/her actions and therefore they may respond without thinking and therefore without caution or control.

Entitlement and Grandiosity Schema

Someone who is afflicted with this schema possesses a strongly held belief in their superiority over others, an exaggerated focus on the need to be the best, who believe that they are entitled to special privileges, rights, or exceptions. As far they are concerned, "normal" social and/or societal rules do not apply to them and so they are liberty to do as they please. They are not concerned with, or affected by, the negative impact of their actions on others, either considering them collateral damage or not noticing the destruction they generate, which is a by-product of their narcissistic and self-absorbed ways. They are obsessively preoccupied with seeking power, control, attention, and approval and are likely to force their viewpoints upon others. Abusers with this schema are intent on trying to control others' behaviours for self-serving purposes and will go to great lengths abusive and/or criminal to ensure their needs are met and to satiate or indulge their wishes and desires.

Behavioural Analysis of an Abuser

The behaviour of an abuser is the outward reflection of the abusers inner dysfunctional emotional, psychological, and cognitive mind.

All human beings, from birth onwards, are absorbing a personal understanding of their environment through the physical surroundings, the conditions in which they live, their life experiences and through their intimate, social, workplace and community interactions and relationships. All information is received through our senses touch, taste, smell, hearing, and sight; this data is then processed both consciously and unconsciously by the brain via these senses to form significant cognitions (thoughts) and emotions about our experiences. How we respond, and how we metabolise our experiences, will depend on our age and our cognitive, psychological, and emotional level of development at the time of the experience, therefore, every experience that we undergo has an impact, and is linked directly to our brain's evolution.

As our brain develops, it needs to form significant synaptic connections to co-create with other brain function and to develop a healthy and balanced range of emotions which we require to manage our behaviour so we can co-exist harmoniously with other human beings. Having healthy levels of remorse, guilt and shame will work to temper the more rational mind and therefore keep any harmful behaviour towards others in check. However, if we experience neglect at any time in our life whether to a mild degree or a severe degree this can impact on our psychological, emotional, cognitive, and physical development, depending of course on our age at the time when the neglect occurred and the nature and duration of the neglect. The negative impact of harmful interruptions during our early childhood and adolescent developmental years will cause varied levels of dysfunction or for some a complete cessation to the development of emotional, psychological, and cognitive elasticity and evolvement.

This lack will ultimately be reflected in a person's limited behavioural competency, the deficit becoming apparent by anti-social, abusive, and criminal behaviours. The ability to empathise with or understand others and the ability to temper baser emotions or needs is limited or non-existent, and so the cognitive, psychological, and emotional capacities of an abuser can be significantly impaired particularly for hardened criminals. This renders rehabilitation for habituated and unrepenting criminals improbable and therefore not an option to be considered when sentencing but rather a yardstick for the type and duration of their punishment.

We have already established that there exists a behavioural continuum on which all abusers exist, the worst kind of predator being, a psychopathic, sociopathic, violent and sadistic abuser such as a rapist, serial rapist or killer, human trafficker or paedophile. Even though I personally am an advocate for "neural plasticity" (the belief that you can re-wire your brain), I also believe that it is rare for the type of high-risk abuser mentioned above to be capable of making the necessary positive cognitive, psychological and/or emotional changes or growths that will be needed for successful rehabilitation. In order to alter the psychosis that underlie and influence the adverse behavioural patterns of these types of criminals, there will need to be a significant transformation of their neural function.

This is because the brain of the sociopath, psychopath and sadist is "hard-wired" so to speak to the point where they are unable to absorb new learnings, nor do they believe they need to, particularly those abusers who are afflicted with a narcissistic disorder. Some of these abusers are hindered by the fact that they are lacking in the intellectual and cognitive capacities needed in order to understand the necessity for change and therefore are considered incapable of growth or change and/or are unlikely to want to change themselves.

All abusers are afflicted with varying degrees of emotional, psychological and/or cognitive developmental deficiencies, some to a lesser degree than others. They share in many of the same incapacities found in their more dangerous counterparts who sit at the extreme end of the abusive scale. The ability to learn anything new is also either diminished, is not wanted or is not possible as they have adapted to having their physical, emotional, and psychological needs satisfied through narcissistic, self-serving, and abusive actions.

Perpetrators of abuse will without doubt go to extreme lengths to have their whims and desires met using verbal and physical threats, coercive and controlling behaviours, brute force, intimidation, bullying, economic manipulation and/or psychological and emotional abuse. We have established that abusive behaviour can range from mild at one end of the continuum to extremely abusive behaviour at the other, having said that, it is obvious that there is a huge gap between the two extremes and so perpetrators of crimes on this continuum will vary in the severity of their offences. However, it does not alter the fact that whatever end of the scale the abuser is on minor or major they are all guilty of acts of abuse and let us not forget those on the minor end of the scale, could very well evolve into becoming a serious offender.

All abusers possess some level of sociopathy and/or psychopathy even though it will vary in degree of severity which they express through their antisocial, abusive, and criminal behaviours. Some perpetrators can easily expose themselves using obvious, conspicuous verbal and/or physical actions as they are unable to control or hide their intentions or behaviours. Other more practiced abusers have learned to be quite stealthy and are devious and surreptitious with their intentions and actions. However, all perpetrators of abuse have learned with varying degrees of success, to survive and even thrive in their chosen environments by steadfastly avoiding the thoughts and emotions that will hinder, inhibit, or derail their intended goals and desires. To understand abusers and what motivates their behaviours, we must also understand defence theory, it is what drives all human behaviour and is at the heart of our psyche. We all possess a particular set of behavioural defences that influence every decision we make and every action we take.

Defence Theory

Behavioural defences are a set of individual automated psychological, emotional, and physical responses that are predominately unconsciously activated that determine how we interact with others and the world at large. They initially come in to being to protect us from any real or perceived threat to the stability of our psychological equilibrium and our emotional and physical wellbeing, with the aim of reducing the distress that arises from potentially harmful stimuli and unacceptable thoughts and impulses. When a psychological defence is activated, it may respond in several distinct ways, it may manipulate, deny, or distort reality in its attempt to defend against disempowering feelings such as anxiety, fear, terror, shame, guilt, pain, worthlessness, or failure. Defence mechanisms are essentially designed to protect our vulnerabilities, maintain our sense of self (our identity or ego-ideal), support our self-esteem, and keep unwanted and unacceptable thoughts and feelings at bay.

They are part of the human condition and are a natural progression of our mind-body evolvement from infancy to adulthood motivated by our instinctual need for survival. They are a distinctive set of strategies and coping mechanisms created out of necessity as we grow and develop that are initially formed without conscious effort or cognitive connection. Every person's "psyche" goes through a varied number of transformative defence mechanisms throughout their lifetime a natural progression of one's psychological and emotional evolution. For healthy psychological and emotional attainment to occur, our defence mechanisms need to evolve as we grow, making the necessary changes through the various stages and experiences of our lives by discarding obsolete defences and embracing the new more adaptive and mature defences. A defence mechanism becomes maladaptive when it has suffered some level of "arrested development" and as result has failed to be outgrown or allowed to evolve into a mature defence. This maladaptive defence will operate in an adverse, destructive, and malignant manner and may become pathological in nature (harmful to oneself and/or others).

Defence mechanisms form part of our psyche and become our mind-body defence system, they essentially influence if not govern how we respond to our life situation (home, work, and social environments) and how we interact in our interpersonal relationships (those closest to us) and towards others in general. There are many schools of thought recorded throughout history by leading theorists on defence mechanisms and their origins, their purpose, the effect they have on our personal development and the influence they have on our behaviour. Carl Rodgers in the late 1950s was an influential American humanist psychologist whose defence theory is based on the belief that "the failure to follow one's authentic inner voice, leads to an incongruity between the real self and ideal self". In other words, a conflict arises between the genuine experience of who you are and the socially influenced construct of who you think you should be. This conflict between the two is difficult to bear causing fear and anxiety, which in turn triggers defensive manoeuvres by the "psyche" to counteract the distress caused by the discord.

Among the most influential defence theory pioneers was the renowned psychoanalyst, Sigmund Freud whose defence theory stems from the belief that the psyche consists of three parts, the "id," "ego" and "superego" all developing at different stages of our lives:

- "Id" – Is the instinctual (libido) part of our psyche responding directly and immediately to satiate our basic urges, needs and desires and is primal and infantile in nature. Id maintains this infantile status throughout our lives, operating unconsciously not affected by reality or logical thinking and is motivated purely from impulse, its only concern is immediate gratification.
- "Ego" – Is the realistic and practical part of the psyche whose job it is to devise realistic strategies for "Id" to achieve its needs, wants and desires (pleasure). The ego has no concept of right or wrong and works from reason only, working out realistic ways of satisfying id's demands. To avoid the anxiety that can arise as result of id's impulsive actions the ego takes into consideration the social realities and rules that govern one's

external life by employing delaying tactics such as compromise or postponement of satisfaction in order to avoid conflict with others.

- "Super-ego" – Is the moral compass of the psyche, it operates with conscious participation taking into consideration the values and morals one has learned from their parents and society. The superego's role is to control id's immoral and aggressive impulses by punishing the ego through feelings of guilt, shame, or remorse. However, the superego can also reward when we behave "properly" through feelings of pride and satisfaction.

When the "ego" fails to keep a reality check on "id's" impulsive bad behaviour, it may generate feelings of distress or anxiety in an individual. In order to avoid these unpleasant feeling, the psyche automatically triggers unconscious defence mechanisms to activate which will help keep these unwanted feelings at bay. Ideally, the "superego" should step in to keep id's impulsive bad behaviours in check with its moralistic yardstick, urging the ego to adhere to the rules or be punished. For most abusers, their "super ego" is underdeveloped or elastic in nature, however for heinous sadistic, sociopathic, psychopathic abusers it is likely to be distorted or non-existent.

We all possess varied defences that were formed according to how we were parented or the lack there-of along with other significant factors such as our environment, our relationships, and our experiences. Karen Horney (a Freudian disciple – late 1930s) believed that parents who were neglectful, abusive, or merely indifferent towards their children created early psychological and emotional problems by provoking anger and anxiety in them. She believed that to defend against the pain of dealing with others, the child may choose one of three common strategies, they may learn to "dominate others," to "please others" or to "avoid others." She postulates that without positive intervention these children will develop into adults with these same dysfunctional motivations. However, according to Leon Festinger (American cognitive psychologist 1950s) his defence theory is based on the concept of "cognitive dissonance", wherein we innately strive to find harmony between our actions and our attitudes. A lack of agreement between the two leads to feelings of tension – a dissonance (disharmony) which we are then motivated to relieve by either changing the attitude to fit the action or the action to fit the attitude.

Defences come into play to manage the psychological stress caused by contradicting beliefs, ideas and/or values by employing rationalisation, justifications, and avoidance tactics to restore the balance and internal emotional and psychological harmony.

George E. Valliant (born in 1934) also a renowned American psychiatrist well known for his extensive work with defence mechanisms, whose defence theory further expanded on Freud's ideas regarding defence mechanisms. He suggests that there is a hierarchy of psychological development in which all human beings participate beginning in infancy and advancing through to adulthood. They range from the unhealthiest at level (1) to healthiest at level (4), he believes that those who use lower-level defence mechanisms in later life reflect significant emotional and psychological impairment.

Level one – Pathological defences

They are the most harmful of all the defences as they are rigid in nature, have a predilection to distort reality and may also be described as narcissistic defence mechanisms as they preserve the most idealistic version of the self. When these defences are activated, a person can appear to be irrational and insane to others, displaying overt psychosis. They include the following:

- Delusional projection – which are delusions created about external reality, usually of a persecutory nature.
- Denial – the refusal to accept the unpleasant aspects of external reality because it is too threatening.
- Distortion – a gross reshaping of external reality to meet one's internal needs.

Level two – Immature defences

These defences are aimed at lessening the distress and anxiety produced by threatening people and/or by an uncomfortable reality. Excessive use of these defences may be experienced as socially undesirable, in that they are immature, difficult to deal with and seriously out of touch with reality. These defences almost always lead to serious problems in a person's ability to cope effectively and are often seen in major depression and personality disorders. They include the following:

- Acting out – this entails a strong display of emotions or behaviours in order to hide the unacceptable underlying feelings or thoughts.
- Hypochondria – an excessive pre-occupation or worry about having a serious illness.
- Passive aggressive behaviour – Indirect expression of hostility.
- Projection – an attempt to reduce anxiety by unconsciously attributing one's own unacknowledged, unacceptable, or unwanted thoughts and emotions onto another.
- Schizoid fantasy – the tendency is to retreat into fantasy in order to resolve inner and outer conflicts.
- Introjection – identifying with an idea, object, or another person so deeply that it becomes part of that person.
- Idealisation – the tendency to perceive another individual as having more desirable qualities than he or she may actually have.
- Somatisation – the transformation of uncomfortable feeling towards others into uncomfortable feelings towards oneself (manifesting physical and/or psychological illness).
- Wishful thinking – to make decisions according to what might be pleasing to imagine instead of by appealing to evidence, rationality, or reality.
- Avoidance – the inability to accept responsibility for one's own actions through deflection (blaming others), repression, denial, dissociation, or compartmentalisation.

Level three – Neurotic defences

These set of defences have short-term advantages in coping, but can often cause long-term problems in relationships, workplace, and social arenas particularly when used as the primary style of coping with the world. They include the following:

- Displacement – this defence mechanism shifts sexual or aggressive impulses to a more acceptable or less threatening target, by redirecting emotion to a safer outlet. In other words, the emotion has not changed but the target of the emotional outlet has changed (the primary emotion is not masked, only redirected).

- Dissociation – this defence involves the separating of a part of one's personality or behaviour from the self or reality, in order to avoid conflict between contrasting beliefs and emotions.
- Intellectualisation – this defence is a form of isolation in that when one focuses on the intellectual aspects of a situation only, they are in effect distancing themselves from any associated anxiety-provoking emotions. It is an avoidance tactic to re-direct frightening or threatening emotions to a safer outlet.
- Reaction formation – by converting unconscious emotions or impulses that are perceived to be dangerous or unacceptable into their opposites. It is the acting out of the opposite of what one really feels or wants or taking the opposite belief because the true belief causes anxiety.
- Repression – in this defence an unpleasant feeling or thought is unconsciously forced out of consciousness (also known as dis-associative amnesia), this differs from "Suppression" where the thought or feeling is both consciously and unconsciously forced out of awareness.
- Rationalisation – Is a way of offering a rational explanation to justify an attitude, belief or behaviour that is unacceptable. It is an unconscious attempt to avoid addressing the underlying reasons for the attitude, belief, or behaviour.

Level four – Mature defences

These defences are commonly found in psychologically and emotionally healthy adults, they have been adapted through the years in order to optimise success in human society and relationships. These defences help to integrate conflicting emotions and thoughts, whilst remaining effective.

- Altruism – helping others to feel better about themselves brings personal satisfaction.
- Anticipation – realistic planning for future discomfort.
- Humour – expressing uncomfortable feelings (in the form of jokes, witticism, or self-depreciation) without causing oneself discomfort.
- Sublimation – the transformation of unwanted or unacceptable emotions or impulses into healthy actions/behaviours.

- Suppression – the conscious decision to delay paying attention to a thought, emotion or need in order to cope with the present reality. It is the only defence mechanism to have some sort of conscious effort although partial.

Defence Theory – Abusers

As you can see, defences can have a positive and negative impact on our life, the positive being that when the defence came into being its original purpose was to protect our emotional, psychological, and physical vulnerable selves needed for our survival at that time. The negative aspect of course is that a defence that was once necessary, that served to protect us at some earlier time in our life is no longer needed and has subsequently become defunct and is now working to suppress the development of an authentic self and is hindering the attainment of fulfilment.

Defences can become detrimental to our wellbeing when they have outgrown their usefulness and as a result become inhibiting to the degree that it may lead a person to live a life that is ruled by fears, phobias, doubts, psychosis and can lead to impaired judgement taking the form of omnipotent and risk-taking behaviours. The list of defences that exist and the combinations of these defences and how they affect our behaviour are unique to every individual only to be determined by the individuals own personal journey in life. However, through the exploration and study of human behaviour it is possible to surmise the types of defences that both abusers and victims have in common and the unique way in which they affect their psyche.

Clinical mental illness will explain the behaviour of abusers who are born with a neurological and/or biological disease/disorder causing diminished physical, emotional, and psychological capacity. For all other abusers, the nature of their personality and their character developed after birth suggesting that at some point in time, they would have experienced some level of physical, emotional and/or psychological trauma that has resulted in triggering or causing developmental dysfunction. Whether minor or major, the dysfunctional deficiencies will have impacted the abuser in a negative and lasting way. At the psychological core of an abuser, beneath the layers of cynicism, narcissism and egotism, there exists a much "younger self" that is acutely insecure, afraid, needy, and possessed of a sexual immaturity.

This younger part reflects the stage at which the abuser has suffered a mild to severe level of psychological and emotional arrested development, which was responsible for and acted as the catalyst that caused the development of life altering, powerful but negative defences. The goal of a defence generated at that moment in time was to prevent a fragile and developing "psyche" from experiencing what it may have perceived as destabilising or catastrophic emotions such as fear, terror, anxiety, powerlessness, shame, guilt, worthlessness, or failure. By understanding how behavioural defences and their associated beliefs operate within the "psyche," we can gain an insight into the drives of the abuser.

Following, you will find a list of the types of behavioural defences commonly found to be present in abusers, predators, and bullies, they may possess any combination or all these defence mechanisms to some degree.

Defence (Abuser): Dissociation

Dissociation (may also be referred to as "splitting off") is an unconsciously activated defence, it does not act out of choice and occurs without your logical (conscious) mind registering that it has occurred. When an experience arises that triggers a flood of overwhelming unwanted emotion, it can cause a reaction in the brain wherein, the part of the brain responsible for logical thinking separates from the part of the brain responsible for regulating your feelings. The intended purpose of this defence is to protect us emotionally and psychologically by lessening the impact of a frightening or traumatic experience. In some cases, it can be experienced as if an event is happening in slow motion. In other words, the experience may have been perceived as taking minutes when in fact it was only seconds long.

There are times when defensive dissociation can be triggered and it may last for hours, days, months, years, or it may be enduring depending on the individual's response to the trauma. The severity of the trauma, the age at which the trauma was experienced and the psychological and emotional maturity of the individual are all contributing factors that determine the impact and duration of a dissociative experience. Dissociating is part of every human being's natural defence system; it is an innate mechanism that activates to protect us from a real or imagined threat to alarm or danger.

It is the mind distancing itself from what the body is experiencing, an example of this is when the "fight, flight or freeze" response is activated. For example, a person may freeze out of terror when confronted with danger out of instinct and without conscious thought as their ability to act (reason) is suspended. However, dissociative responses can also be triggered when a person experiences, overwhelming and unwanted feelings such as grief, shame, guilt, or anxiety and is unable to cope at that time. When these overwhelming emotions flood the body, it sets in motion a chain reaction causing the thinking and feeling parts of the brain to delink.

Dissociation can work in dual ways when de-linking, a person can respond by either going into all "thinking brain" without the ability to feel, or go into all "feeling brain" without the ability to think. When abusers act without thinking, they are known to respond in an instinctually defensive and reactive manner, who are solely responding from a heightened feeling state, wherein the abuser acts with unregulated emotion and without thinking enabling them to commit abusive, violent, and heinous crimes.

The abuser's response may also be linked to previous earlier experiences of these same overwhelming emotions, which when combined with the inability to manage these emotions, can trigger unregulated and irrational behaviour in their current circumstance. They may react to a "minor slight" unconsciously perceiving it as a major insult or affront, an over-reaction that by normal standards is considered a disproportionate response to the slight that was originally perpetrated. In other words, a situation that for most people only merits a mild reaction such as irritation or reasonable anger may for a person who dissociates trigger an unmerited response such as rage. When this happens, there is no reasoning with an abuser as they literally "see red," in other words, they have "split off" from thinking and the more rational self and are acting solely from the feeling and the less rational self.

Conversely, when abusers act without feeling, they are known to respond in a scheming, retributive, merciless, remorseless, violent, or cruel ways. When in this state, there is an inability to empathise with others as they are completely cut off from their emotions, enabling them to commit acts of abuse of lesser nature through to extreme acts of brutality without conscience or remorse. They may react to a real or perceived insult or threat to their control in a cold, calculated or vengeful manner, putting thought into extracting retribution from a victim.

Defence (Abuser): Compartmentalisation

Compartmentalisation is similar to but a lesser form of "dissociation," wherein parts of oneself are separated from awareness of other parts, it is the process of dividing something into different categories or compartments, whereas "dissociation" is a state of complete separation/disunion.

Compartmentalisation is an unconscious psychological defence mechanism principally used to avoid "cognitive dissonance" (inner disharmony or conflict) by allowing two opposing cognitions (thoughts), emotions or values to co-exist in separate compartmentalised states. Cognitive dissonance is responsible for creating acutely uncomfortable mental and/or emotional internal tension, causing an undesirable and anxious state of mind and body. By compartmentalising, you are able to keep the two worlds from colliding, in other words compartmentalisation is a way to resolve the tension of two or more inner conflicting viewpoints by isolating the inconsistent views or behaviours from each other.

It ultimately forces a person to favour one view over a less comfortable one, even if the more comfortable view is wrong or dangerous. By keeping things separate, we can avoid unpleasant feelings and maintain or restore our psychological and/or emotional status quo. We all engage in some type of compartmentalisation in everyday life by "redirecting our focus," this is essential at times and is psychologically adaptive, allowing temporary respite from stressful thoughts and emotions. Adaptive compartmentalisation can be achieved either "intentionally" as we purposefully segregate our thoughts and feelings from each other for example, to get through your work day you may need to distance yourself from the upset of an argument you had with another person earlier that day. Or you can "unintentionally" compartmentalise by inadvertently becoming absorbed in or distracted by other activities that cause you to put certain worries aside without your conscious participation.

Healthy compartmentalisation is a process that creates mental partitions that aid in preventing psychological and emotional strain from overwhelming or dominating our everyday life. It allows us to free our mind to other experiences. However, there is a dark side to compartmentalisation which occurs when an individual disconnects from their humanity, decency and morality leading to abusive and criminal behaviours including extreme violence and homicide, secrecy and lies.

Compartmentalisation allows an abuser to alter the behaviour to fit the thinking or alter the thinking to fit the behaviour and if necessary, can adopt a new disposition or belief altogether to alleviate the inner conflict they may feel. For example, to avoid unpleasant mental conflict, a substance abuser will engage in self-deception, making excuses to continue sanctioning the dangerous habit, they may deny and/or rationalise the self-destructive behaviour. In fact, all abusers whether they employ conscious or unconscious participation will co-enlist other defensive measures to keep the walls of compartmentalisation from cracking.

The need to eradicate the inner conflicting turmoil is not only paramount but also essential to maintain their inner dysfunctional psychological equilibrium. They will ignore, deny, rationalise, and minimise information that conflicts with their existing belief or action, choosing to compartmentalise the cause (abusive action taken) from the effect (harmful results of the action taken). By separating themselves from their actions, the abuser can avoid or minimise (diminish) his/her personal accountability, giving themselves a kind of detached vindication.

Defence (Abuser): Denial

Denial is an unconscious defence mechanism that prevents the conscious mind from accepting the reality of an experience. It is an avoidance tactic that denies acceptance of a true event, thought, emotion or occurrence as if it never happened, despite obvious and overwhelming evidence to the contrary. The theory of denial was first extensively researched by Anna Freud, a psychanalyst and pioneer in child psychology, who postulated that "denial was the instrument of the immature mind, because it conflicts with the ability to learn and cope with reality." Some typical examples of denial are when a smoker denies the reality of the health risks associated with the act of smoking or gambler with a gambling addiction who only remembers their wins and denies the existence of their losses.

However, denial can also be a semi-conscious act in the form of "minimising" which is the act of redefining events to downplay their significance and/or one's participation in those events for example, a person may whitewash a role in a crime in order to lessen their culpability for that crime despite being confronted with irrefutable facts to the contrary. Abusers are experts at using denial as a defence mechanism in order to diminish personal responsibility for their abusive and criminal actions. They achieve this by either outright denial or by "minimising" their answerability and/or participation in the abusive act that they have committed.

By denying involvement and deemphasising abusive and criminal harmful actions, they can either ultimately absolve themselves of any wrongdoing, or at the very least reduce the level of their personal accountability. This enables them to avoid experiencing what they believe to be disempowering emotions such as fear, guilt, shame and remorse and it is also an attempt to mitigate their behaviour to avoid punishment. Abusers/criminals when caught will undoubtedly try to distance themselves from their actions, diminishing their involvement and some may even show significant regret for their actions. However, the regret is not for the abuse or crime they committed but rather for themselves, they regret getting caught and having to face atonement for those crimes.

Historically, there are many documented criminal cases where a perpetrator is caught and confronted with overwhelming evidence that they had without doubt committed the crime they were accused of and yet continued to vehemently deny liability for their criminal actions even after their subsequent conviction and incarceration.

Denial is a defence that is difficult to refute as those that use denial to defend abusive behaviours are irrational and dogged in the pursuit to recant or negate their felonious activities. The abuser may recall an argument with a victim and when confronted later cannot seem to recall that their actions towards the victim were abusive or excessive. In the perpetrators recounting of the incident, they acted accordingly suggesting that the victim is exaggerating or lying about the severity of the incident. Perpetrators of abuse rarely admit to themselves or others that their actions have been harmful, and in cases where there is an admission of guilt or culpability it will be minimised or trivialised by the abuser citing their actions as either accidental or they blame the victim or extenuating circumstances.

Nearly all human beings at one time or another have experienced, or will experience exercising some type of denial in their lifetime in order to survive an overwhelming physical, psychological and/or emotional occurrence. This defence mechanism is designed to step in, when necessary, to lessen the immediate impact of a traumatic event. However, if the effects of the trauma are not addressed at some point post its original initiation, then the use of the defence of denial will become a deficit to that person. The short-term use of denial may leave you feeling temporarily isolated, apprehensive, worried, anxious, fearful, unhappy, or sad. The long-term use of denial has a more serious detrimental impact on one's life, it becomes harmful not only to oneself but also to those significant others that one associates with, creating habituated dysfunctional thoughts and patterns of behaviour that are adverse, limiting, destructive and toxic in nature.

Following is a list of the types of "denial" that may be employed as defensive measures by an abuser:

- Denial of fact – denial by lying, using lies in order to avoid facts that may incriminate them, they may leave out particular details of a story to lessen the impact or tell outright lies.
- Denial of responsibility – denial by blaming, minimising and/or justifying. This is an attempt to shift attention onto another, lessen the impact of one's actions by diminishing accountability or as a rationalisation of culpability.
- Denial of impact – denial of impact is the avoidance of thinking about or understanding the harm the abuser's behaviour has caused another (thereby avoiding guilt, shame, and remorse).
- Denial of awareness – denial by citing that they were in an altered state of awareness, (under the influence of drugs or alcohol or mental health related) thereby minimising accountability and shifting blame.
- Denial of cycle – denial of cycle is the avoidance of acknowledging the decisions that lead up to an event and/or not acknowledging the pattern of decision making and how harmful behaviour is repeated.
- Denial of denial – denial by self-delusion, the avoidance of the need to change ones negative and harmful thoughts, actions, and behaviours.

Criminals of all types including serial killers and serial rapists use denial via minimisation and rationalisation to mitigate their culpability, detaching or distancing themselves from their adverse actions by citing that "it wasn't me who committed the crime, it was this other self," another part of them that was driven by momentary insanity or instead of "I shot the gun" they will say "the gun went off." All abusers engage in the defence of denial to one degree or another as it helps to compartmentalise or separate emotion and conscience from harmful behaviour and immorality. In other words, they deny acknowledging the physical, psychological, and emotional harmful impact that their actions have on the victim themselves, the victims loved ones, "their" own families and society at large. Thus, giving them permission to continue with life free from experiencing guilt, shame and/or remorse, allowing them to believe that they are in control, providing them with a false sense of security and possible vindication or justification of their actions through their warped and brittle morality.

Denial may also exist in many large public and private organisations; the denial and ignorance of abusive behaviours can start at the top of an establishment and may be perpetrated by senior staff, management and/or board members. Their ignorance of the psychological, emotional, and physical harmful impact it has upon victims can have major negative repercussions on the overall morale and productiveness of that organisation. In these organisations, bullying is rife and condoned by those who are in a position of seniority and influence, an example of where this takes place is within some university campuses by university students who disguise "induction procedures" as "rites of passage," an attempt at invalidating the associated abusive behaviour, that includes acts of abuse perpetrated with debasing, humiliating and sometimes dangerous rituals. Denial by those in authority is also commonly found in large organisations such as the army, navy, and large companies/corporations with multiple employees in the form of "hazing." This type of bullying is disguised as a "prank" a form of victimisation which has been unofficially encouraged, ritualised, and then minimised as a sort of "joke" or harmless "initiation ceremony."

Defence (Abuser): Projection

Projection is a defence that is triggered unconsciously; it is a response that redirects unwanted and unacceptable emotions and thoughts onto another. Projection is a common enough defence which all human beings experience throughout different times in life for varying reasons and to varying degrees. According to (Karen R. Koenig, M. Ed, LCSW) by "projecting something you don't like about yourself onto another protects you from having to acknowledge a part or parts of yourself you don't like." Projection can be a significant psychological hurdle and may need to be addressed either consciously through external therapeutic intervention or it may be unconsciously addressed through a person's natural growth (maturity) and/or through positive life experiences, quite often without realisation from the person affected. Projection by nature can complicate and limit one's life having an adverse effect that can be personally injurious, however not necessarily always have a harmful impact on the other person/s that are the object of the projection.

For an abuser, projection onto another consists of variations of a series of disowned or unacceptable and unwanted feelings formed through adverse experiences, leaving the abuser with an inability to accept or process thoughts and emotions. The foundations upon which the projections were formed likely occurred during the abuser's early childhood and/or adolescent developmental years and were possibly cemented into their "psyche" by similar experiences in later life. Projections like many other defences reflect the limited emotional range of the abuser, they can process positive affirming emotions that support their ego-ideal of themselves, however, are unable to process life's undesirable but necessary emotions such as embarrassment, shame, guilt, remorse, rage, grief, failure, or fear. By projecting these undesirable and unresolved feelings onto others, the abuser can completely alleviate or avoid the discomfort associated with the unwanted thoughts and feelings.

You will find that perpetrators guilty of crimes of a personal nature (crimes committed against a person or persons) will have projected one or more of their unresolved feelings onto a victim, believing that they are deserving of the mistreatment directed at them. By projecting their unresolved thoughts and/or feelings onto another, the abuser can commit the most heinous acts of abuse imaginable and at the same time dismiss those rising unwanted and unacceptable feelings and thoughts. Anger and/or rage are quite often found high on the list of emotions that the abuser projects onto a victim to counteract their own personal feelings of fear, failure, guilt, shame, disappointment, and inadequacy. Which they express in many ways from psychological, emotional, and verbal abuse through to physically violent acts including rape, torture, and murder.

Projection is not limited to those who are known to the abuser but can also be directed towards larger and more general groups of people defined by a particular demographic including race, culture, religion, or those of a particular political or sexual orientation. According to (Michael Brunstein, PsyD), "People who suffer from feelings of inferiority and low self-esteem can fall into the habit of projecting their own feelings of not being 'good enough' onto others, manifesting into the broader form of racism or homophobia." Projections regardless of the nature and/or context are all counterproductive, however they become abusive in nature when directed towards others and are psychologically, emotionally and/or physically harmful.

A "projection," if never challenged, can become ingrained and may eventually form part of a person's personal belief system, which can lead to generalisations being established about oneself, others, and the world at large. For example, an "all men cheat" generalisation is a projection onto men that may have resulted from a women's personal and possible single experience of a cheating partner. A male abuser may project onto women an "all women are inferior to men" generalisation, which is projection onto women that resulted from a possible personal experience of growing up in a misogynistic household and/or may have been perpetuated by religious and/or cultural endorsement.

Defence (Abuser): Control

As human beings, we all have a natural need to feel that we have some level of control over our lives allowing us to set goals and make personal choices that express and define our individuality, sexual orientation, career, social environment, and lifestyle. The ability to be reasonable, rational and take responsibility for ourselves and our actions usually reflects a healthy level of psychological and emotional evolvement. The "need for control" and how to manage the associated emotions that accompany "the loss of it" are tempered through the coping mechanisms and strategies that we learned as we developed through our early formative childhood/adolescent years and subsequently through general life experience.

We were taught to accept responsibility for ourselves, our actions and how to cope, deal with and overcome life's set-backs and the feelings of disappointment, disillusionment and failure that may have come with those set-backs. Unfortunately, a person who becomes controlling of others in an abusive manner is incapable of accepting responsibility for themselves and their actions. They have at some point in life experienced an impediment (developmental trauma) to the healthy evolution of adaptive coping mechanisms causing limited psychological, emotional and/or cognitive elasticity. There are several distinct dysfunctional scenarios that can generate defensive controlling behaviours to manifest in children/adolescents:

- Violent and abusive parenting – this is when the child/teen has undergone any or all the following: physical, sexual, verbal, emotional and/or psychological abuse.
- Symbiotic parenting – this is when the parent/s see the child as an extended part of themselves and not a separate being, in other words the child's failures and accomplishment belong to the parent as much as the

child. Therefore, the child is parented with an over-intensity in which they are micromanaged by overbearing, bullying and personally intrusive methods.

- Extreme parenting – this is when a parent/s have placed extremely high, unrealistic, and unreasonable goals and expectations on their child. The child is parented with overbearing, bullying and manipulative methods.
- Neglect – this is due to poor or non-existent parental guidance (absent parents/caregivers).
- Modelling – this is when the child models one or both parents. While growing up, the child is a witness to and embodies the controlling, dominating, coercive, manipulative, and overbearing ways of the parent/s believing that to be the ideal or norm.

These scenarios and others like it can lead to an experience of feeling anxious, fearful, inadequate, incompetent, defective, ashamed and/or tormented, which to the young developing psyche can be encountered as psychologically and emotionally overwhelming or catastrophic. This translates to feelings of impotence, helplessness and vulnerability and a profound need to feel powerful and in control again is born. This creates a chain reaction that kick starts over-compensatory, reflexive defensive action to be taken by the psyche for self-preservation, to restore psychological and emotional equilibrium and to counteract the feelings of disempowerment.

Defensive negative and dysfunctional beliefs are created that support controlling, coercive and manipulative behaviours to keep unwanted feelings and thoughts at bay, and unless challenged in a significantly altering way, will become a way of life. The need to maintain control over others and one's environment becomes paramount in the "psyche" so when a real or perceived threat to that control is experienced it can trigger instant and possible disproportionate responsiveness.

Control and the need to "attain it" and "maintain it" are the most important defining factors that underpin every action the abuser takes and every decision they make. It can become all-consuming as they are unable to bear the lack of it, and therefore their need to sustain it at all times crosses over into all areas of their life (personal, social, and professional). The over exertion of controlling behaviours by the abuser reflects the inability to accept a situational outcome that differs from their own expectation and highlights their incapacity to process the possible resulting negative and disempowering emotions that may have resulted from this outcome.

Often controlling behaviours hide a confused and chaotic mind, they are a front that mask the abusers emotional and psychological immaturities, insecurities, and vulnerabilities. The abuser often projects their shortcomings onto a victim using them as an outlet for their disowned and/or unresolved emotions, allowing the abuser to achieve a sense of superiority over the victim while fulfilling their need for control. However, even though abusers will continuously endeavour to strive for or aspire to be in control in every area of their lives, does not necessarily mean they can achieve their desired goal.

In fact, not all abusers have control in every area of their life, an abuser may have control over their professional life and not their personal life or visa-versa. As a result, it is possible that if the abuser is at any time experiencing a real or perceived loss of control in one area of their life, they will likely attempt to compensate this imbalance by pouring more energy into micro-managing this need for control in another area of their life. For example, an abuser who feels out of control in his/her personal relationship or home life who perhaps feels dominated or bullied by an intimate partner or another family member, might compensate by exerting controlling behaviours in a place they know they can, such as their workplace for example.

When dealing with perpetrators of abuse, it is important to note that they possess a fundamental need for control over their "internal and external" environments. This is expressed through narcissistic, self-serving, dominant, controlling, manipulative and coercive behaviours which they fortify with a deep sense of entitlement. When I refer to their "internal environment," I am referring to the conscious and/or unconscious psychological, emotional, and cognitive "states of being." When I refer to their "external environment," I am referring to the actual lived experience of their life which is defined through work, home, social and community environments, personal relationships, and interactions with others. Remember, when an abuser experiences a loss of control it may be perceived by their "fragile psyche" as being catastrophic and can incite the abuser to immediate retaliatory or restorative action in order to re-establish their real or perceived loss of power. This may result in mild to extreme acts of emotional, psychological, verbal and/or physical abuse including homicidal violence by the abuser in order to achieve this reinstatement.

Defence (Abuser): Rationalisation

Rationalisations are reasons created by the abuser to justify their behaviours, allowing them to blame others or extenuating circumstances for their abusive and criminal actions and thereby avoid taking responsibility. Rationalisations in effect give the abuser permission to commit crimes and acts of abuse without conscience according to their distorted and self-serving belief systems. Predators/abusers/bullies all share common immature, prejudiced and unfounded beliefs and misconceptions about themselves, others, the world at large, particularly about money, sex, and gender equality. These beliefs and misconceptions are the driving force that define how they interact within intimate, familial, social, and working environments and relationships and form the basis for the rationalisations (justifications) for their actions. Those that rationalise criminal and abusive behaviour possess narcissistic tendencies and exist in a world where their own personal needs and wants are a priority above all others.

The high-functioning abuser (refer to p14 high-functioning abuser) has a narcissistic nature which is usually combined with a great need to be in control and to reflect success whether its financial, personal, social, career or all four, keeping up appearances of this success is essential. They will go to great lengths to maintain this façade as they believe that it defines who they are to others and supports the ego-ideal that they hold of themselves. The lower-functioning abuser (refer to p14 lower-functioning abusers) is also narcissistic in nature, however his/her needs even though self-serving are less sophisticated and revolve around using any means to get their needs met including overt abusive and criminal behaviours. However, regardless of whether the abuser is high or low functioning, rationalisations play an integral role in the way they live their life as it gives them permission to act as they please with validation.

Even though rationalisations are influenced by one's core beliefs, they are driven by psychological and emotional immaturities and incapacities. They come into play to help the abuser defend against experiencing feeling shame, guilt, remorse, personal vulnerability, being vulnerable to others, failure, appearing like failure to others and/or experiencing feeling a loss of control in their personal, social, or working environments and relationships. Over time rationalisations are cultivated by the abuser and become second nature giving them permission to act without conscience or accountability. Abusers are expert at exonerating themselves from any wrongdoing, their first course of action is to avoid taking responsibility, however if caught red-handed they will always minimise their culpability using rationalisations to justify their behaviour and blame others or extenuating circumstances that were beyond their control. As a rule, he or she likes to think that they are a good person, convincing themselves that they are a victim of sorts and therefore reasonable in their actions.

Ironically, despite the heinousness of the perpetrator themselves or the severity of the crimes they have committed, in order to survive they still have a deep need to maintain some sort of personal integrity or personal value. They will use rationalisations to either minimise, vindicate, or justify their actions. Serial killers are known to blame victims for placing themselves in harms-way, by accusing the victim of having culpability in their own demise. Rapists rationalise by minimising personal accountability, blaming the victim who according to them "asked for it" because they believe she dressed or behaved in a provocative manner.

Following are some examples of commonly used rationalisations by perpetrators of abuse that justify, exonerate, minimise and/or excuse their abusive actions:

- If there is no evidence of physical violence on the victims' body, then they (the abuser) have not committed an act of abuse. (This is particularly true for perpetrators of domestic abuse).
- Pushing, shoving, holding a victim against their will, or leaving a bruise is not a notable act of violence.
- Verbal insults and threats are not abuse.
- They (the victim) "deserve" the abuse that was perpetrated on them (the abuser blames the victim for inciting the abuser to abuse them).

- They (the victim) are stupid; therefore, the abuser must take control of them and the finances. (abusers most often assume that they are more intelligent than the victim).
- They (the victim) are responsible for the abusers' happiness and therefore failure to do so deserves mistreatment.
- My partner is my possession, (therefore I control them and I make the all the decisions in our relationship), they will do as they are told, I have the right to do as I please with them.
- My partner must provide me with sexual gratification.
- My partner is responsible for fulfilling all my needs (emotional and physical).
- It is the victim's fault for placing themselves in harm's way.

Defence (Abuser): Superiority / Grandiosity

Feeling superior to others is the negative way in which the "psyche" has learned to feed itself in order to support a fragile ego identity and is directly linked to the narcissistic character structure. Normally a person who displays superiority over others in reality experiences the opposite even though they are highly unlikely to be consciously aware of it. Thinking and acting superior is usually a way to overcompensate for real underlying feelings of self-doubt, shame, failure, unworthiness, powerlessness, and inadequacy. However, possessing feelings of superiority does not necessarily equate to a person being abusive unless of course the need to feel superior is accompanied by psychological, emotional, and physical abusive behaviours towards others in order to support feeling superior.

The predator/abuser/bully can possess an unhealthy sense of grandiosity (having an exaggerated belief in one's importance) in which they believe themselves to be better than those they associate with and other people in general. They believe that they are "a cut above the rest" and perhaps notable or exceptional in some way, this may be in any arena such as intellect, cunning, popularity, career, social status, creative or sporting ability, physical prowess and/or personal appearance. This works to help elevate the ego-ideal that they hold of themselves, giving them a sense of loftiness, authority, power, dominance, control and/or omnipotence.

The need to feel superior is fulfilled through personal, social, and professional relationships and achievements and is exposed through a display of a range of mild to serious abusive behaviours towards their victims. Which at the mild end may appear as arrogance, snobbery, condescension or being dismissive and at the extreme end can translate to being psychologically, emotionally, and physically harmful. This can include for example private and/or public humiliation, degradation, undermining and demeaning tactics or physical displays of violence.

Abusers who aggrandise themselves are also likely to either minimise their culpability if caught in a wrongdoing or exaggerate their accountability for successes that do not necessarily belong to them (this behaviour is common in the workplace and/or career advancement scenarios). They are easily provoked into taking defensive action if they experience a real or perceived threat to their position of loftiness, so even when a well-intended suggestion is put towards them, they may regard it as a criticism or a personal insult of their abilities. As a rule, they will deny the true reality of a situation, especially when it differs from their own perceived reality and particularly if it paints them in a negative light. They will discount those whose opinions and/or beliefs are contrary to their own, believing that "others" are less intelligent, beneath them or envious of them.

This type of abuser is easily slighted and capable of feeing a deep resentment towards those he/she believes are thwarting or challenging their career advancement or jeopardising their personal, social, or professional standing and/or relationships. They are unable to accept feelings of failure or defeat, so when confronted with an inevitable set-back whether personal or professional may respond with indignation or "righteous anger," believing that the world is unjust, rather than accept that they may be less than who they believe themselves to be.

To maintain this sense of superiority/grandiosity over others, the abuser is likely to enter a continued and possible unrelenting campaign of abuse aimed at undermining the confidence and self-esteem of the intended victim, while reminding them of their dependence on the abuser and/or re-enforcing who is in charge. If challenged, they usually engage in shaming, bullying and intimidatory tactics, however this can escalate into overt physical acts of violence particularly if they become enraged or are feeling vengeful.

Many victims of family and domestic abuse for example, will attest to the fact that their abuser has without doubt mercilessly verbally, emotionally, psychologically, and physically abused them with the intention to belittle, subjugate and intimidate, fuelling their need to feel dominant, in control and superior. Abusers who possess this defence will likely establish at least one primary source (can be multiple) from which they are able to derive their sense of superiority/grandiosity. It may be via their intimate partner relationship and/or other family members or through their peer, social or workplace environments and relationships.

Some abusers do not necessarily need to have a particular reason to exert superiority over a victim other than it has become an ingrained habit, a continued and assured source that feeds their need to feel imperious, self-important and in control. These abusers have an over-inflated self-confidence only needing to express their superiority (abusive behaviour) over others on an intermittent basis. However, there are other perpetrators whose insecurities require reassurance on a more consistent basis, needing to support the belief that they are in fact superior to those significant others in "their" life.

They need to reassert their supremacy over others through continuous acts of abuse to sustain their exalted position and fortify their dominant position. A challenge to the abuser's position of power by their victim (primary source) will not be tolerated or permitted and may be perceived as an attack or an attempt to dethrone the abuser from his/her seat of power in the relationship and a threat to what they believe to be their dominant and controlling position. This can trigger retaliation from the abuser equal to the perceived threat, which for some victims can have serious consequences to their wellbeing. An abuser's sense of superiority can also be challenged or threatened indirectly by an experience in another area of their life outside of their primary source.

For example, let us assume that the perpetrators feelings of superiority and/or grandiosity are derived primarily from the intimate-partner relationship and home environment then this is where they feel their most powerful, in control and confident. However conversely, they may be experiencing the complete opposite in another area of their life perhaps a workplace or social environment where the sense of superiority/grandiosity is either non-existent or unattainable. Let us now assume that in this environment, the abuser is experiencing opposite and adverse emotions such as mediocrity, inadequacy, or inferiority, triggering a strong need to reassure themselves that they are who they think are and compelling them to reassert their superiority/grandiosity with their primary source where they know they can easily re-gain feeling powerful and in control.

Being resentful, envious, or covetous of the intelligence and/or success of either an intimate partner, peer or work colleague is common by those who believe they are superior to others and is a prime motivator for their abusive actions. The abuser will be struck with a deep need to belittle, undermine, and discredit any significant other person or persons who they believe are threat to their own feelings of superiority/grandiosity.

They like to believe that they are better than everyone they associate with and tend to boast about their skills, abilities, achievements, and physical attributes sometimes under the guise of humour. The most noted significant misconception they hold of themselves is that they think themselves to be smarter than everyone they associate with, believing that they are intellectually more superior. Criminals typically are afflicted with the belief that they are consummate and more cunning than the authorities; however, ironically it seems that prisons are full of criminals with this affliction.

Feelings of grandiosity lead the abuser to think that they are special or unique in some way, they may boast of future achievements or exaggerate their personal qualities or undertake unrealistic and ambitious projects and then find themselves unable to complete them. Grandiosity can also engender feelings of omnipotence (to feel godlike) causing the abuser to commit risk-taking offenses and to behave in an unrestrained manner as they are unable to properly anticipate danger and do not fear the consequences. They feel powerful, untouchable and think themselves above the law and therefore unstoppable, remember their "superior intellect" allows them the luxury to think they have everyone fooled.

The need to avoid shame, guilt or remorse is at the heart of nearly all defensive action whether it is consciously or unconsciously triggered

For most of us, experiencing healthy levels of remorse, shame and/or guilt will act as a behavioural yardstick letting us know if we have overstepped a boundary and harmed another. These emotions help us to hold ourselves accountable for our actions and tempers our behaviour towards others, however for an abuser, these emotions either do not exist or are avoided at all costs, permitting the abuser to commit unconscionable acts of abuse. The ability for an abuser to feel real shame, guilt, or remorse towards others or for their own actions is minimal and for many non-existent.

The inability to allow themselves to feel these emotions will have stemmed from earlier personal, negative life experiences and is a considered to be a defence against feeling disempowered and vulnerable while protecting them from experiencing undesirable feelings. This defence likely would have come into being at some point during the abuser's early childhood or adolescent emotional and psychological developmental years, emerging when they were faced with experiencing overwhelming emotions that they were unprepared for and not mature enough to resolve in a healthy manner.

Some experiences can be viewed by the "psyche" as catastrophic causing us to react in a defensive manner to protect ourselves from a real or perceived attack to our psychological and emotional stability and at the same time triggering the need to protect against a fracture to an immature and fragile ego-self. One way in which we attempt to circumvent re-experiencing distressing emotions is through avoidance, (the need to avoid destabilising emotions at all cost). It can be activated either as an automated unconscious response or a conscious response, however the aim is the same, and the intention is to avoid unpleasant feelings, thoughts or any personal moral censorship that may hinder our objectives. It comes into play for an abuser when the overwhelming emotions threaten to undermine his/her self-confidence, self-esteem or when it induces feelings of vulnerability.

Any threat to derail the established dysfunctional psychological and/or emotional status-quo must be avoided at all costs especially if it interferes with an abuser's goals, needs, or desires. The abuser may respond with several varied defences not only to avoid uncomfortable emotions and thoughts but also to avoid answerability for their abusive actions.

For example, an abuser may employ the unconscious automated defence of "dissociation" which causes them to unconsciously "split off" from feeling mode into all thinking mode or from thinking mode into all feeling mode, by-passing those emotions or thoughts that may temper their behaviour before it has an opportunity to take root. When the defence kicks in, the abuser can act without morality or feeling, with a single-minded purposefulness, lacking the ability to reflect over their past actions and thereby avoid shame, guilt, or remorse. Another defensive measure commonly used by perpetrators of abuse to avoid these uncomfortable emotions is to use of "deflection" which is a reflexive tactic that aids in the evasion of answerability and the possible unwanted emotions and thoughts that accompany wrongful behaviour. This is achieved by the abuser vehemently avoiding taking responsibility for themselves or their actions, deflecting by blaming others or alternately they may deflect by playing the victim themselves. There are many perpetrators who believe themselves to be a victim in a crime or act of abuse that they themselves have perpetrated. Some have mastered the art of deflection by turning the tables on the one who is challenging their behaviour by employing an attack rather than defend tactic, by challenging the challengers' credibility and/or undermining their confidence with insults and disparaging remarks.

An abuser that possesses a reasonable level of social and cognitive intelligence will tend to fit into the "higher functioning" category, (refer to higher functioning abusers p14) they understand the importance of showing a modicum of shame, guilt or remorse to others when needed even if they remain unaffected themselves. However, it will be performed for self-serving reasons only, guilt, shame and remorse can be turned on and off like a tap and is mostly drawn upon when they need to manipulate others for their own gain. Perhaps they need to portray remorse to the authorities in order to reduce the severity of sentencing for a crime they committed or maybe a guilty party is caught committing adultery and needs to show contrition to appease or manipulate the injured partner.

Even though predators and abusers possess a limited or underdeveloped emotional range, it does not mean that they cannot quite successfully learn to mimic the emotions they know are expected of them by others in society. Abusers who lack reasonable social and cognitive intelligence are in the second category and considered to be "low functioning" abusers, (refer to lower functioning abusers – p14). They cannot easily manipulate others or a situation to their advantage and are unable to mimic or draw on emotions such as shame, guilt, or remorse as they may have no remembered experience of or understanding of these emotions. This type of abuser cannot hide their intent or behaviour and is very visible as a result, they usually act without restraint or consequence led by their baser instincts and needs.

Whether high or low functioning, both types of abusers can commit the most heinous crimes imaginable without conscience. We must consider every abuser an individual as to whether they have the capacity for rehabilitation or possess the real desire to redeem themselves can only be determined by how early in childhood they were wounded, the severity of the wounding and length of time that have lived their life with core fallibilities. However, the probability of any significant enough psychological and emotional rehabilitation is quite low particularly for sadistic, narcissistic, or psychopathic/sociopathic abusers, hence the term "repeat offenders."

Recognising an Abuser

Let us first establish that you are not likely to recognise an abuser simply by their appearance, vocation, or public persona as is currently evidenced in the news with allegations and/or convictions against high profile predators and abusers of sexual and predatory misconduct and abuse. The truth is we have predators and abusers in powerful and influential positions using their popularity, position, power, money, or a combination of all four to either hide behind and/or to manipulate and intimidate with the aim of avoiding retributive justice. Abusers can be found across all levels of our familial, social, workplace, political and religious arenas and they are not defined by age, gender, race, culture, religion, social status, political standing, or sexual orientation. They can be a high-income earner or a low-income earner, highly educated or uneducated, appear to be a respected member of the community such as a politician, doctor or teacher or they might be your average "Joe" such as a desk clerk or sales person. They can be your employer, your co-worker, your close friend, your neighbour, your teacher, your sibling, your parent, or your grandparent. In other words, they can embody anyone in our society making it very possible that we likely cross paths with abusers and potential abusers in our daily life.

However, without doubt abusers have specific, habitually defining behaviours that can be placed into sub-categories that are identifiable. Many abusers will through default use specific familiar manipulative, controlling and coercive mediums to either attain new victims or control existing victims. These modes of behaviour have been tried and tested by the abuser and have worked successfully for them in the past, however how they choose to operate will vary with each individual. There are many categories of predators, abusers and bullies whose needs, wants and methods will vary according to the level of emotional, psychological, social, and cognitive intelligence that they and the intended victim possesses.

Following is a list of the various types of Predators, Abusers and Bullies and how they operate.

The Bully

I think it would be fair to say that bullying would be one of the most widespread forms of abuse in any society in the world today encompassing a range of destructive and damaging behaviours which extend from being mild at one end to violently abusive at the other. It occurs in our intimate, familial, social, and working relationships, environments, and organisations, perpetrated by people who we trust, respect and even love. Bullying may be easy to recognise when it is overt in its nature taking the form of obvious behaviours such as verbal abuse, physical intimidation, or physical violence. However, even though these are methods known to be principally used by bullies, there are many who indulge in covert (concealed) forms of bullying, taking the form of manipulative, coercive and passive aggressive tactics. This type pf bullying is insidious in nature and is commonly used by perpetrators because it can be difficult for victims to discern or detect and is often a very effective method in which a bully can achieve whatever it is, they intended. The bully who is adept at using passive aggressive manoeuvres to manipulate, intimidate and control others will most surely be using these same narcissistic and self-serving methods in their personal, social, and professional lives, particularly to further a career, gain personal popularity or improve social status or political standing. They will have a personal history that has taught them how to use this instrument of persuasion and they successfully and advantageously will without doubt justify and or rationalise injurious behaviours towards others, holding the belief that they are deserving and entitled, giving them permission to victimise vulnerable targets.

Bullying behaviours are likely to have developed in early childhood or adolescence as a result of abusive and dysfunctional parenting/caretaking and/or damaging and adverse social and schooling environments. These early negative experiences engendered psychological and emotional developmental issues that reflect negative self-image, attachment insecurities and an inability regulate emotions such as disappointment, frustration, and anger.

Resentment, jealousy, and envy drive bullying behaviour and are based on the bullies own unconscious, disowned, and unresolved feelings of anxiety, fear, unworthiness, helplessness, inadequacy and/or shame and guilt. To compensate for their short-comings and to mask a rather fragile ego, they develop an exaggerated or inflated ego-ideal of themselves, which does not cope well with disappointment or failure whether it is real or perceived. They may display feelings of disdain and contempt towards their victim in order to fortify their self-worth and to counter their underlying feelings of inadequacy and/or powerlessness.

They may engage in using covert and subversive behaviours not easily discernible by their victims or obvious overt behaviours in the form of threatening, demeaning and subjugating words and actions. Regardless of whether a bully is overt or covert with their actions, they intentionally target victims that display physical anomalies and/or emotional and psychological weaknesses. It is important to note that not all bullies should be characterised as coming from backgrounds that reflect a visibly abusive upbringing, whose current actions reflect a negative attitude towards authority figures and societies constraints in general. Some bullies may reflect success and popularity among their peers or work colleagues, possibly coming from backgrounds whose parents were over-indulgent or narcissistic in nature however, nevertheless just as dysfunctional.

For some bullies, their actions and interactions are a way of life inured in a belief system that has its origins based on mantras such as "all is fair in love and war," "it's a survival of the fittest" or "they (the victim) deserve it" and so on, endorsing and/or validating selfish and adverse practices. The need to achieve their goal, overrides feelings of empathy, understanding and reason giving them license to act as they please. As intimated earlier bullies often engage in bullying behaviours as an overcompensation to counteract negative and underlying feelings of powerlessness, failure, inadequacy, and worthlessness etc. For example, those who suffer from feelings of shame and incompetency can often project shaming behaviour (bullying) onto others to avoid their own personal feelings of shame.

However, they may also engage in bullying tactics as an overcompensation if they feel bullied themselves in some other area of their life. For example, a person who feels dominated, controlled or inadequate in their home or personal life may compensate by becoming the bully in another area of life such as their work environment or vice-versa. Many bullies exhibit coercive, controlling, and manipulative behaviours in order to gain or maintain power, dominance, and control in their social, workplace or intimate relationships and environments, and to appease the need to feel superior and/or grandiose. However, there are some bullies who solely indulge in passive aggressive behaviours who may be in part ignorant of the seriousness of the harmful impact that their actions can have upon the victim it is directed toward.

This type of bully is extremely self-absorbed and so their world is centred solely towards having their own needs met, without thought to others but also without conscious malice. They tend to see themselves in a positive light and because of their narcissistically driven tendencies, they think they are a good person, often harbouring ulterior motives while appearing to be kind and helpful or offering to do good deeds. Social acceptance, personal and professional success and keeping up appearances means everything to them and is of the upmost importance, guiding their selfish actions.

Do not be fooled by a bully's disguise, they can appear to be meek, quiet, or shy in temperament or they can be the opposite appearing to be gregarious, outspoken, and confident. Bullies never take responsibility for their actions and have a habit of excusing, minimising, justifying, and rationalising their negative and adverse actions. Bullying is not limited to an individual versus and individual, it can, and often is perpetrated by a "collective" or group of individuals, it may be in the form of a circle of one's "workplace or social peers" or it may be an assembly of strangers referred to as a "mob." In this scenario, the primary or "head bully" enlists the aid of one or more "lieutenants" to support them in their endeavours, giving the head bully an inflated feeling of importance, power, and omnipotence. This type of bullying also referred to as "mobbing," it is common-place in medium to large institutions and workplaces where "speaking out" is frowned upon, ignored, or actively discouraged.

These types of cultures are commonly found to exist in organisations such as private or public, schools, colleges, universities, social clubs, sporting clubs or workplaces, social groups, prisons, and neighbourhoods anywhere where there is a consistent gathering of people. When the bullying takes place in the presence of a large group of by-standers (witnesses), it may lend support to the bully's illusion that they have the backing of the majority, particularly when the witnesses remain silent. Quite often, witnesses will not speak out against the bully, because they feel intimidated and do not wish to draw attention to themselves for fear of becoming the bully's and/or the bully's accomplice's next target.

Bullying is not a single act of abuse, nor is it social rejection or dislike. It involves deliberate and repeated attempts by another individual, a group of individuals, an organisation, or an institution, who may or may not be known to the victim, whose aim is to cause physical, emotional, psychological, or social harm to another or to create dislike of the victim in others in the form or "social bullying."

The motivation that drives bullying may include any or all the following:

- To feel powerful.
- To gain attention.
- To alleviate boredom.
- For financial gain.
- To attain or maintain a strategic or superior hierarchical, familial, social, workplace or political position.
- To appear to be powerful to others for strategic reasons.
- To attain or maintain dominance and/or control over an individual/s or environment (home, workplace or social).
- In response to feelings of jealousy or envy towards an individual or group.
- Because of ones bigoted, racist, or sexist beliefs against an individual, group or nation.
- To compensate for one's personal disowned feelings of anger, guilt, shame, or unworthiness by projecting these feelings onto others.
- To satisfy a perverse need to feel superior or grandiose.
- For retaliatory reasons in response to a perceived threat.

The Social Bully

Social bullying also referred to as "relational aggression" is a more subtle form of bullying as it is generally accomplished in a covert (veiled) manner and therefore not always easy to detect. It may be defined as a series of repeated negative behaviours by a member of a group (the bully), aimed at socially isolating another member of that same group (the victim) from others in the group. They may also hope to ruin or damage the victim's personal or professional credibility or reputation, devalue them in the eyes of their peer group and/or undermine their confidence, self-esteem, and self-worth. This type of bullying can occur in families, mothers' groups, social cliques, religious assemblies, the workplace, anywhere where people gather in consistent and familiar surroundings such as, educational institutions, professional training facilities or clubs.

Social bullying is perpetrated by someone who has reached an age where they understand how to use manipulative, coercive and subversive tactics to achieve a desired outcome and to get their needs met. It has shown itself to be the most popular and successful form of bullying as the perpetrators can hide behind façades of innocence or ignorance, claiming that they do not know who started the rumours or cannot remember where they came by the defamatory information. When they are caught out, they may use the excuse that they did not mean anything by it, or they were "joking" or what they did or said was being taken out of context, to negate or minimise their abusive behaviour. Their refusal to accept responsibility acts to further perpetuate the bullying by implying that the victim is being overly sensitive or deserving of the bullying.

There are also some social bullies who are careful to cover their tracks, not wanting to let anyone know that they are the instigator of the bullying and so they use their peers (other members of the group) to which the victim also belongs, to perpetrate the bullying in their stead. In this way, and if it suits, the instigator can deny any involvement in the bullying, feign ignorance, blame someone else, and/or avoid punishment.

For some, the preservation of the anonymity allows the instigator to avoid detection and maintain a relationship with the victim, particularly if they work with or for the victim wherein the anonymity may be essential. For others, the anonymity provides them with an opportunity to be up close and personal with victim to witness the effects of the bullying, simply because they receive a perverse kind of enjoyment from the victim's distress and it gives them a sense of power over the victim. Regardless of the reason for remaining anonymous, the instigator is in a position to exploit the situation taking advantage of the victim's vulnerability.

Social bullying may be achieved through several means:

- Social exclusion/isolation – by ignoring or excluding the victim from social gatherings and events, and/or encouraging others in the peer group to the same.
- Spreading defamatory or embarrassing rumours and gossip – this is an attempt to destroy the victim's social status, peer relationships and to undermine their self-esteem. It may be perpetrated either in person or via electronic means (cyber or mobile phone).
- Embarrassing or shaming – sharing confidential information, by making public, privately disclosed personal and sensitive information about the victim.
- Taunting or insulting – directly or by using the pretence of a "joke" with underlying malicious and derogatory intent. Perpetrated either in person or via electronic means (cyber or mobile phone).
- Embarrassing or shaming – deliberately embarrassing or shaming the victim directly in front of others.

The Student/Teacher Bully

Student or "schoolyard" bullying is not limited to an age group and may be perpetrated by children (male or female) who are as young as pre-schoolers, progressing through to primary school, high-school, college, or university. Children, adolescents, and young adults of all ages, may participate in bullying; however, it may vary in degree in the level of injury and violence perpetrated according to the age and maturity of the bully. Bullying behaviour from those whose ages range from pre-pubescence to early adolescence is usually overt (unconcealed) in nature and usually takes the form of verbal abuse such as taunting, ridiculing, threatening, or insulting a victim and/or includes some of the lesser forms of physical abuse such as pushing and hair pulling. The behaviour, however, may escalate as the children grow into their mid to late teens becoming steadily more aggressive with physically harmful behaviours that may include biting, scratching, punching, slapping, kicking, shoving, tripping, spitting at, throwing objects at, or pouring liquids over a victim.

When children enter their late teens or young adulthood, their bullying behaviours may be perpetrated both "overtly" (openly) or "covertly" (secretly) as they are "maturing" into an age where they can think about and plan their actions. At this stage, a bully may engage in the more serious bullying crimes with behaviours such as stalking, violent physical abuse, intimidation, and threats to commit violence, inappropriate touching, sexual harassment, and sexual assault. Some of these bullies operate on their own without the support of a group, perhaps being a bit of a loner themselves or feeling as if they are a social outcast. However, most bullies tend to operate in a small group or a pack, giving the members in the group/pack, particularly the senior members a sense of importance, power, and omnipotence and at the same time supporting their need to feel superior and dominant. However, as mentioned earlier, the bullying behaviour is simply masking their true unacknowledged, underlying feelings of shame, fear, envy, jealousy, unworthiness, inferiority, failure, powerlessness, and unresolved rage.

Unfortunately, educational institutions are still facing troubling numbers of "sexual and gender-based bullying" (including transgender and non-binary victims). This is still occurring despite the progress modern society has made and the increase in awareness of the issues surrounding sexual equality, sexual abuse, and the acceptance of those that exist outside the gender "norm." Sexual and gender-based bullying is defined as "any adverse and harmful behaviour whether physical or non-physical that is based on a victims, sexuality or gender." This type of bullying can occur in primary school among pubescent children onwards to students participating in college and university courses. It may include behaviours such as unwanted touching, sexual assault, being forced or coerced to witness or submit to acts of a sexual nature or being ridiculed and shamed through the circulation of sexually explicit photos via social media (computer or mobile-phone).

When students have reached an age where they have come to understand that if they are caught their evident and unconcealed bullying actions will incur personal detrimental consequences for them (in the form of punishment or social exclusion), they may elevate their bullying tactics to include secretive, unsuspected and camouflaged forms of bullying known as "social bullying" (refer to social bullying p66) which is a more surreptitious form of bullying usually perpetrated via electronic means i.e., social media forums. Their aim is to undermine, ridicule, humiliate, torment, or punish their intended victim and at the same time avoid direct confrontation by hiding behind their anonymity.

Below is a list of the most common "overt" and "covert" bullying tactics used by school bullies to harm their intended victim:

- Leaving someone out on purpose – either directly by telling the victim they are not wanted in the group or by indirect means, telling other children to exclude the victim from the group or walking away or ignoring the victim when they attempt to join the group.
- Telling other children not to be friends with the victim – either indirectly using manipulatory tactics such as telling others in the group that you do not understand why they would want to be friends with the victim or

directly by telling the victim that you and the rest of the group do not want to be friends with them anymore.

- Social exclusion – either directly by not inviting the victim to social events such as gatherings and parties or indirectly by encouraging other peers not invite the victim to their social events.
- Spreading rumours about the victim – either directly through word of mouth or indirectly via social media and mobile phone messaging, with the intent to malign their character, damage their reputation or social standing, undermine their academic or sporting achievements or jeopardise their personal relationships.
- Verbal and physical harassment and persecution – embarrassing, humiliating or shaming the victim publicly with the intent to denigrate and malign the victim's character by directly mimicking, making fun of, or playing nasty jokes on the victim or indirectly by enlisting the aid of others to mimic, make fun of or play nasty jokes on the victim.
- Written and/or visual harassment and persecution via electronic means – by posting written or visually derogatory, shaming, or debasing remarks and images about the victim with the intent to denigrate and malign the victim's character through social media platforms or mobile phone messaging.
- Stalking the victim – either physically by following the victim before, during and after school hours and/or electronically via the internet.
- Physical intimidation – to directly insult, intimidate, dominate, humiliate, or subjugate a victim through menacing stand-over tactics with the threat to commit violence.
- Outright violence – using physical violence to abuse the victim either individually or jointly by enlisting the aid of another individual or a group.
- Sexual harassment/persecution/assault – by committing acts of sexual abuse such as, unwanted touching, sexual harassment, sexual coercion (forced to witness acts of a sexual nature), sexual assault (including rape) or being victim to sexual blackmail or shaming via the exposure of sexually explicit photos or audio-visuals via electronic means (internet and mobile phone) on public forums via social media platforms.

Bullying at school is not confined to students bullying students, it may also include students bullying parents, teachers, staff, and other authority figures or conversely it may be teachers and staff bullying students. Teachers may be perpetrators of bullying in either of two ways, they may observe and ignore (failing to act on what they are witnessing) or they may be the perpetrator of the bullying directly themselves. Teachers who mistreat students do so because they have a past that includes their own dysfunctional childhood where they were once a victim of abuse or a witness to abuse themselves, who are now re-enacting bullying behaviours to counteract residual underlying feelings of inadequacy and powerlessness. Other abusive teachers are subject to their narcissistic, psychopathic, or sadistic character traits and simply enjoy feeling powerful, dominant and in control, they relish using tactics such as public humiliation of students in the classroom, auditorium or on the sports field.

They may exploit a victim's vulnerabilities by exposing a real or perceived ineptitude or incapacity so that onlookers, particularly the victim's peers may hear or bear witness to their humiliation. Other tactics employed by teachers may include disclosure of sensitive private or confidential information about the victim they are targeting, to other teachers, students, or parents of students in the form of gossip. They may verbally berate a student with the intention to denigrate, undermine or embarrass a student under the guise of "constructive criticism," or they may engage in out-right physical intimidatory and threatening behaviours.

Some teachers fixate on a student for seemingly no apparent reason, looking for a reason to punish them, by giving them low grades, humiliating them, or making an example of them in front of their classmates. This is likely the result of the teacher's conscious and/or unconscious projection onto the student of their own unresolved feelings of anger, disappointment, defectiveness, and shame triggered by a past dysfunctional youth and/or subsequent experiences of failure and disillusionment. Some teachers may be experiencing feelings of prejudice, jealousy or vindictiveness towards a student and will try to inhibit, suppress, or undermine the student who is showing the promise of excelling artistically, academically, musically, or physically through their sporting prowess.

This is a result of the teacher's inability to witness, accept and cope with the student's natural talent and potential for success that they had at one time aspired to and never achieved. There also exists those teachers who at some time earlier in their life had experienced feeling unattractive, unpopular or who were socially inept who project feelings of envy, resentment, and spite towards a student simply because the student is especially physically attractive and/or highly socially popular.

Conversely, teachers can become targets of bullying by aggressive, disgruntled, and entitled parents and students. Teachers are often made the target of bullying by parents who believe their child has not been marked fairly, failed a subject, asked to repeat a subject or whole year of schooling, not chosen for a significant classroom or school role, or not chosen to participate in a coveted sporting team, music, or drama role. Parents will either verbally berate, physically intimidate, consistently harass the teacher or they will use subversive tactics by entering a campaign that may involve spreading malicious and denigrating rumours to undermine the teacher's credibility.

Students will do the same, however they tend to use cyberspace to attack or humiliate a teacher via social media, some posting surreptitiously taken classroom videos to post on-line. Other common bullying techniques used by students is to; cause disruption in the classroom by creating chaos in order to distress the teacher, verbally abuse the teacher with threats, insults and taunts in and out of the classroom, physically abuse a teacher (spit at and commit acts of violence onto), vandalise a teacher's personal property particularly their cars (scratching, denting or causing flat-tyres) or they may stalk a teacher either online or physically follow them out of school hours.

The Work Place Bully

Workplace bullying may present itself in either an overt or covert manner, perpetrated by just about anyone in any working environment and is defined as a "consistent pattern of mistreatment in the workplace that may be psychologically, emotionally and/or physically harmful" to another. The bullying may be perpetrated by business owners, directors, managers, senior or supervisory staff, general staff or by co-workers. It may be found in any field of employment and is not defined by, or limited to someone's gender, age group, race, disability, sexual orientation or religious, cultural, or political disposition.

Workplace bullying can occur in any environment where workers co-habit on a regular basis such as an office, warehouse, manufacturing plant or on a job site and may involve two or more people. There are several divisions and classes of worker, however, for all intents and purposes let us refer to the two main divisions of the "white collar worker" and the "blue collar worker." White collar workers are also known as the "shirt and tie set" and are usually employed in professional, desk, managerial, or administrative work, who as a rule do not perform strenuous manual labour.

Blue collar workers are identified as those who perform some type of physical or manual labour, and may be employed in industries such as mining, maintenance, building/construction, agriculture, manufacturing, and service (including firefighters and police officers). Workplace bullying perpetrated by blue collar workers is more likely to be overt in nature and tends to be centred around sexual harassment and racial or gender identity discriminatory actions, with females being the most prevailing targets as these industries are predominately male. These bullies are known to openly, verbally racially or sexually harass, taunt, ridicule, debase and insult a victim and are likely to be physically abusive with behaviours that include menacing intimidation, physical sexual harassment, and assault, shoving, tripping, playing jokes on or hazing.

The other prime target of bullying in the "blue collar" sector are apprentices (regardless of gender), who have had to deal with being scapegoats for poor performance or negligence by incompetent supervisors or "supposed" experienced senior staff. They are frequently made targets of nasty, embarrassing and humiliating "practical jokes" or "initiation pranks," perpetrated by their co-workers and ignored or sanctioned by senior staff. These acts of abuse are all performed under the guise of "harmless fun" or regarded as a requisite "toughening up" or "acceptance into the crew" processes. There are many "senior" experienced blue-collar workers particularly tradesmen who see bullying of apprentices as mandatory to allow them the "right of passage" into their industry.

However, workplace bullying perpetrated by white collar workers is more likely to be covert in nature and therefore not easily detectable and often missed by supervisory or senior staff, even though it might be common knowledge by many others throughout the organisation. However, conversely, it may also be perpetrated by supervisory or senior staff or by business or company owners. White collar bullies are known to be self-serving individuals who possess narcissistic tendencies, they will go to great lengths to fulfil their personal needs or to attain their professional goals. They lack empathy for others, using considerable charm to manipulate and/or undermine their fellow-workers in order to avoid any work-related negative repercussions and have no qualms throwing a co-worker or underling under the bus.

White collar workers with high career aspirations who are lacking in ability, knowledge and experience may resort to underhanded exploitative tactics to fast-track job advancement or to gain a senior position. Workplace friendships will be strategic, in that there will always be a personal and/or professional ulterior motive for the relationship, to either further their career or use this person as a scapegoat without them realising. There are many workplace bullies in positions of power who ruthlessly abuse their positions to take advantage of an employee and/or undermine those working under them whom they may feel threatened by. There is also another type of abusive behaviour that workplace bullies consistently and advantageously engage in referred to as "workplace gas-lighting," this is when a work colleague or a more senior staff member (manager/supervisor) purposefully invalidates what the victim believes to be true, causing them to question the facts, their capabilities and themselves.

It is found to be commonplace in many work environments, whether in small business or much larger industry, it is a cunning and devious type of bullying that is not easy to detect and very difficult to regulate. The abuser's aim is to undermine or usurp a victim (work colleague or employee) causing them to question themselves, their credibility and their actions in a way that is detrimental to their career. The perpetrator uses subtle and scheming techniques that are designed to exclude, discredit, subvert and invalidate the victim and their abilities whilst destabilising their confidence and causing them to experience self-doubt and confusion. Gaslighting by a perpetrator who is in a position of authority or power is particularly disturbing because it gives them added manipulative and coercive influence over the victim and the workplace environment.

Gaslighting in the workplace may include any or all the following behaviours:

- Outright denial of the truth and/or telling lies – The abuser never takes responsibility for their mistakes however; they will take the credit for work completed by someone-else.
- Deny making agreements or promises in order to get a co-worker or underling to put in extra time either working for them, or instead of them, and they never pay up.
- Fly off the handle – If challenged, they will lash out at the challenger, to deflect responsibility for their own laziness, negligence, or wrongdoing.
- Show a modicum of positive reinforcement – When they realise that someone, they depend on in the workplace is showing signs that they have had enough poor treatment and may leave their employ, the "gas-lighter" will turn on their charming/manipulative side offering them enticements (more pay or time-off – that may never come to fruition) or just enough praise to keep them from leaving.

Bullying in the workplace creates an unhealthy and undesirable work environment and will undoubtedly lead to a drop in work performance and productivity, a decline in morale, an increase in employee absence (sick leave), high staff turnover and create an atmosphere of mistrust and a culture of secret alliances. Victims of bullying suffer from high levels of fear, stress, anxiety, and depression which inevitably leads to an increased rate in the incidence of physical illness, depression, eating, anxiety and behavioural disorders, substance abuse, addiction and in the worst-case scenarios suicide.

The Cyber Bully – Internet Bullying

Out of all the advanced technologies that exists today, the "Internet" has become the most integral, and may almost be considered the life force of our modern-day society bringing with it a positive and negative impact. The internet has unintentionally become a medium for what appears to be prolific passive aggressive bullying and it is extremely difficult although not impossible to monitor or at least reduce the incidence of this type of predatorial and abusive activity. Cyber space provides an avenue for bullies such as "internet trolls" to bask in their anonymity without fear of consequence or retribution allowing them to perpetrate bullying with the safety of distance and within the comfort of their own homes.

They will use social media with the intent to victimise, bully, harass, torment, belittle, castigate, undermine, and manipulate, they can be any age, sex, race, religion, culture, or sexual orientation. I am sure there are many social media bullies out there who lack the cognitive and emotional intelligence to fully comprehend the harmful impact that their actions perpetrate on their victims and the fact that it can inflict seriously injurious and irrevocable psychological and emotional impairment.

As soon as an individual places themselves on the internet in either a personal or professional capacity however necessary, they are at risk of opening themselves and their business to unwanted scrutiny, trolls, and dissatisfied clients. Using social media accounts to promote oneself and/or one's business for professional reasons makes sense and is almost essential in our current automated society, however it also exposes us and our businesses to the internet bully whose intention is to undermine, intimidate or belittle someone personally or professionally. If the bullying is for personal reasons, then the abuse may well be a projection of the abuser towards the victim, stemming from the perpetrator's own feelings of inadequacy, jealousy, or envy.

However, if the bullying is for professional reasons, then it may stem from the abuser's intention to sabotage or undermine their business opposition. It is therefore important to remain extremely vigilant for this type of criminal activity and make it a priority to report it to the appropriate authorities immediately. It is due to the lack of reporting of cyber bullying that we are not garnering accurate figures on the incidence of these crimes and therefore as a society, we are not responding with equal action.

Cyber-harassment or cyber-stalking is a crime that can have legal consequences and may involve hefty fines and/or incarceration depending on the seriousness of the offence. This includes mobile phones as well as computers whether it is via email, text message or through social media websites such as face-book and Instagram. Cyber-space has become an avenue for bullies wishing to hide behind their obscurity, using an indirect means to vent their dissatisfaction with themselves and/or their lives by projecting it onto others without having to face them.

Internet Predators

As much as the internet is used for legitimate, honest, positive, uplifting, informative and connective reasons, it is also used for the opposite reasons in the form of illegal, dishonest, negative, predatory, and abusive activities. The internet has become rife with criminals either looking for potential victims with financial gain in mind, via illegal means or they are predators searching for potential victims with more evil personal intent, such as domestic and family abusers, bullies, sexual offenders, paedophiles, stalkers, sex traffickers, cults, and adulterers.

The internet provides a perfect environment for every perverse type of predator to use to source potential victims or monitor and control existing victims. It provides them with a certain degree of safety and concealment while they cultivate relationships with intended unsuspecting targets. These abusers are quite confident and brazen in their search for prey as they have access to an inexhaustible number of potential victims and it simply becomes a numbers game for them. Online predators can be anyone they think you want them to be, their advantage is that they are prolific sociopathic liars who possess a series of practised scripts that include questions that can illicit information enabling them to determine how they will approach their intended target.

The experienced predator is adept at garnering important information such as age, emotional and psychological maturity, cognitive intelligence, and level of life experience while paying particular attention to a victim's current personal problems or issues. All the while, they are planning how they are going to exploit the target with the information they have collected. They purposefully identify with the victim, giving them attention, feigning interest, and understanding in their problems, offering empathy and support while establishing a rapport, and cultivating a climate of trust. These perpetrators zero in on targets that have inadvertently exposed a psychological, emotional, physical, intellectual, or financial vulnerability.

Online predators who are successfully obtaining victims via chat rooms and dating sites on the internet are highly skilful and can hide their true intent. They would have honed the necessary specific duplicitous skills over time, through trial and error and as a result have gained a great deal of experience with grooming techniques used to disarm, charm, and manipulate potential victims. Many of these predators can detect inexperience, naivety or innocence in a target and use this to ferret out vulnerabilities with the sole purpose of using these fallibilities to their advantage to gain the victims confidence and trust.

Internet predator's lure unsuspecting prey by giving them the impression that they possess the much-desired personality traits that victims who are searching for an intimate relationship, a friendship or who feel lonely, misunderstood, or different are likely to want. They provide the victim with what they discern the victim needs, such as focused attention, caring, empathy, sympathy, understanding, kindness and consideration whilst at the same time cultivating a relationship, intimating that they are harmless and lulling the victim into a false sense of security.

Following is a list of the types victims who are priority targets for Internet predators because have expressed one or more of the following vulnerabilities.

- Feel lonely – perhaps a single parent, an elderly person, a widow, or widower.
- Feel as if they are social outcast – these victims feel different from, or misunderstood by their family, peers and/or society in general.
- Have few or no friends – may be shy, introverted or socially awkward or inept.
- Are separated from family and friends – may be isolated from family and friends by geographical distance.
- Are estranged from their family and therefore are less likely to have protection or someone who will take an interest in their wellbeing.
- Are homeless – these targets may be anyone, however the majority are adolescents or young adults.
- Have little life experience – victims who are sheltered and perhaps naïve, including young children and adolescents.

- Are currently or have been a victim in the past of bullying either at school, home, workplace or socially.
- Are currently or have been a victim of abuse, whether a random act or ongoing abuse (sexual and/or non-sexual).
- Are grieving the loss of a loved one.
- Possess an eating, behavioural or anxiety disorder.
- Suffer from depression.
- Possess a physical or mental handicap/disability.
- Need financial aid.
- Possess an addiction – this may include sexual, gambling, alcohol, and drugs (licit or illicit).

The Abuser in a Position of Authority
This Abuser is in a Position of Power and/or Influence (social, religious, cultural, or political)

This type of abuser uses their power, fame, political, religious, or societal influence to manipulate, bully, dominate and/or control a victim. They may have financial or legal backing or they may be a high-profile figure such as a politician, religious leader, sporting hero or a famous movie, television, or music star. These perpetrators are likely to possess feelings of superiority, grandiosity and omnipotence drawing on their fame and status to manipulate a situation to their benefit. These types of abusers inhabit a world where they have been made to feel special, leading them to believe that they are powerful and/or invincible and beyond societal law. Who, if caught committing a wrongdoing, they will without doubt use their considerable influence, power, or authority to manipulate, coerce invalidate, discredit the legitimacy of, or intimidate a victim into being silent, should the victim decide to take action against them. These abusers possess an air of supremacy and are typically narcissistic, believing that that they are untouchable.

The Unassuming Abuser

Most people when they hear the term predator, abuser or bully conjure up images that suggest that the perpetrator possesses some notable if not unpleasant physical traits that sets them apart from others in the community. In reality however, nothing could be further from the truth in fact, predators, abusers, and bullies who have thrived over long periods of time have used their obscurity to their advantage, cleverly hiding behind seemingly innocuous and unassuming facades. They may be pleasant, charming, act polite, be helpful and friendly or they may appear to be introverted, timid, reserved, and shy, either way they give the impression of being non-threatening. Perhaps it is the elderly neighbour next door, your quiet and shy work colleague or a happy-go-lucky friend, remember an abuser can embody any persona, displaying what they want the world to see, keeping their dark nature well hidden.

This type of abuser typifies a "wolf in sheep's clothing" and can be the most terrifying predator as they are able to lead a double life, carefully and purposefully separating out the private but dark, abusive, and criminal persona from their public non-threatening and unassuming persona. In fact, some of the most prolific killers and sexual predators in the nineteenth and twentieth centuries have managed to evade being caught, remaining active for incredibly long periods of time because of their carefully cultivated facades, blending into neighbourhoods, some with a family that had no idea that a monster lived in their midst. Perpetrators of domestic and family abuse must be counted among the most notably prevalent types of abusers in society today, many of whom have well-crafted public veneers, adept at separating their private world from their public world managing to conceal an abusive, dissolute, and malignant persona from extended family, friends, work colleagues, the community, and the authorities.

The Physically Attractive Abuser

This type of abuser has most certainly cultivated a charming persona over time to accompany their good looks, more than likely honing their manipulative skills from a very young age. They may appear to be attractive, captivating, and charismatic despite having hidden dark natures. Some have managed to acquire profound wealth and/or a successful career and lifestyle such as a business owner, political leader or a high-profile sport, music, or television industry personality. However, physically attractive, perhaps charming abusers may also come from lower socio-economic backgrounds also and they do not necessarily possess successful careers, great wealth, or lavish lifestyles in fact the opposite might be true for some who have simply relied on their good looks and charisma to attain their victims.

One must not be fooled by a person's appealing appearance and charismatic persona as it has the potential to hide a monster beneath the surface. An abuser (female or male) can be attractive to extremely attractive with an equally appealing physique, which they know gives them the possible advantage of standing out among their peers. As is typical of abusers who are possessed with good looks, they will have learned very early on in their youth how to use their good looks to entice intended victims. If you combine good looks with a "high functioning" (refer to p14), charming and manipulative character structure, then you have the potential for an accomplished predator.

The Domestic and Family Abuser
Includes all Intimate Relationships Regardless of Sexual Orientation

Next to bullying, domestic and family abuse could quite possibly be considered the most widespread of all abusive crimes facing society today. The crimes associated with family and domestic abuse can be the direct result of specific clinical conditions (mental illness) such as schizophrenia, paranoia bi-polar or borderline personality disorders. However, they are more often a direct result of dysfunctional childhood and adolescent upbringings and ingrained negative patterns of behaviour, that are based on personal ideologies rooted in gender inequality, misogyny and influenced by antiquated religious, social, and cultural beliefs. The other major attributing factor or cause of domestic abuse is substance abuse or addiction, most commonly drug, alcohol, sexual or gambling related, all of which aggravate, heighten, or provoke the abuser's actions.

Domestic and family abuse can occur in any relationship regardless of age, gender, sexual orientation, socio-economic status, social standing, religious orientation, or cultural background. It is not restricted to abuse occurring in the home between two people who are in an intimate relationship; it also includes conduct occurring outside the physical confines of the home. It can be perpetrated by any member of a family towards another member of that same family such as parent to child, adolescent to parent, sibling to sibling etc., and it includes those individuals who are estranged from each other (separated or divorced). Perpetrators of domestic abuse are like all other abusers with the same profile as I have discussed in earlier chapters sharing the same histories, character structures, defences, and patterns of behaviours. As their profile suggests, they can be anyone who perpetrates psychological, emotional, and physical abuse on another through, dominant, controlling, coercive, violent, and intimidating actions.

Please note; that even though there is a growing number of male victims in this category of abuse, it is widely globally acknowledged that women and children hold the highest statistics as victims of family and domestic abuse and homicide.

Perpetrators of domestic abuse are different to an abuser whose behaviours are solely motivated by a behavioural disorder or consumed by a substance abuse or addiction problem in that not all of them are completely at the mercy of their pathologies and addictions. There are many domestic and family abusers who can make calculated decisions about when, where and how they will perpetrate their abuse. This is demonstrated by the fact that they are not usually indiscriminately violent, showing that they have enough cognitive and social awareness not to expose their baser sides in public, allowing them to act with restraint in a community, workplace, or social environment. These perpetrators do not want to risk exposure to the outside world and will go to great lengths to ensure this does not occur. For this abuser, it is absolutely paramount that they maintain a façade to protect themselves so that they can continue on with their abusive activities behind the scenes without interruption or consequence.

Perpetrators of family and domestic abuse resent interference from outsiders particularly the authorities, other family members or family friends as it can weaken the position of dominance and control that they hold over their victim/s. This type of abuser is smart enough to fear law enforcement and the penal repercussions (incarceration) that may result should a victim act against them. However, they are not fearful enough to stop being abusive, in fact, "not getting caught" is a priority and motivates the abuser to act in a more devious and secretive manner to avoid detection. Perpetrators of domestic abuse like all human beings crave approval and acceptance from others and dislike, if not fear falling from grace or being ostracised and/or alienated from those who hold them in high regard or those whom they hold in high regard.

Exposure therefore can be particularly devastating for those abusers who need to maintain a popular or revered public persona that aids them financially, socially, or politically such as business owner, musician, artist, actor, politician, or religious leader etc. Many perpetrators of domestic abuse put an extended effort into cultivating and maintaining a public image that portrays them as appearing in a positive and/or successful light. They like to be thought of as being kind, caring, generous, pleasant, altruistic, non-threatening and incapable of committing violence towards those they say they love.

However, even though there are perpetrators of domestic and family abuse who are seemingly controlled and calculated and are able to show a modicum of restraint when abusing their victims, there are also those who cannot. As statistics reflect and according to Mission Australia (2018–2019) report on average, one male victim is killed per month, and one female victim is killed per week by a current or former partner. Some perpetrators of domestic violence show us that they possess the ability to exert control over their actions by making deliberate decisions about how, when and where they perpetrate abuse. They display this by:

- Being cognizant and controlled enough to choose where on a victim's body they will inflict the abuse so that it remains hidden from prying eyes, choosing specific areas of the body that they know can be covered by clothing and therefore not easily detectable.
- Being able to suddenly change behaviour from abusive to congenial in the middle of an abusive episode, if they are interrupted by a visitor or a phone call and then resume their abusive behaviour again afterwards.
- Being able to choose whether they wish to abuse the victim privately at home, or in a public place and/or in front of friends or family, should it suit them.

Those who commit domestic abuse share the same character traits as the "psychopathic/narcissistic abuser" (refer to p21–32) in that they project blame onto the victim and rarely take responsibility for their actions. They may accuse the victim of provoking them to act in an abusive manner towards them, justifying their actions by citing that the victim "pushed their buttons." By projecting the blame, they can shift accountability from themselves onto the victim to minimise or acquit their participation in the abusive event. They will rationalise their abusive behaviours, sometimes blaming extenuating circumstances such as I was drunk or stressed etc., suggesting that their actions were beyond their control. In cases of domestic and family abuse, the primary goal of the abuser is to gain control over a victim in order to fulfil the need to feel powerful and dominant.

These perpetrators operate under a wide spectrum of behaviours, which include being verbally, psychologically, emotionally, and physically abusive. A perpetrator will often use verbal and physical intimidation (bullying), including threats to commit violence to the victim or the victims' loved ones in order to gain or maintain submission from them and control over them. The abuser will engage in verbal abuse in the form of insults to belittle, demean, humiliate, and denigrate the victim to intimidate and undermine their self-esteem and confidence whilst giving the abuser the opportunity to vent their unresolved frustration and anger.

They will batter a victim with physical abuse through acts of violence such as shoving, slapping, punching, kicking, biting, choking, sexually assaulting, breaking bones, maiming, or murdering a victim. They will use deliberate manipulative and bullying tactics to consolidate supremacy over them, instil fear and feelings of helplessness and at the same time establish the victim's dependency on the abuser. This is achieved over time by slowly and systematically wearing down a victim's defences until they become compliant and pliant.

Some abusers like to use a strategy whereby they randomly "change the rules" or their expectations from the victim, causing the victim to experience constant anxiety and confusion therefore keeping them emotionally and psychologically unbalanced and fearful. One of the most successful tactics used by family and domestic abusers as a coercion tactic apart from the threat of violence or the violence itself, is for the abuser to remain "consistent and unrelenting" in their pursuit to attain dominance and control.

As a result, the victim becomes exhausted with the constant battle for their emotional, psychological, and physical survival, reluctantly giving in to the perpetrators demands which in turn provides "the" perpetrator with the leverage they seek. Those who are among the most dangerous of domestic and family abusers will undoubtedly engage in high-risk behaviours to gain and maintain control such as, threats of homicide against the victims and/or the victims loved ones. They may use weapons to threaten and intimidate and/or commit extreme acts of violence that include sexual assault or permanent bodily injury or disfigurement. The abuser who is afflicted with a psychopathology (mental disorder) or substance related addiction will definitely be in the more dangerous and unpredictable category, classed as a high-risk abuser.

Domestic and Family Abusers as Parents

Please note that my reference to children includes biological and non-biological children such as step-children, adopted children and foster children.

There are many ways in which abusive parents/caregivers harm their children, the most recognised and obvious type of abuse is perpetrated via direct and overt acts of abuse ranging from verbal and physical intimidation, coercion, and violence to crimes of a sexual and/or sadistic nature. The impact of course is not only physically harmful to a victim but also emotionally and psychologically just as damaging, contributing to the development of anxiety, eating, sleeping, psychological and behavioural disorders, physical illness or alcohol and substance abuse/addiction. Many abusive parents/caregivers do not care how their behaviours affect others and are also likely to be labouring under the misconception that the abusive actions committed against their selected victim directly impacts on their chosen victim alone.

They are completely ignorant to the fact that they are also indirectly abusing any witnesses who may be present when they commit these acts of abuse. For example, a child can be faced with conflicting emotions when confronted with witnessing the abusive actions of one parent/caregiver upon another parent/caregiver, they may be feeling as anxious, frightened and as helpless as the victim or they may feel anger, dislike, or hatred towards the abuser, while simultaneously being torn by their feelings of affection, loyalty, and love for the abuser. This leaves the child feeling a distressing and disorientating combination of emotions towards the abuser which they are not mature enough to understand or resolve and may be a constant source of both conscious and unconscious apprehension and anxiety for them.

These children will most likely experience feeling psychologically and emotionally tormented by the constant pull of loyalty and affection that they feel for both the primary victim and the abuser. On the one hand, they know the abuse is wrong and may feel the need to protect the battered parent, however on the other hand, they may also feel resentment towards the battered parent for "putting up" with the abuse. To maintain a position of overall power and authority over their family and in their home, abusers also engage in several varied psychological and emotional, bullying, and scheming tactics with their intimate partners and children.

One of which is to encourage their children into aligning with them and against the primary victim (intimate partner or ex-intimate partner) in order to control and intimidate the primary victim and to cement their connection to, and influence over the child. Abusive parents will manipulate their children into being puppets for their use in order to have their needs met and to fulfil whatever agenda they have at that time.

Not all abuse is overt and easily identifiable, their also exists a more widespread, covert, and insidious type of abusive exploitation and negligence being committed by parents and caregivers which on the surface appears as socially and culturally acceptable, if not normal forms of parenting. This type of abuse is subtly perpetrated under the guise of committed, attentive and caring parenting styles and is not easily discernible by others in society, but is just as damaging to a child's healthy development as if the child was physically abused.

The abuser whether male or female, is driven to fulfil their self-serving needs first and foremost, who will exploit their children without thought to the possible negative effects of their actions. The abuse usually begins in infancy and continues throughout adolescence and into adulthood, wherein the parent employs a range of manipulative and coercive psychological and emotional acts of persuasion to achieve their desired ends. These acts of abuse are perpetrated both consciously and unconsciously by inept, ignorant, immature, selfish and misguided parents/caregivers.

Following is a list of the categories an abusive parent/caregiver may belong to:

The Apathetic Parent

This type of parent possesses an apathetic (callous and indifferent) attitude towards their children, treating them with complete indifference, showing little interest or participation in their lives and who are only moderately concerned about their child's wellbeing. This leads to adverse emotional and psychological developmental issues for a child, including feelings of insecurity and worthlessness, acting out, eating, sleeping, anxiety, behavioural and attachment disorders, lowered self-esteem, and mistrust of others.

This in turn can manifest into other maladaptive responses such as alcohol and substance abuse issues and addictions as they get older. When a child is ignored or unacknowledged, it sends the message that they "don't matter," which is deeply harmful and a form of neglect as it purposefully undermines their psychological, emotional, and physical wellbeing and becomes responsible for the development of the core negative belief about themselves that they are "unworthy and/or undeserving of being loved."

This abuser considers themselves a "good enough" if not a very good parent, particularly if they are providing essential care in the form of food, clothing, shelter, and education believing nothing else is required from them. This is because they are incapable of forming a real human connection or bond with their child/children and therefore they may become just another possession to the abuser. Their lack of attachment to their offspring causes them to treat them with disinterest and detachment, allowing them to treat the child/children as an object for their personal use.

They may use them in several adversely damaging ways, the most common being as a pawn to manipulate either an intimate partner, an ex-intimate partner, or another family member. As a scapegoat to compensate for the abuser's own shortcoming and failures and/or as an opportunity to reflect success to their social or workplace peers via the child's/children's sporting, academic, musical, or artistic talents and achievements. The main focus for the abuser is always themselves, a narcissistic aspect of their psyche that prioritises their self-serving needs and desires above all others. The apathetic parent/caregiver is self-absorbed and selfish in nature and if in a relationship they need to be the centre of their intimate partner's world, demanding their partner's complete and focused attention to be on them as a priority and therefore may resent the inconvenience, distraction, and interference that they believe children represent.

The Antipathetic Parent

This type of parent possesses a deep and perverse "antipathy" (malevolence and dislike) towards their children, treating them as the enemy and projecting their own unresolved childhood hostility onto them. The children are regarded as objects not human beings, and so they become an outlet for the abuser's spite, bitterness and malice and are treated accordingly, either with insignificance and disdain and/or with emotional, psychological, and physical torment and cruelty. The abuser may hide his/her true nature from their intimate partner, other family members and friends by projecting an image of a caring, concerned, and loving parent, while they are in fact engaging in covert, abusive behavioural tactics to manipulate, undermine, destabilise, and exploit the children or a past or present relationship through the children. These abusers may also possess a general overall dislike for all children regardless of whom they belong to, or what their relationship is to them.

The Narcissistic Parent

This type of parent possesses an emotional detachment from their children, they view their children as an investment, a possession, an extension of themselves expecting to be admired, respected, and loved unconditionally. On the surface, these abusers appear to be the ideal parent who have their children's best interests at heart. However, the reality is that this so-called professed "love" comes with many expectations and conditions and is generated from the abusers, narcissistic sense of entitlement and the need to project an image of success and accomplishment in all areas of their life including their children. A child can only gain the abusers approval and acceptance if they fulfil the high standards in the scholastic, sporting or creative endeavours demanded of them by the parent/caregiver. They need their children to stand out from the crowd or excel in a field chosen by the parent/caregiver, that they themselves may have possibly wanted to but failed to succeed in themselves or conversely, that they did achieve success in and expect their child to follow suit. The narcissistic parent also views his/her children's real or perceived failures as their own failures and may respond in inappropriate and disproportionate abusive punitive or retaliatory behaviours, either directly towards the child themselves or towards those individuals whom they believe have directly or indirectly brought about their child's failure.

These abusers are likely to use the same controlling behaviours towards their children that they apply to their intimate partner; they can be rigid and demanding, expecting obedience without resistance. They are known to be harsh disciplinarians quite often lacking in restraint which can lead to disproportionate responses when meting out discipline. They regularly place high and unrealistic expectations on children, lacking in understanding and sensitivity to the emotional, physical, and psychological stages of development of a child and their capacity to bear the burden of the expectation placed on them. They believe their children to be an extension of themselves and therefore they do not afford them their individuality, habitually engaging in subversive, manipulative and coercive tactics to achieve their desired outcome. When faced with failure and disappointment from their children, they may likely respond by withdrawing attention, care, love, financial support and/or they may respond by punishing the child with verbal abuse, shaming, guilt tactics or possible physical violence.

Summary

There are only slight differences between the three parenting styles above, children of parents/caregivers regardless of whether they are apathetic (uncaring), antipathetic (hostile) or narcissistic (self-centred) are not cared for or loved in a nurturing or adaptive manner. The common theme of course is that the parents themselves possess a limited range of emotions which exclude sensitivity, affection, empathy, compassion, tenderness, and warmth. Their inability to give and receive these nurturing emotions is most likely based on their own past negative and damaging childhood and/or life experiences. However, the fact remains that any one of these parenting styles regardless of how they came about can have long-lasting and adverse effects on the child/adolescent who is exposed to them. Unfortunately, without some positive input or therapeutic intervention the negative impact of this type of parenting on the child/adolescent will likely follow them into their adulthood, causing much unhappiness and dissatisfaction in their lives and possibly being responsible for producing either a future victim or perpetrator of abuse.

Domestic and Family Abusers Who Exploit Their Children/Step-Children to Undermine an Intimate Partner or Ex-Intimate Partner

Sometimes a perpetrators coercive and abusive behaviour towards their intimate partner or intimate ex-partner sends the message to their children that it is okay for them to treat that partner/ex-partner (the victim) in the same manner. The abuser may use tactics such as disregarding or overriding the victim's decisions, inferring that they are an inadequate parent with no real authority. The perpetrator's goal is to undermine the intimate partner/ex-partner and lessen his/her influence over their children to help cement the perpetrators authority and control in the household and over the children.

Some abusers use children to fulfil their emotional needs, particularly in cases where they have experienced a separation or divorce expecting a specific child or all their children to fill an emotional void left by the absent partner. They will expect the children to be available when needed, often overwhelming and burdening them with problems and responsibilities that are beyond their emotional and psychological capacity at that time. This is done without consideration and with complete disregard to the child's/children's own needs and conflicting emotional struggles, leaving them feeling neglected and used. In cases where the abuser is separated or divorced, they will prioritise their own needs first and foremost, and are likely to use their children without a qualm to further personal agendas.

These abusers are usually motivated by:

- Jealousy – they resent their intimate partner moving on without them or onto a new relationship.
- Vengeance – they felt cheated in some way and want to pay their partner/ex-partner back.
- Greed – they resent paying child maintenance and want to make life difficult for the ex-partner and/or remind their ex-partner of their financial dependency on the abuser.
- Spite – some abusers are vindictive in nature, wanting to punish the partner for leaving them.

These abusers may manipulate and intimidate an ex-intimate partner with threats to harm or abduct their children, withdraw financial aid, disrupt visitation rights with false accusations about their partner to authorities or threaten to seek sole custody. Perpetrators of domestic and family abuse possess these four distinct core beliefs that motivates their abusive behaviours:

- They believe that they "own" their intimate partner/ex-intimate partner and any children or step children they may share. All are considered to be "possessions" of the perpetrator just like the perpetrator's car, home, etc.
- They believe that they are "entitled" to do as they please with their "possessions," to use and abuse as they see fit, without external interference and without consequence.
- They believe that their intimate partner/ex intimate partner and/or children/step-children are the "cause" of any or all his/her disappointments, failures and/or unhappiness and therefore to blame. This stems from the perpetrators inability to take responsibility for the choices they make. Perpetrators of abuse will always shift blame onto a victim as they are unable to accept accountability for themselves or their actions.
- They believe that the victim deserves the abuse, punishment, and retribution that they receive from them (the abuser). This allows the perpetrator to absolve themselves of shame or guilt, minimise their accountability and to rationalise (justify) their abusive behaviours.

Domestic and Family Abusers Who Are Vengeful and/or Retaliatory Towards Their Ex-Intimate Partners

Domestic and family abusers have great difficulty letting go of their ex-intimate partners as they believe that they still have ownership over that individual and any children they may have had together. They harbour resentment and are angry or furious towards the partner that has left the relationship, with many wanting to exact revenge against them. Vengeance is common among domestic abusers and habitually overrides common sense, they develop a burning desire to "get back at" the ex-partner who they believe is responsible for all their problems and unhappiness and who is now no longer at hand to be a receptacle for their abuse.

They can become overwhelmed with rage as they struggle with having lost the "control" they believe they had over their intimate partner and children, triggering a need to retaliate with possible indiscriminate violence and abuse or in extreme cases disfigurement, maiming or homicide. Perpetrators of domestic and family abuse never expect a victim to stand up for themselves, take steps to free themselves, or take legal action against them. They believe the victim to be sufficiently cowed, never daring to make a move against them, so when a victim separates from an abuser, they will undoubtedly receive some form of punitive and retaliatory response from the abuser.

In many cases, these abusers view the separation or divorce as a major threat to their financial security, perhaps believing that they should keep the "lions share" of the marital/de-facto assets. They do not want to part with any property (split assets), pay child-support or diminish their overall financial standing who must change their lifestyle as a result, or as in cases of adultery that has resulted in a new relationship, they may desire more than their share of the assets to start a new life. The need to avoid a financial loss can cause the abuser to enter a campaign of intimidation and coercion in order to manipulate their estranged partner into accepting less than they are entitled to and in extreme cases, it may lead to the homicide of the ex-partner.

Unfortunately, in some cases of domestic and family abuse, the abuser does not restrict retaliatory backlash to the ex-intimate partner and his/her children, they may threaten or exact vengeance on other family members or friends of the victim. Some abusers purposefully target those close to the victim if they believe that they are influencing or supporting them in any way, the intention is to either weaken the victim's position (a coercion tactic) or because they want to indirectly hurt the primary victim by harming those whom the victim loves.

The abuser has little or no regard for the harm they perpetrate on secondary victims (innocent by-standers, friends of the victim or other family members) in pursuit of vengeance against the partner who they feel has betrayed them, viewing the secondary victims as collateral damage. The perpetrator believes that their victim (ex-intimate partner) deserves being subjected to the abusive treatment that they are receiving as a punishment for leaving them. They often do not accept the break-up and may project the totality of the blame for the break-up onto the partner who has left the relationship. This causes a build-up of animosity and rage in the abuser and may manifest into retributive action towards the ex-partner via harm to those the ex-partner loves.

A horrifically notable incident of the kind of vengeful act by a partner towards his estranged wife occurred in Melbourne Australia, on the 29 January 2009, by Arthur Freeman, a 37-year-old father of three, who after a weekend visitation with his three children, was on his way to deliver his four -year-old daughter Darcy and their two sons to his estranged wife, who was waiting in the school grounds to mark what should have been Darcy's first day of school. While driving over the Westgate Bridge in early morning peak hour traffic, he pulled over into the emergency lane and asked his daughter to climb into the front seat.

He then calmly carried her to the railing and dropped her 80 metres to her death as his sons, aged two and six watched. He called his wife and told her, "Say goodbye to your children, you will never see them again." After killing his daughter, he drove his two sons to the Federal Court Complex where he was arrested. He pleaded not guilty to murder on the grounds of mental impairment, however during his trial, his state of mind was scrutinised by accomplished psychiatrists, of which five out of six psychiatrists found him to be of sound mind.

He was subsequently found guilty of murder and sentenced to life in prison; however, this does not compensate for the loss of an innocent child, who became collateral damage in a father's quest for vengeance against his estranged wife.

Domestic and Family Abusers Who Monitor, Stalk and Bully

Perpetrators of domestic and family abuse can be just as persistent with their abusive actions after separation from a partner as they were when they were together. They may use electronic devices to harass, coerce, bully, threaten or stalk a victim, and are known to send a barrage of text messages and/or email messages including threats to harm the victim and/or those the victim loves. Perpetrators may also threaten to disclose a victims private, personal confidential information, photos, or films through social media with the intent to either directly humiliate and embarrass them, or as a form of blackmail. Obsessive and controlling abusers (female and male) often feel compelled to consistently monitor their current intimate partners or ex-intimate partners every move, where they go, who they spend their time with and how they spend their money.

Many have been known to stalk an estranged or ex-intimate partner by physically following them trying to intimidate or confront them by randomly showing up at places they know the victim frequents such as their children's school, workplace or a friends or relatives place of residence. However, with the advancements in modern technology, it is much easier and more popular to stalk a current partner or ex-partner via the internet, using devices connected to the same iCloud or Wi-Fi network, gathering information about their activities through surveillance. These abusers are also known to stalk a victim's every move with the use of hidden cameras, tracking devices or spyware installed into the victim's home, car or in a child's favourite toy or iPad or phone provided to the child by the abuser. It is common practice for a domestic abuser to call, text or email a current or ex-intimate partner whenever they feel the need to express their disapproval, gain compliance for any demand they may have or to castigate their victim for a real or perceived slight.

However, those who obsess over an ex-partner or failed relationship may spend an inordinate amount of time incessantly calling their ex-partner to vent their dissatisfaction and rage, as they were used to venting their dissatisfaction and rage at their ex-partner when they were together and readily at hand. Unfortunately, this does not change when the abuser and the victim separate as the abuser believes they still have some level of ownership over the victim despite the separation and are entitled to continue to treat them in the same abusive manner as they did before. Rarely do abusers take ownership of their own faults, failures, or wrongdoings, which results in a projection of the associated unresolved or displaced emotions of disillusionment, frustration, anger, and disappointment onto the victim whether they are a current partner or ex-intimate partner.

Ex-partners are often bombarded with high volumes of electronic communication from an abuser usually demanding the victim's immediate attention or because the abuser simply wants to "vent their spleen." They may contain disparaging, demeaning and belittling remarks that are aimed at undermining the victim's self-confidence or to destabilise the victims newly found freedom and fragile sense of safety. They criticise the victim's behaviour and/or parenting abilities, ridicule their decision making, cast aspersions on their character and malign and discredit their friends, family and/or co-workers. If, however, the abuser believes that their attempts to communicate are being purposefully ignored, they can become enraged and are likely to turn up physically, to confront the victim. If they have decided on a face to face with the victim, then the risk of a volatile situation occurring rises exponentially and may result in violent retribution from the abuser.

Abusers often enter relentless campaigns of electronic harassment aimed at keeping a victim (ex-partner) in a constant state of anxiety, fear and panic with the threat of intended punishing or retributive action towards the victim themselves or those closest to the victim. Whether or not the abuser intends to carry out the threatened violence is not the point of their incessant attempts at communication. What they want is for the victim to listen to what they have to say, no matter how many times they want to say it (no matter the duration of that contact). This goes on until the abuser becomes tired of venting, is distracted by another activity or until he/she have received the attention or acquiescence they sought from their victim.

It is important to note that the perpetrators of domestic and family abuse tend to regard themselves as the victim in a failed relationship despite their abusive behaviour, (a consequence of psychopathic/narcissistic character traits). They have one major priority and it is themselves and their own needs, they will do whatever it takes to ensure these needs are met. These perpetrators do not tolerate dissention in what they perceive to be their controlled and ordered world, which is maintained through their abusive actions. So, it is no surprise that when this order is disrupted that they are going to deal with the situation with the same or elevated levels of abuse, looking to exact vengeance against the partner who leaves the relationship. Many victims of domestic and family abuse are silent about their abuse for fear of provoking the abuser, who they know is a ticking time bomb with a very short fuse.

Domestic and Family Abusers Who Commit Homicide

In cases of domestic and family homicide, it is mainly but not exclusively perpetrated by males who murder their female counterparts. The AIC (Australian Institute of Criminology) the organisation responsible for National Homicide Monitoring in Australia through actual statistical studies have concluded (as per studies completed 2015, 2016, 2017) that males accounted for the majority of perpetrators of domestic and family homicide at around seventy-five percent. To further add to these statistics in a study published in the United Kingdom, by Dr Jane Monckton Smith (forensic criminologist – University of Gloucestershire), 5 August 2019, on Intimate Partner Femicide (IPF – The killing of women), found that women globally, account for eighty-two percent of victims of Intimate partner homicide, with most of the victims coming from heterosexual relationships involving a male perpetrator.

According to the Government National Homicide Monitoring program, domestic and family violence is divided into these sub-categories:

- Intimate Partner – The victim and perpetrator are in a relationship and are either married, de-facto, fiancés, or girlfriend/boyfriend.
- Filicide – The victim is a child of the perpetrator, this includes biological, adoptive or stepchild.
- Parricide – The victim is the parent of the perpetrator, this includes biological, adoptive of stepparent.
- Siblicide – The victim and the perpetrator are brother/sister, brother/brother, or sister/sister, this includes biological, adoptive or step-sibling.

- Other Family – The victim or perpetrator can be either/or nieces, nephews, uncles, aunties, cousins, or grandparents, this includes biological, adoptive or step-relatives.

Statistics reveal that IPH (Intimate Partner homicide) is the highest occurring of all the domestic and family violence homicides, and that these homicides were likely to occur in the evening between 6 pm and midnight. This may be due to the fact that this is when couples are generally forced in a sense to spend time together as it is usually post daytime working hours for the majority of society. When you combine this fact with the understanding that emotions such as depression, stress, anxiety and unresolved anger or frustration can often be heightened during the evening hours, particularly after a stressful day, can be a match ready to be lit for perpetrators of domestic abuse.

The abuser believes that their home is their domain over which they rule, and once they arrive home, they are free from the behavioural constraints required of them by the outside world (work, social and community environments). In their homes, they allow any pent up and volatile emotions to have free reign, giving themselves permission to express themselves and act without regard and/or restraint towards their victim/s.

There is a higher risk of homicide in homes afflicted with domestic and family violence when there is alcohol and/or substance abuse involved as it has the potential to heighten the abuser's behaviour to lethal levels. Circumstances can easily escalate and are a common recipe for dangerous and volatile behaviour by the perpetrator. It is during these hours that victims feel their most vulnerable and perpetrators feel their most powerful as there are fewer witnesses about during the evening time. Whether the perpetrator has committed a homicide in response to a spontaneous incident (a crime of passion) or they committed a purposefully planned homicide, both situations are conducive to the cover of nightfall in terms of manipulating a crime-scene or moving a victim to another location.

Intimate Partner Homicide

Intimate partner homicide is the most common of all domestic and family homicide's and usually takes place when the "psyche" (mind-set) of the perpetrator has shifted from a position of wanting or needing to sustain the relationship with the victim, to the mind-set of wanting to punish or kill the victim for wanting to leave it. We have already established the overwhelming majority of intimate partner homicides are committed by males, who are in heterosexual relationships with the victims being female.

This is specifically known as IPF (Intimate partner femicide), the links between IPF and domestic abuse are powerful, and a history of domestic abuse is a key marker in those who are IPF killers (Dawson and Piscitelli, 2017). There are three distinctly evident reasons that are present that can induce the perpetrator into murdering their intimate partner and/or murdering those that the victim loves and cares for.

Passion: This type of homicide is attributed to a loss of control of emotion wherein the perpetrator acted without restraint and "in the heat of the moment" (passion). The killer is seeking to claim diminished responsibility by citing passion (responses beyond their control) for their lethal actions in order to diminish his/her accountability for their crime. They act without thought and without limitation based on emotions such as rage, hate, grief and jealousy. Perpetrators of domestic violence do not need a specific reason to become enraged, most of the time they are seeking an outlet to vent or project their frustrations, fears, anxieties, disappointments, insecurities and real or perceived failures onto the victim as they are incapable of resolving these emotions themselves.

However, in some cases these volatile emotions can fester, becoming pathological in nature, lying dormant just beneath the surface, and it takes only the slightest real or imagined threat to shatter the fragile hold that the perpetrator may have had on their unpredictable emotions causing them to erupt into homicidal violence. There are several common threads that lead to passion fuelled homicides in intimate relationships. Any of the following scenarios can incite an abuser into committing unrestrained violence, either stemming from feelings of jealousy or "the" abuser believes they are being betrayed, neglected, abandoned, or disrespected:

- If a victim has threatened to leave the relationship or has separated from the abuser. The abuser feels betrayed and/or abandoned responding with lethal violence, with an attitude of "if I can't have you, no one can," the abuser will not allow the victim to live a life without them in it.

- If a victim either threatens to, or reports an incident of abuse to the authorities (the abuser feels betrayed/disrespected).

- If the victim discloses an incidence of abuse to someone outside of their intimate relationship i.e., other family members, friends, or co-workers. Abusers do not cope well when their abusive behaviours are made public (they feel betrayed).

- If the abuser has reason to become jealous, perhaps believing the victim is acting or dressing in a way that the abuser deems provocative, they believe the victim has committed an infidelity or if the victim committed an infidelity (they feel betrayed/disrespected).

- If for any reason the abuser believes that the victim has caused them to "lose face" or be "shamed" in the eyes of the abusers other respected family members and/or the wider community to which they belong. This may be a result of the abusers cultural and/or religious background (the abuser feels disrespected).

Greed: This type of homicide is attributed to the abuser's sense of entitlement and the fear of diminishing his/her financial standing and/or holdings, (money, property, and assets). Regardless of how the abuser attained their financial status, whether they are the bread-winner, the partner (victim) is the bread-winner or whether it was inherited through the partner's family line or their own, the abuser regards the financial holdings as belonging to them. The money and possessions are more valuable than the life of their intimate partner and they are not prepared to part with it. A homicide that is committed solely for financial gain is perpetrated with varying degrees of pre-meditation and not considered a crime of passion. Greed is a powerful motivator for homicide and there are cases of what appears to be a seemingly "harmless intimate partner," perhaps without a history of domestic abuse who has been moved to commit murder when threatened with financial loss due to an imminent separation or divorce. The most common reasons for a homicide of this nature stem from the following:

- The abuser views his/her possessions/assets as a reflection of their personal, business, or social standing and success, they cannot bear the loss of power and status that comes with the financial loss that may result from a divorce or separation.

- The abuser does not want to split the assets, pay child support or any type of financial maintenance that comes with a divorce or separation, they are either miserly or do not believe the ex-partner deserves financial support or recompense.

- The abuser may have a new partner and/or family to start over which may provide the incentive to contemplate homicide to keep their finances intact.

- The abuser may be afflicted with an unhealthy sense of "entitlement" believing that the "money and assets" accumulated throughout the relationship belongs to them alone, and that the ex-partner or soon to be ex-partner does not deserve any of it.

- The abuser experiences feeling a "loss of control" due to the threat to his/her financial position which cannot be tolerated (a psychopathic/narcissistic trait) inciting a retributive response towards the victim in the form of murder. This particularly applies to those abusers that have been controlling the finances throughout the relationship.

Revenge: this type of homicide can be attributed to the perpetrators inability to accept that the victim has ended the relationship and moved on without them. They may experience feeling betrayed, abandoned, used, resentful and/or envious of the ex-partner. Particularly, if they witness the ex-partner moving on with their life, either with a new partner or just simply being happy with their new circumstances. Some perpetrators feel especially vengeful when their financial status has been compromised by a separation or divorce, believing the ex-partner does not deserve any compensation from the partnership. Many of these perpetrators harbour a deep resentment towards the ex-partner as they are oftentimes under the misconception that the maintenance and child-care compensation that they are required to pay to the ex-partner is being used by the ex-partner on themselves and not on the welfare of the children and so they begrudge every payment. Homicides committed out of revenge can be committed in "the heat of the moment;" however, homicides committed out of greed are likely to be a pre-meditated and planned homicide.

Sexual Predators/Abusers

Sexual predators exist in all societies across the planet, they can be any race, nationality, gender or sexual orientation, culture, religion, education level, socioeconomic status or be of any physical appearance. They may hold a low profile in society, this includes anyone who does not have a public persona or a high profile in society such as a Politian, actor, singer, reality star or sports icon and so on. In other words, they can be anyone and as a result are not always easily identifiable, and if clever enough, they manage to hide behind carefully constructed discerning façades.

Crimes of a sexual nature come under the umbrella of "sexual violence" which includes; rape (also known as molestation), marital rape, sexual assault, sexual harassment, unwanted touching, sexual coercion, sex trafficking, sexual slavery, enforced prostitution, forced pregnancy, child sexual abuse, child marriage, enforced sterilisation (female genital cutting), incest, child pornography and exploitation, stalking and indecent exposure (flashing). Sexual violence can also be perpetrated on line or via digital technologies and includes on-line stalking, gender-based hate speech, image-based sexual abuse, on-line threats of rape and on-line sexual harassment.

It may be performed by an individual or by a group of individuals, in the group scenario the sexual violence is commonly perpetrated randomly by groups of males. Group sexual violence is usually incited by a lead male who is supported (seconded) by someone who may be considered the leaders lieutenant, side-kick, or admirer, who both rally the group into a sexual frenzy. Sexual violence can also be perpetrated by armed forces on large scales during times of armed conflict or war against innocently captured civilians, the majority being young girls, women, and children of both sexes.

It is universally statistically proven that most acts of sexual abuse and violence are perpetrated against the world's female population (mainly women and girls), and are mostly perpetrated by males (men and teenage boys). Sex offenders are likely driven by a combination of biological, behavioural, and anti-social factors and are predisposed with having a difficulty in controlling their sexual and/or violent impulsivity.

They are known to possess elements of, or be completely absorbed by sadistic, psychopathic, sociopathic, or narcissistic tendencies or personality disorders where they have increased levels of callousness, selfishness and remorselessness who also display an inability to empathise with others. These predators engage in anti-social, impulsive, and risk-taking behaviours, driven to seek self-gratification with little regard to the consequences, this is combined with a minimal to no capacity to control or inhibit their behaviours.

There are some predators however, that may exhibit a façade that is controlled and does not appear to be threatening, in fact this type of predator may even come across as pleasant, friendly, harmless, or non-descript. Crimes of sexual violence have less to do with the sexual gratification itself but rather more to do with the perpetrators need to express their unresolved, displaced, and projected feelings of rage, frustration, disappointment, inadequacy, unworthiness and/or failure.

They are driven by a deep need to overcompensate for feelings of powerlessness, to feel dominant and powerful, to elevate their underlying feelings of low self-esteem, to bolster their existing but superficial feelings of self-importance or superiority (aggrandise themselves), or to fulfil a deviant or fetish driven fantasy. The need to dominate and assert power over a victim is not about fulfilling a sexual need as there are many perpetrators of sexual violence who are married or in on-going intimate relationships with active sex-lives, who commit crimes of this nature.

Sex offenders may in fact have minimal actual sexual experience and those that do are inclined to be inferior in their experience. They receive gratification through possession and dominance the idea is to dominate, intimidate and/or frighten their victim into compliancy or submission. Perpetrators of sex crimes regard their victims as possessions or objects and therefore easily used, abused, and discarded. By objectifying a victim they can compartmentalise or deny them their humanity, indulge their self-serving needs and desires and experience no remorse, shame or guilt as a result. Some sexual offenders commit crimes of a deviant sexual nature that do not have actual physical contact with their victim such as those who participate in exhibitionistic behaviours. They may participate in committing acts of indecent exposure which involves the perpetrator exposing their genitalia at random or on purpose to others, hoping to either entice the victim into a sexual act, receive an admiring gaze or shock a victim.

Other predators of this nature include electronic or physical stalkers, "peeping toms" who engage in voyeuristic behaviours and intimate apparel thieves who engage in stealing underwear from the homes and backyards of their victims. New studies have shown that these types of predators along with burglars that rob homes are pre-disposed to graduate into committing the more personal crimes of sexual assault and rape. They have found that the lesser deviant sexual acts that were performed from a distance are likely to at some point lose their gratifying impact on the perpetrator and can eventually lead to an increased need for gratification through actual physical contact with a victim.

Predators with a psychopathic, sociopathic, sadistic, or narcissistic character traits enjoy the deception, the challenge, and the chase as much as they enjoy ensnaring their intended prey. Some invest a calculated amount of time planning their crime, perhaps stalking a victim for a period of time to ensure they have fewer obstacles in their path and a lesser possibility of getting caught. Other perpetrators with less self-control commit random crimes of a sexual nature as a result of unchecked sexual impulsivity, out of anger or rage or because they are drug or alcohol affected. The narcissistic predator can take retributive or aggressive sexual action towards a victim if their advances are rejected, purely out of their sense of entitlement as they may consider themselves to be important, successful, dominant, and desirable and they usually do not accept a refusal to what they believe to be "their" privilege.

There are many sexual predators who gorge on violent, deviant, fetish, or illicit pornographic material to either, compensate for their inability to connect with other human beings in a normal and healthy manner, compensate for their own real or perceived shortcomings and failings or to indulge their hedonistic and deviant thoughts and feelings. The over-indulgence or over-exposure to this type of extreme pornographic material can create a psychological, emotional, and physical link between sexual gratification and violence and may lead to perpetrators acting-out violent and abusive sexual acts. Adolescents who have continued exposure or an over-indulgence to pornography are influenced by the subliminal sexist messages affecting views on intimacy and ultimately inhibiting their ability to form healthy and satisfying relationships or at the very least it helps to create or support misogynistic thinking and perpetuates objectification of women.

Please note: Sexual offenders can consider themselves to be in a relationship with a victim after having spent as little as a few hours on a single occasion with them.

Reoffenders and Serial Abusers

Including Serial Killers and Serial Rapists

There is often much confusion and debate surrounding the issue of whether pathologically violent offenders are insane or sane when committing acts of perfidy, especially in cases concerning violent psychopathic, sociopathic and/or sadistic serial sexual offenders and/or serial killers. The confusion over which category to put them in exists because of the extremely violent nature of the crimes perpetrated by these offenders that are very difficult if not impossible for non-violent human beings to fathom. It is therefore understandable and even quite natural to deem everyone who commits crimes of this nature to be "not of sane mind."

However, the fact is that it is possible for them to be both in a sense, as they can commit insane and sane actions simultaneously. Serial offenders such as these can blend into society, leading what we consider to be normal lives as in, they may have a family, a partner, children, they may be low-profile (working and living among us) or high profile such as a business mogul, politician, religious leader, actor, singer etc.

Geoffrey Epstein a "billionaire" and convicted sex offender, accused of multiple heinous crimes, who was believed to have used his wealth to create a façade to fund and hide his abusive activities which included the trafficking of women and minors on a large scale, with the express intention of sexual exploitation. These women (including adolescents and minors) were bought and sold explicitly for sexual purposes, they were manipulated and coerced into prostitution, psychologically brainwashed, and emotionally conditioned similar to the process of the indoctrination tactics used by a cult or sect.

They were emotionally, psychologically, and physically abused and intimidated into being pliant, compliant and to keep silent about their activities. Epstein created a public persona that engendered an appearance of an accomplished, charismatic, intelligent, philanthropic, and benevolent figure, to successfully camouflage his monstrous intentions and abuses. He is the epitome of the "high functioning" (refer to high functioning abusers p14) psychopathic, sociopathic, and narcissistic predator.

He and his cohorts exploited the unprotected and vulnerable without conscience, for their own personal financial gain and/or their sexual and possibly fetish or deviant driven gratification. He like all other predators and abusers was incapable of feeling empathy towards his victims, treating them as objects or possessions, while justifying and rationalising his actions. He created a business around the buying and selling of human beings as if were selling a product in a shop window, acting without conscience. These types of abusers, thrive on feeling powerful and omnipotent thinking they are not only above the law but also untouchable.

Let us look at two of America's infamous serial rapist/killers who had committed multiple heinous crimes over long periods of time "Ted Bundy" and "The Golden State Killer," we must ask the question how did they remain undetected for such a long period of time. The answer is that these two men had enough social, emotional, and academic intelligence (Ted Bundy held an above average IQ) to co-exist within their communities for decades before being caught. They both managed to create carefully crafted façades that helped them to blend into their environment, disarm potential victims, fool family, friends, and co-workers and for the most part appear unassuming and harmless. Regardless of the question, "are these perpetrators insane or not?" the fact remains that they are most definitely possessed of a criminal pathology. However they managed to successfully operate for decades and only because of the little missteps made by the perpetrators, advances in forensic science and a hell of a lot of dogged and persistent detective work were these predators finally brought to justice.

Contempt

Perpetrators of Abuse Regard Their Victims with Contempt

Contempt is disapproval tinged with disgust, disdain, scorn, and the belief that a person or thing is beneath one's dignity and is unworthy of notice, respect, or concern. The contempt that perpetrators of crimes of a sexual and violent nature (including homicide) hold for their victim enables them to commit any number of atrocities. For the perpetrator, the victim is not regarded as possessing humanity, but rather an object or a possession they own, want or desire which they regard without empathy and therefore are easily discarded or disposed of. They give themselves permission to batter, main or kill a victim (possession/object) whether it is in "the heat of the moment" or whether in a calculated and planned manner. Their intention is to satiate their baser sexually deviant, sadistic and/or violent desires, indulge their need for power, control, and domination and/or as a projection of their own displaced feelings of self-disgust, unworthiness, or rage.

By projecting contempt outwardly onto the victim, the perpetrator is in fact re-directing their own inner unacknowledged and unresolved contempt for themselves and their abusive behaviour. Contempt is a useful tool that gives the perpetrator the green light to act without conscience towards a victim and at the same time allows them to absolve themselves of guilt, shame, and remorse for their actions. Most perpetrators of abuse and violence who are habituated behaviourally are likely afflicted with either a sadistic, narcissistic, sociopathic, or psychopathic personality disorder or psychosis and therefore incapable of making the significant enough growths or changes necessary to their emotional and psychological framework to be considered rehabilitative.

It is beyond comprehension for the majority of society to accept let alone understand the motivations behind abusive, violent and homicidal criminals and the heinous and abhorrent crimes they commit. There is a need by society to want to accredit the perpetrators of these types crimes to have acted from either a "treatable criminal pathology," "momentary insanity" or a "chemically induced" (drug or alcohol) act of violence and therefore candidates for possible rehabilitation or medical and/or psychological intervention.

Wishing the world safe or believing that every human being innately possesses the capacity for redemption may have foundations stemming from religious or spiritual teachings and however well intended is not a realistic approach to criminal intervention or crime prevention. Unfortunately, many offenders can function in society without detection because they do know the difference between right and wrong behaviour and do understand the harmful impact of their behaviours, even if they do not possess empathy or the ability to care. There are many perpetrators who can hold jobs, have families, and interact with others without giving away their perverse and dysfunctional ideologies, personalities, and addictions. Society is often divided by two conflicting and opposing schools of thought when it comes to perpetrators of crimes of this nature.

The first is one of "forgiveness and rehabilitation" based on the belief that every human being possesses or is capable of some degree of humanity, and the second is one of "deterrence and punishment" with a no mercy endorsement. In general, there are many in society who believe that there is good or the possibility of good in every human being and therefore those criminals not classed as insane are capable of an acceptable degree of reform. A belief that is advocated by mainstream religions or new age spiritual dogma, recommending that the act of forgiveness is a divine pursuit. Those that are in favour of deterrence in the form of harsh and unrelenting punishment for all criminals also has its origins founded in religious dogma and comes from the school of thought that no criminal has the capacity for redemption or rehabilitation supported by an "eye for an eye" belief.

The Modus Operandi of a Predator/Abuser

There is a distinctive pattern of thoughts and behaviours that most predators/abusers appear to follow, a kind of footprint that exposes how they operate. It is defined by this six-step system of operation: Hunt, Groom, Separate, Isolate, Dominate and Control, all in that order.

Step one – Hunt

The predator/abusers first step is to find and choose a target victim.
They use their predatory skills (some with much more experience than others) to search (hunt) for someone that possesses a vulnerability that they can easily exploit. The target victims may be any of the following:

- A person who is estranged from their family and has few or no friends that actively participate in their lives.
- A person whose family and friends live apart from the victim, perhaps interstate or overseas and so the victim may be isolated by distance.
- A person who is going through a traumatic event, perhaps grief at the loss of a loved one.
- A person who has gone through or is going through a divorce and suffering from, loneliness, grief, sadness, or depression as a result.
- A person who may be experiencing financial hardship.
- A person (adult or adolescent), with a substance abuse issue or addiction including drug, alcohol, sexual or gambling.
- A person (adolescent or adult) who is experiencing homelessness.
- A person of any age who has little life experience who is innocent, naïve, and trusting.

- A person of any age who is experiencing bullying and feels depressed and/or lonely.
- A person who feels as if they are a social out-cast and is feeling isolated or lonely.

- A child or adolescent who is left regularly unattended, without parental supervision before or after school hours, perhaps they are the child of a single parent or parents who are working, absent due to illness, or negligent due to substance abuse/addiction.
- A person who possesses some level of being intellectually or physically impaired or handicapped.

The predator will use any or all the following methods when hunting to disarm and entice their victim, they may:

- Act caring, concerned and offer support and/or pretend they have gone through, or are going through the same circumstances as their target victim.
- Act charming – using witticism, humour, or perhaps old-fashioned gallantry, in other words they will want their victim to think that they are charming, pleasant, and harmless.
- Act generous – they may act as if they are generous by offering to pay for drinks, meals or buy gifts, send flowers etc.
- Act wealthy (whether true or not), implying that they offer financial security.
- Pretend to be whoever or whatever they believe the target victim would like them to be: this includes pretending to be, any age, gender, sexual orientation, religion, political or social disposition, employment or career inclination or relationship status (married, single, divorced or widowed).

Step 2 – Groom

The predator/abusers second step is to groom the victim into a state of complacency (feeling safe and comfortable) and into accepting them. The underlying primary purpose of the grooming is to either normalise

inappropriate behaviour and/or to gain the trust of their intended victim.

This is achieved by exploiting the vulnerabilities that they have already determined in their target victim during the "hunt." For example, a sexual predator may groom an emotionally and psychologically vulnerable child, adolescent, or adult by providing the understanding, affection, and focused attention that they believe the child, adolescent or adult covets.

They may use any of the following techniques:

- An experienced predator becomes whom they think the victim wants them to be to gain the victim's acceptance.
- The predator will use his/her manipulative skills to create the illusion of safety, comfort, and care.
- The predator will work diligently to gain the trust of the victim, by identifying with and/or empathising with the victim's problems/issues and/or by offering advice and supposed "unconditional support."
- The predator will exploit the victim's emotional, physical, psychological and/or financial vulnerabilities with the intention to create a possible co-dependency.
- The predator will want to become the most important and influential person in the victim's life and so they encourage the thinking that they are "a team" or it's "the two of them against the world."
- The predator may shower a victim with gifts, focused attention, and flattery.
- The predator will delude the victim into believing that they (the victim) are the most important person in the predator's world.
- An experienced predator will work to desensitise a victim to their physical advances and/or inappropriate sexual touching through progressive boundary-probing, while at the same time developing a foundation of trust.
- Predators who target child victims will act covertly, seducing the intended victim with focused attention, while at the same time they are working fervently to cultivate a climate of trust and familiarity. The child is manipulated from the beginning into keeping their developing relationship a secret, deluding the child into thinking, and feeling as if they are special to the predator.

- Predators who target child victims will often introduce and climatise a child through non-sexual touch such as hugging, tickling and physical play. If the child is responsive, the abuser introduces the child to sensual touch followed by consistent efforts of boundary probing until they achieve their goal.

Step 3 – Separate

The predator/abusers third step is to separate the target victim from the people they think have any significant influence on them.
Step three is the turning point for a predator as they have chosen their target victim and will want to test whether they have, or can truly become the most influential person in the victim's life. The predator's aim is to separate the victim from the people they think may have any significant emotional and/or psychological influence on them, this could be their friends, work colleagues, family members or religious affiliations. The aim here is to become the most important person in the victim's life and the central point of reference in all matters including all decision-making processes.
They may use any of the following techniques:

- The predator will lead the victim to believe that they care for or love their victim more than anyone else including the victim's closets friends and family.
- The predator will lead the victim to believe that they alone have the victim's best interests at heart.
- The predator will influence the victim to spend more time alone with them or perhaps demand it.
- The predator will influence the victim to spend more time with those people that they (the predator) approve of, perhaps the abuser's own family and/or strategically chosen friends.
- The predator will use psychological and emotional manipulations to gain leverage over the victim's trusted friends, work colleagues or family by casting seeds of doubt as to their sincerity. For example, it is not uncommon for the predator to say things like "they are jealous of our relationship" or "they don't understand us" or "they don't care about you like I do."

- The predator will involve themselves in every aspect of the victim's life including family, social, career and workplace asserting their opinions and manipulating outcomes that favour their personal intentions,
- The predator will persistently, use every opportunity to find fault with the victim's family and friends hounding the victim until the victim to appease or please the predator, reduces their contact and personal interactions with those closest to them.

Step 4 – Isolate

The predator/abusers fourth step is to isolate their victim: By isolating a victim, the predator has taken a major step towards gaining the power and control that they are ultimately seeking in their relationship with their victim.

The abusers aim here is to isolate the victim from all other external influences so that they become the most important and influential person in the victim's life. By this stage, the predator has worked diligently to alienate (separate) the victim from influential work-mates, friends, family, or religious affiliation expecting the victim to defer to them in all things.

They may use any of the following techniques:

- The predator will encourage the victim to move in with them, or they will move in with the victim, they do this to keep a close eye on the victim and to ensure that any possible external influences do not interfere with the control they have established in the relationship.
- The predator strategically moves both themselves and the victim to a location that is far from those the victim is close to, sometimes interstate if they deem it necessary.
- The predator strategically moves themselves and the victim to a rural and/or remote location that is far from community interaction and/or aid from social or policing bodies.
- The predator will discourage contact with those closest to the victim and may even limit, supervise or ban the victim from having contact with those closest to them. The abuser usually perpetrates this process

gradually as the relationship develops so that the victim remains unaware of their underlying motives.

Step 5 – Dominate

The abusers fifth step is to exert dominance over their victim with the intention to cement their position of power in the relationship.
Once the predator has established dominance over the victim, they will not tolerate interference from an outside party or disagreement from their victim. By this stage, any opposition from the victim can result in the predator needing to reassert their authority.

They may us any of the following techniques:

- The predator will monopolise the victim's time and expect the victim to prioritise the predator's needs and/or demands above all else and at all times.
- The predator will create parameters for the victim under which the relationship will function, for example, the predator may make the decisions that control with whom, when and for how long the victim can socialise. They will have a strong influence over the victim's dress code or in the more extreme cases a predator will want to accompany the victim wherever they go.
- The predator may expect the victim to keep in constant contact with them when they are apart.
- The predator is likely to electronically monitor and/or control (phone and internet) who the victim communicates with, the content and the duration.
- The abuser will become extremely verbally and physically assertive or forceful to ensure the victim remains pliant and compliant.

Step 6 – Control

The abusers sixth step is to manage and maintain the dominant position that they have established over their victim using controlling behaviours
The predator now expects complete obedience from the victim, an adherence to the rules and parameters that have been set out for them. They consider the victim to be their possession, who must defer to their decisions in all things the predator deems necessary.

They may use any of the following techniques to ensure the victim remains pliant and compliant:

- Engage in intimidation tactics, using the threat to commit violence either directly to the victim or to the victim's loved ones with the intention to instil fear into the victim to discourage them from leaving the relationship.
- Threaten to commit homicide either to the victim or to the victim's loved ones.
- Commit acts of verbal and physical abuse including sexual assault upon the victim.
- Use psychological and emotional manipulations by exploiting the victim's vulnerabilities and insecurities for example, withdrawal of "love, care or attention" triggering a victim's possible fear of abandonment issue.
- If the abuser is the sole provider and only source of income in the relationship, they will most certainly use this as tool for manipulation and control (using the threat of withdrawal of financial support).
- Control and/or monitor the victim's movements and interactions with others via electronic means using cameras and tracking devices.
- Control and/or monitor the victim by screening their mobile phone (text messages and voice calls), social media and/or internet usage i.e., they regulate who the victim communicates with, for what period of time, and they check the content of the conversations.
- Deny the victim access to electronic communication devices telephone (landline), mobile phone or computer.

- Deny the victim access to family, friends, or others in the community, or at the very least, they will inhibit or regulate the time spent with anyone other than themselves.
- Limit or prevent access to television to regulate usage, ensuring the victim remains ignorant of the realities of the world at large.
- Prevent the victim from seeking employment.
- Inhibit or prohibit a victim from attaining an education, they are either not permitted to receive an education or are allowed limited education attainment.
- Physically restraining the victim and/or keeping them in enforced confinement, to control their movements and/or to prevent them from leaving.
- Forcefully medicating or addicting a victim to licit or illicit drugs and/or alcohol.

Can an Abuser Really Change
Their Behaviour?

All predators, abusers and bullies, behaviour will stem from some type of underlying psychological and/or emotional trauma linked to their personal history (excluding those diagnosed with a genetic or biological mental illness or clinical disease/disorder). They possess a unique history that has been shaped by earlier life experiences, varying in the degree of complexity depending on the type and severity of the dysfunctional influences they had undergone. For a great many perpetrators of violence and abuse, rehabilitation is marginal and for some it is impossible as evidenced by the increasing numbers of repeat offenders and hardened criminals currently serving time in our prisons. There is an ever-increasing rate of crime in general, particularly crimes of a sexual nature and those of domestic and family abuse. In order for rehabilitation to be successful so that the perpetrator may be allowed to assimilate back into mainstream society without being a threat, they must be able to meet the following required criteria.

- Be able to sincerely take responsibility for their actions and understand how their actions have impacted on the victim, the victim's family, and society at large.
- Be able to feel remorse for their actions and empathy for their victim.
- Be able to show an acceptable capacity for the cognitive, emotional, and psychological growths, changes and learnings required for assimilation back into society.

There are several influencing factors that need to be present for a perpetrator to make the necessary changes that will be required for rehabilitation and reassimilation to occur successfully. Firstly, they must possess a strong need, want or desire to make these changes and secondly, they must have the capacity for the psychological and emotional advancement, combined with an acceptable level of social and cognitive intelligence to make the changes that are needed.

For those perpetrators who possess a diminished cognitive, emotional, and social learning ability, mental illness and/or a pathological clinical disorder, their rehabilitation will range from minimal to improbable. For other less violent offenders, there is a possibility for rehabilitation to an acceptable degree or at least to a notably improved level, this modification to their behaviour may allow them to assimilate back into society, however, it must be under supervision. For perpetrators who exhibit habituated, long term, sadistic, sociopathic, and psychopathic tendencies, it is unlikely that they are capable of any significant growth in their psychological and emotional capacities.

The reality is that many offenders are not likely to want to or are able to change themselves or their behaviours especially but not exclusively, if they fall into any of the following categories:

- Those who have experienced extreme early childhood and/or teenage developmental physical, emotional, and psychological adversity and/or abuse without intervention resulting in borderline, narcissistic, schizoid, paranoid or antisocial personality disorders.
- Those exhibiting serious sadistic, sociopathic and/or psychopathic behaviours.
- Those who suffer from psychosis such as schizophrenia or psychotic or delusional disorders.
- Those who possess a violent pathology stemming from a violent pathological history.
- Those afflicted with long standing, habituated substance abuse and addictions issues.

The Victim

There is an innate sense of safety that we as human beings hold and likely take for granted until tested, this no longer exists for a victim of violence and it is not something easily recovered from or regained.

Introduction

Abuse does not discriminate against age, sex, sexual orientation, race, culture religion, socio-economic background, social or political standing or education level and it exists in all societies across the planet.

However, it is a fact that globally women and children are two of the largest groups of victims that are most vulnerable to crimes of domestic abuse (including homicide), sexual assault, stalking, kidnapping, enslavement, and human trafficking as current national and inter-national statistics will support.

There are many in our society who labour under the misconception that being highly educated, holding a reputable form of employment, or having social or political standing in the community excludes you from the victim or perpetrator pool. In fact, nothing could be further from the truth there are many high-profile figures who have been convicted of or are currently awaiting trial for committing crimes such as kidnaping, human trafficking, sexual assault, paedophilia, domestic abuse, and murder in any of the following arenas political, religious, policing, sporting, social and the arts such as the film or music industry.

It is a mistake and a naïveté to think that most victims come from lower socio-economic, uneducated, impoverished, or criminal backgrounds just as it is a mistake and a naïveté to assume that most abusers come from those same backgrounds. There are many victims of abuse who are highly educated, may be high income earners and/or may also be holding positions of social, religious, or political standing who are experiencing some form of abuse from an intimate partner, or from a family member, peer, co-worker, or employer and as a result are experiencing feeling powerlessness, humiliation, and debilitating shame. These victims are affected by the same fears as all other victims of abuse. However, they may be exceptionally reluctant to admit that they are working or living within an abusive environment or relationship, terrified that exposure will jeopardise their career or compromise their professional credibility and some may fear being publicly ridiculed.

There are many erroneous and misogynistic beliefs still held by some male members of our society due to their certain religious, social and/or cultural backgrounds. These misogynists may be highly academically educated and hold reputable and even elite employment positions or they may be poorly educated with average employment positions and little social standing. However, they all have a few things in common which is that their beliefs are steeped in archaic dogma that perpetuates male dominance and superiority, and at the same time objectifying and stereotyping women.

They possess a psychological and emotional immaturity in their understanding of women, sex and relationships and unfortunately have a propensity to empathise with their own sex with a sexist preconception towards women. As a result, they possess both conscious and unconscious misplaced compassion for male abusers who have committed crimes of a domestic or sexual nature and will always rationalise the abuser's behaviour to some degree if not completely exonerate abusive behaviour.

There is a great need to take a closer look at why domestic abuse, sexual assault, bullying, child abuse, denigrating and sadistic pornography and human trafficking, is prevalent in our society and is continuing to escalate. Obviously, statistics can only reflect the crimes that are reported to the authorities and the associated organisations that deal directly with perpetrators and victims. However, I do not believe that those statistics are even close to accurately reflecting the reality of the pervasiveness of these types of crimes. There are numerous victims that cannot report that they are or have been a victim of crimes of this nature and the reasons are varied and complex. My personal experience, my training and my research will hopefully bring to light why these crimes are not reported and why we live in a society that is rife with this type of abuse.

The Anatomy of a Victim

All forms of abuse whether, verbal, physical, psychological, or emotional are a violation.

Violent and abusive behaviour whether it is a random act or short or long term in its duration will most certainly leave a victim with varied levels of trauma. Physically the impact of abuse is obvious as the injuries speak for themselves however, psychologically, and emotionally the consequences of abuse and the recovery from abuse can be complex and distinct to each individual. Rehabilitation is influenced by four major variables the severity of the impact of the abuse, the longevity of the abuse, the victims present physical, emotional, and psychological state of being and the victims personal psychological and emotional history (refer to "Our Map" p10).

Each of these factors differs for every victim and will ultimately influence if not determine how equipped they are to respond to intervention and treatment. It is therefore important to understand the individuality of every case of abuse and the need to treat each circumstance with singular care as every victim and how they metabolise the abuse they have undergone is also singular. Some may take weeks, months, or years to recover, others may be afflicted with permanent psychological, emotional and/or physical injury.

There is no one specific method, type of treatment or particular time frame that can establish recovery periods for victims of abuse. For some, the road to recovery can be achieved by receiving the appropriate psychological and medical treatment, along with a safe place to live, for others the need to bring the perpetrator to justice can aid in the healing process. There are many influencing cognitive, psychological, and emotional factors that need to be addressed to achieve a healthy level of recovery. A victim of a random act of violence may need prolonged rehabilitative intervention equally as much as a victim of short or long-term abuse. Ultimately, however, recovery will be determined by the individual's capacity to respond to treatment.

Just like the abuser victims are influenced by their personal history, character structure, schemas, defence mechanisms and their cognitive, emotional, and psychological capacities, particularly those who have subsequently entered long-term abusive relationships. Character structure and the accompanying defences and schemas can be responsible for emotional and psychological dysfunction sometimes keeping a victim trapped in an abusive relationship, preventing them from moving forward and inhibiting their recovery. In order to gain insight into the anatomy of a victim, we must understand the key factors that influence their victimology and understand the impact that an act of abuse whether considered mild or severe in nature can have on a victim.

It is possible that a victim of abuse may possess a singular or a combination of the following character structures, schemas, and defences mechanisms. Please note; as mentioned earlier maladaptive schemas are an influential part of the abuser's psychological anatomy and are also considered to be just as influential on a victim's psychological anatomy. There are eighteen documented schemas, some are adaptive and some maladaptive in nature, however either way we all possess a combination of at least several of these schemas. Maladaptive schemas are based on ones' negatively held core beliefs about oneself, others, and the world at large, they are formed during childhood and adolescence and influence our thoughts, emotions, actions, and relationships.

Negatively held, maladaptive schemas develop in early childhood or adolescence generated from poor, non-existent or neglectful parenting and abusive adverse social or schooling environments and experiences. Children who are repeatedly told they are "lazy," "stupid," "inept" or "incapable" will grow up believing they are, despite their achievements to the contrary. These schemas can cause victims to develop disconnection, social alienation and mistrust issues, attachment disorders, feelings of inadequacy, eating disorders, identity, and dependency issues which if left unchecked can lead to more serious psychological disorders in the form of psychosis or complexes.

These maladaptive beliefs work to prevent a victim from having their needs met in healthy and adaptive ways and can reinforce falsely formed rationalisations that minimise, justify, or absolve abusive behaviour. Following, you will find a list of the possible character structures that victims of abuse may possess combined with a list of the corresponding schemas that support if not drive them.

Character Structure Victim – "Schizoid"

The Schizoid Structure also known as "sensitive – withdrawn," is often referred to as the "unwanted child," a result of not feeling wanted by hostile parents and is activated from within utero to first six months of life. This individual fears contact with others and is unable to form healthy adaptive relationships, believing they have no right to exist physically, a result of early infantile experiences of either interrupted, insufficient or neglectful parenting/caretaking. When the experience of extreme stress or fear is severe enough, it causes the infant to remain in a heightened state of arousal wherein the nervous system is unable to relax or balance itself out. If it is compounded with the consistent absence of the parent/caretaker who is needed to regulate or return the infant to a relaxed state, it may lead to the development of defensive dissociative responses and emotional numbness. Without therapeutic intervention, the effects are long-term or even life-time, carried throughout adolescence and into adulthood.

Those afflicted with strong schizoid tendencies are unable to form normal or healthy attachments to their physical bodies, a defensive action that was taken in order to avoid experiencing the remembered fear and terror of their early infancy and childhood. The detachment from their physical body and the associated emotions encourages a dependency on the use of their "thinking mind" creating an existence in the cerebral or spiritual realms, becoming "all dealing and no feeling." They may be perceived as being "highly sensitive," shy, inhibited, reserved, and are often referred to as "loners" who are usually socially clumsy or inept. They can be highly intelligent, creative, and imaginative and tend to gravitate to fields of employment or careers where they can work alone or independently. For example, you will find the schizoid structure or elements of this structure particularly in those who choose to work with computer programming and/or software development or design, a job where one works alone most of the time.

Victims with a predominant schizoid structure have a limited emotional range who may feel lonely, perhaps different, and possibly socially awkward as they are unable to make the necessary personal and emotional connections required to cultivate and maintain friendships and/or intimate relationships with others. They tend to avoid negative overwhelming emotions and inter-personal conflict and are likely to suppress how they really feel about what is happening to them. This makes them more vulnerable to predators who can exploit a victim who they know has few or no friends or inter-personal relationship experience and may be naïve as a result. The schizoid type has tendency to supress strong feelings such as anger, rage, and frustration mainly because their instinct is to resist embodying these emotions, and to avoid conflicting with others. They will inhibit overwhelming emotions such as shame, distress or grief turning these emotions inwards towards themselves in the form of self-hatred, which they may express through, self-harm, substance abuse, addiction, or physical illness.

Victims of abuse with the schizoid structure are likely to stay in an abusive relationship for lengthy periods of time, because even though they fear intimate connection with other human beings, there also exists an opposing, instinctually driven but unacknowledged part of themselves that craves human connection, ironically keeping them unconsciously attached to their abuser. The other possible scenario is that they may be experiencing anxiety and/or terror at the prospect of being rejected by their abuser, which is directly linked to their early childhood abuse and their first experience of abandonment. The inability to cope with the high level of distress that arises at the thought of being abandoned, consequently results with the victim keeping a firmly committed relationship to their abuser despite the abuse.

The Possible Associated Schemas to the Schizoid Structure:

Emotional Inhibition Schema

This schema is driven by the belief that you must suppress spontaneous emotions and impulses, especially anger. Those afflicted with this schema have learned to supress all heightened emotion to avoid embarrassment, retaliation, censure, or criticism, fearing that they will harm others or that they will be disliked, rejected, or abandoned.

Their demeanour may be viewed as being cold, rigid, indifferent, uninterested, or uptight and therefore they will find spontaneity difficult if not impossible. They tend to resist change, embracing rigid thinking patterns that inhibit their innate natural responses and/or impulses. This schema likely originated in childhood or adolescence in an abusive environment where it was either not safe for the child or adolescent to experience emotion and/or the parents or caregivers were such that they discouraged or suppressed any show of emotion in those under their care.

A victim afflicted with this schema may remain in an on-going abusive relationship or situation because they do not allow themselves to feel the full impact of the emotional, psychological, and physical abuse being perpetrated on them. They tend to engage in fixed thinking patterns based on rigid rules and standards that they doggedly adhere to. They do not cope well with change and even the threat of change can cause fear or anxiety and so they will engage in minimisations and rationalisations to avoid having to change their life situation regardless of how harmful it is. Eventually, long-term use of this schema may result in the manifestation of physical illnesses, substance abuse and/or addictions or eating, anxiety and behavioural disorders.

Defectiveness/Shame Schema

This schema is driven by the belief that one is fundamentally flawed in some way and if they allow others to get close to them, they will realise this and withdraw from the relationship. This person believes that they are entirely, or in some capacity physically, emotionally, intellectually, or psychologically incompetent or defective rendering them unacceptable and unlovable to others. These feelings of innate inadequacy will ultimately lead to a strong sense of shame and unworthiness which may have stemmed from early childhood or adolescent dysfunctional parenting and/or abuse. A result of overly critical and/or punitive parents or caregivers who had unrealistic expectations of their offspring. Victims with this schema may become either socially avoidant believing that others will recognise their flaws or alternately create situations that will make them feel constantly flawed. They may pursue approval seeking, perfectionistic or self-sacrificing endeavours in an effort to counter feelings of imperfection and shame that are associated with the defectiveness.

It is not uncommon for those with this schema to gravitate towards relationships, organisations, and environments whether personal, social or workplace related that contain elements of abuse, that may be highly critical, humiliating, punitive or debasing reinforcing the victim's negative beliefs about themselves. Victims who are afflicted with schema may be unconsciously drawn to a partner who is physically, emotionally, and psychologically abusive towards them confirming their feelings of inferiority, inadequacy, and defectiveness.

Social Isolation/Alienation Schema

This schema is driven by those who believe that they are fundamentally different from other people, feeling isolated from the world at large, disconnected from others in their community, with no sense of social belonging. They have difficulty making friends and maintaining relationships resulting in social isolation and/or alienation, they feel misunderstood and lack a solid sense of self, suffering from feelings of low self-esteem, loneliness, shame, and social anxiety. The isolation makes this individual more vulnerable as they lack interpersonal relational experience and may be naïve to the dark natures of human beings, putting them at a higher risk of becoming the target of a predator who is able to identify with the victim's vulnerabilities. Alternately, victims afflicted with this schema may consciously or unconsciously gravitate towards a partner (abuser) who wants to isolate them so that they may exercise their controlling, possessive and manipulative agendas taking advantage of the victim's compliant nature.

Character Structure Victim – "Masochistic"

The Masochistic Structure also known as "burdened enduring," develops around two to three years of age and stems from a dominating, self-serving (possibly narcissistic) and/or extremely needy parents/caregivers whose emotional and psychological manipulations have overwhelmed the child, leaving them feeling stifled, ashamed, and needlessly guilty. The child is not allowed the freedom to develop a healthy individuality and does not learn how to set appropriate boundaries with others, leaving them vulnerable to exploitation and victimhood.

The parent/caregiver has taught them that in order to receive the love, care, attention, and approval they must meet the parent/caregivers needs and demands first and foremost while sacrificing their own. Consistent parenting in this manner solidifies the belief that the child's own needs, wants and desires should always be secondary to that of any significant others in their life whether it is parents, caregivers, siblings, friends, work colleagues, intimate partners, or their own children.

As the masochistic child grows into adulthood, they have learned to endure, burdening themselves with unnecessary and sometimes overwhelming responsibilities. Their need for approval, acceptance, love, and affection cannot be achieved directly and so is received vicariously by being in constant service to others or through pursuing altruistic endeavours. The masochist will have difficulty saying "no" to another's request, even though it may be inconvenient or burdensome, without feeling a deep sense of guilt or becoming anxious over losing approval or popularity.

However, underlying this dysfunctional structure are unconscious, deeply repressed emotions such as anger, frustration, rage against other and rage against the self that are disowned or unacknowledged. Victims, with a history of long-term abuse, will have this character structure or elements of it and are likely to endure abuse for longer periods of time than other victims of abuse. They tend to be submissive to some degree and possess a propensity to accept responsibility for an abuser's actions; this makes them very attractive to predators.

This defence mechanism separates closeness and freedom, the need to be emotionally connected to or loved by another human being equates to the loss of one's personal choices, and the need to be available or even self-sacrificing in service of those they believe they love. In other words, they will have to endure all sorts of things in order to feel accepted, close to, or valued by another. Their capacity to endure hardship combined with their difficulty to say no to a request or to seek or accept aid, keeps them trapped in abusive intimate, familial and social relationships, and jobs. They tend to supress their emotions, especially anger and rage, however, they are prone to feelings of being dissatisfied and over-burdened resulting in depression, substance and alcohol abuse, addiction and/or physical illness.

The Possible Associated Schemas to the Masochistic Structure:

Approval-Seeking/Recognition-Seeking Schema

This schema is driven by one's innate need to be liked, recognised, and approved of, those who are afflicted with this schema will go to great lengths to gain the admiration and/or recognition from others at the expense of their genuine needs, happiness, inner peace, and authentic self. They tend to set unrealistic goals with an emphasis on social status, career, power, and prestige while making their appearance a number one priority. A victim with this schema may suppress spontaneous emotions, decisions, and impulses to adhere to the rigid rules and expectations set by those they are seeking approval from. They will struggle with conscious and/or unconscious feelings of low self-esteem, failure, and unworthiness, leading to the onset of defensive tactics such as denial, minimisation and/or suppression. A victim with this schema will likely be seeking to preserve the approval of their abusive counterpart despite the abuse, their need to sustain the connection with the abuser with whom their identity and sense of self is linked is paramount, and overrides all other emotions.

Emotional Depravation Schema

This schema is driven by the principal that ones' essential primary emotional needs will never be met by others. Those who are afflicted with this schema believe that they are fundamentally flawed or unimportant and therefore undeserving or unworthy of affection, comfort, happiness, respect, or love and that they should not expect to receive it from others. A victim with this schema feels uncared for or invisible which may trigger a need to over-compensate for this perceived short-coming through endless approval seeking behaviours out of the fear of being rejected or abandoned. They may portray a façade, appearing to be confident, strong and in control, however the reality is that they suffer from loneliness, insecurity, emotional starvation, neediness, sadness, or depression.

They will never ask for emotional support because they do not expect to receive it and may come across as being distant, reserved, or unavailable protecting their true vulnerability. A victim afflicted with this schema will unconsciously gravitate to relationships with partners or friends who are cold, ungiving and emotionally unavailable or they may be self-centred and needy, this in turn helps to perpetuate their schema. Unfortunately, victims who suffer with emotional deprivation are more likely to partner up with an abuser who is attuned to their neediness, only providing them with scraps of kindness or affection to keep them hooked, while taking full advantage of their power over their victim.

Self-Sacrificing Schema

This schema is driven by the excessive sacrifice of one's own needs in order to help others, these individuals feel an unhealthy amount of guilt and/or shame, afraid that they will disappoint others or if they do not meet the other persons needs that that person will suffer in some way. They greatly fear that they may be disliked, rejected, or abandoned by those they seek approval from. This schema was likely generated during childhood or adolescence wherein the child or teen was made intentionally or unintentionally responsible for the well-being of either a sibling or siblings or one or both parents, learning very early on to associate their self-worth and value with supporting others. Being self-sacrificing also works to build one's "ego-ideal" or sense of self, in that the individual who is self-sacrificing feels worthy, important, revered, or accepted.

They would like to be lauded for their loyalty and benevolent acts of care, service, and assistance towards others, even at the expense of their own wellbeing. There is an immoderate focus on going "above and beyond" what would be considered normal or necessary when attending to others needs whether it is for a friend, family member, intimate partner, co-worker, acquaintance, or stranger.

Victims with this schema are likely repressing, supressing, and denying their real thoughts, feelings, needs, dreams, and desires in order to sustain the maladaptive relationship that has its foundations built on their heroic and altruistic actions and commitments. The excessive sacrificing however well-intentioned leads to feelings of being underappreciated, undervalued, unloved, depressed, resentful, exhausted, stressed, empty and anxious. This takes an adverse emotional, physical, and psychological toll on the victim, which in the long-term may lead to the manifestation of physical illness, substance abuse and addiction, or eating, anxiety and behavioural disorders. Those who are afflicted with this schema may possess deep-seated feelings of unworthiness and low self-esteem leading to over-compensatory self-sacrificing behaviours in an effort to become indispensable to the abuser and/or to counter the underlying negatively held beliefs about themselves. Predators are drawn to victims with this vulnerability as the self-sacrificing behaviours associated with it are glaringly apparent, leaving the victim open for exploitation.

Character Structure Victim – "Oral"

The Oral Structure also known as "dependent – endearing" or "self-reliant – independent" is a structure based on an early experience of deprivation and abandonment, wherein the primary parent/caregiver was unable to adequately fulfil the infant's basic needs for nourishment (food), comfort and affection (activated from birth to first 18 months of life). There are many reasons why a caregiver may be psychologically, emotionally, or physically unavailable (or intermittently absent) from their infant's life, such as physical or mental illness, exhaustion, pre- or post-natal depression, addiction, incarceration, divorce, or they may be grieving over the loss of a loved one.

The infant can experience varied levels of emotional, physical, and psychological neglect through deprivation (whether short or long-term), leaving them feeling fearful and anxious, activating their central nervous system into a constant heightened state of arousal. Regardless of the reason for the absence of the caregiver, the infant has suffered some level of dysfunction in their early development creating maladaptive attachment and co-dependency issues that will affect them through childhood, adolescence and into adulthood. A person with an "oral structure" experiences a core feeling of emptiness and longing, seeking fulfilment vicariously through external means and may appear to be either "needy" (dependent/endearing) or the opposite, "needless" (self-reliant/independent).

A victim who has the "needy" (dependent/endearing) aspect of the oral structure harbours a profound hunger for love, affection, acceptance and understanding and may attach themselves to an abuser who exploits the victim's dependency on them and the deep need to maintain their attachment to the abuser despite being abused. **Conversely if the victim is "needless" (self-reliant/independent)** they also have a profound hunger for the same things as the "needy" victim, however it is underlying (unconscious) and therefore not apparent to the person themselves and not visible to others.

A victim who possesses this aspect of the oral character structure is very likely to come across as autonomous, self-sufficient, confident, and self-assured and even though they may appear to be so, they are overcompensating for their true unacknowledged, unconscious, fundamental longing to be loved and cared for. These victims may gravitate towards an abusive partner who is their polar opposite, exhibiting signs of being extremely needy and impossibly demanding or they may seek an abusive partner who is similar in nature to themselves who colludes with the victim's self-reliant/independent character structure. This fits right in with the narcissistic, psychopathic, or sociopathic abuser who lacks empathy, is disinclined to show affection, has a limited emotional range and who is callous, insensitive, and cold-hearted. This abuser will exploit the victim's self-sufficiency, while using their shared emotional disconnection to their full advantage. By preserving distance in a relationship, the abuser can view the victim with a level of detachment that allows them to perpetrate their abusive actions without remorse, shame, or guilt.

The Possible Associated Schemas to the Oral Structure:

Enmeshment/Undeveloped Self Schema

This schema refers to the belief that one cannot exist without a significant other person in which they have placed their love and trust, developing a co-dependency that vicariously allows them to receive a sense of self and self-worth. The other person may be for example, a parent, grandparent, sibling, best friend or intimate partner, the relationship is experienced as intense emotional closeness and excessive attachment where one's priorities are centred entirely on the other person's needs. This schema likely originated in early childhood or adolescence wherein one is parented by controlling, over-protective, abusive, or symbiotic parents/caretakers who discouraged independence and encouraged co-dependence ultimately hindering the child's natural individuation process and development of a separate identity. Those who are afflicted with this schema often suffer from feelings of confusion, sadness and emptiness and an unconscious sense of grief or loss from the lack of possession of an individual identity. This is a result of the bond (symbiosis) created with their co-dependent figure, a relationship that unfortunately prevents them from knowing who they really are.

Victims with this schema will have created a dysfunctional bond with their abuser to the point where it is hard to tell where one begins and the other ends as they have completely enmeshed their identity with the abuser, in fact there is no sense of an "I" for the victim in this relationship. They become a satellite figure to the abuser revolving their entire life around meeting the abusers needs and wants while suppressing, repressing, or denying their own. This bond is usually encouraged by the abuser, feeding into their narcissistic need to feel superior and/or grandiose and to support their dominant, controlling, and manipulative agendas.

The relationship between the victim and abuser is maladaptive and highly detrimental to the victim particularly if the abuser possesses enough emotional and psychological intelligence to be aware of this vulnerability in their victim. Knowing that the victim needs and depends on them even perhaps reveres them, gives the abuser power over the victim making it easier to use and abuse them. Criminals and criminal organisations such as fraudsters looking for financial gain, paedophiles, pimps, cults, sex traffickers and extreme religious orders are known to hone in on potential victims with this schema, targeting the young (runaways or homeless) or those who have lost their partner through death or divorce with the intention to exploit them.

Abandonment/Instability Schema

This schema is driven by the constant fear of relationships ending; these individuals live with the expectation that they will lose their significant other with whom they have formed an emotional attachment. Those who are afflicted with this schema feel anxious insecurity and live with the constant fear of being rejected, betrayed, or abandoned by someone they love, they remain vigilant believing that the relationship could end imminently. There is a pervasive and constant anxiety that underlies their relationships that may cause clinginess, neediness and hypervigilance stemming from feelings of instability and insecurity. Victims afflicted with this schema may cling to a partner despite being abused fearing abandonment or they might mistake a controlling, possessive and manipulative partner as loving and caring keeping their fear of abandonment at bay.

Subjugation Schema

This schema is driven by the belief that one must surrender control to others in order to avoid being rejected or abandoned or to avoid any negative consequences or conflict that comes with objection. Individuals with this schema feel compelled to subjugate their needs and emotions to others who threaten to do something or withhold something if they do not comply. This is coupled with the belief that their own needs, desires, feelings, opinions, and decisions are unimportant or secondary and so they will likely repress, suppress, or deny their innate natural responses. This schema likely originated (not exclusively) during childhood or adolescence from overly controlling and punitive home and/or schooling environments.

Victims with this schema may experience feeling trapped and helpless, finding it difficult to speak out or assert themselves, they lack self-confidence and suffer with low self-esteem and feelings of unworthiness. Narcissistic, sadistic, psychopathic, and sociopathic predators will actively seek out victims with this affliction knowing that they are easier to manipulate, control and subjugate making them a perfect fit for their needs and purposes. A victim of on-going, long-term abuse may possess this schema which acts both consciously and unconsciously to keep them trapped in an abusive situation for long periods of time.

Character Structure Victim – "Rigid"

The Rigid Structure – also referred to as either "industrious – over focused" or "expressive – clingy" develops around the age of three to six years old. This structure forms when the parent/caregiver denies the child their natural and instinctual spontaneity, individual expression, and sexuality, leaving them feeling rejected, guilty, and ashamed. This type of dysfunctional parenting creates a fundamental need in the child to prove to the rejecting parent/caregiver and/or significant others in their life that they are worthy of being loved. In order to gain the much-desired acceptance, approval, and love from those important to them, they have learned to deny, suppress, or repress their own, needs, wants, impulses and emotions to become the desirable perfect and/or accomplished child or adolescent and later the perfect and/or accomplished adult.

Unfortunately, the child develops a split between love and sex; they are unable to surrender to love, fearing the emotional vulnerability that comes with it. When it comes to intimate relationships, they have difficulty connecting emotionally in their intimate relationships even though they are sexually attracted to their partner and are afraid of making mistakes. They are likely to be driven by an unrelenting desire for perfectionism and success, are competitive and tend to be highly critical of themselves and others, expecting those same standards high standards of everyone. You will find that their rigidity is reflected in their posture making it difficult for them to relax, they tend to be inhibited and so may struggle with being playful. Victims with this structure persist with dysfunctional and abusive relationships with the hope that the relationship will improve with time. Their perfectionistic tendencies will not allow them to give up and they desperately need to maintain the façade that they are successful, viewing a relationship break-up or break-down as a failure on their part.

The possible Associated Schemas to the Rigid Structure:

Emotional Inhibition Schema

This schema is driven by the belief that you must suppress spontaneous emotions and impulses, especially anger. Those afflicted with this schema have learned to supress all heightened emotion to avoid embarrassment, retaliation, censure, or criticism, fearing that they will harm others or that they will be disliked, rejected, or abandoned. Their demeanour may be viewed as being cold, rigid, indifferent, uninterested, or uptight and therefore they will find spontaneity difficult if not impossible. They tend to resist change, embracing rigid thinking patterns that inhibit their innate natural responses and/or impulses.

This schema likely originated in childhood or adolescence in an abusive environment where it was either not safe for them to display emotion and/or the parents or caregivers were such that they discouraged or suppressed any show of emotion in those under their care. A victim afflicted with this schema may remain in an on-going abusive relationship or situation because they do not allow themselves to feel the full impact of the emotional, psychological, and physical abuse being perpetrated on them. They tend to engage in fixed thinking patterns based on rigid rules and standards that they doggedly adhere to. They do not cope well with change and even the threat of change can cause fear or anxiety and so they will engage in rationalisations to avoid having to change their life situation regardless of how harmful it is. Eventually, long-term use of this schema may result in the manifestation of physical illnesses, substance abuse and/or addictions or eating, anxiety and behavioural disorders.

Unrelenting Standards or Perfectionism Schema

This schema is driven by the belief that you must meet incredibly high or unrealistic standards in your performance and your behaviour or you have failed. There is an internal demand or unrelenting pressure to meet the highest possible competence level no matter what the endeavour is that this individual takes on. They must always strive harder to do better and expect those who they interact with to do the same and be the same whether it is their children, family, friends, co-workers, or intimate partners.

They hold themselves to impossibly high ideals with excessive attention to time-management and detail, they possess a rigid moral stricture and behavioural code and are hypercritical of themselves and others. This schema would likely have originated in childhood or adolescence wherein love and acceptance from the parents or caregivers was conditional upon the child or teen meeting high and unrealistic goals and standards. Those afflicted with this schema suffer from a constant anxious internal struggle in their pursuit of perfectionism to mask their real underlying feelings of low self-esteem, unworthiness, humiliation and most notably, they fear failure and the shame that may accompany that failure.

They put themselves under constant pressure and as a result suffer from feelings of anxiety, restlessness, agitation, frustration, irritation, and anger when things are not going their way despite the effort they are expending. Long-term use of this schema will ultimately lead to the manifestation of physical illnesses, substance abuse and addiction, eating, anxiety or behavioural disorders and/or clinical psychosis.

Victims who possess this schema are likely to stay longer periods of time in on-going or long-term abusive relationships whether they are intimate, familial, friendship or workplace, unable to free themselves due to their fear of failure. The need to succeed or show they are succeeding to others is highlighted through dysfunctional inter-personal relationships, particularly intimate partner relationships. Consequently, despite being abused, they will employ defensive actions to repress, suppress or deny the abusers actions in order to appease their perfectionistic needs and appear as if they are successful to others. They will engage in rationalisations that may include minimising the abuser's actions or participation in abusive events, quite often taking responsibility for the abuse that was perpetrated on them. They are driven by their unrelenting inner critical voice that blames them for causing problems and urges them to continue to persevere with the maladaptive abusive relationship.

The following three schemas may be linked to (shared by) all the above Character Structures:

Mistrust/Abuse Schema

This schema is driven by the expectation that everyone has an ulterior motive behind their actions and will intentionally take advantage of you in some way, therefore no one can be trusted. This belief was likely formed in early childhood or adolescence stemming from dysfunctional parenting and/or possible verbal, emotional, psychological, or physical abuse. Those afflicted with this schema have a deep-seated belief that others cannot be trusted and expect to be exploited, cheated, hurt, or lied to, suffering from feeling of unhappiness, loneliness, alienation, paranoia, and anger as a result. Victims with excessive mistrust are extremely cynical and doubting of others' intentions and the world in general, finding it difficult to maintain friendships, relate to co-workers or trust intimate partners in romantic relationships.

They may consciously seek out a like-minded partner who shares their mistrust issues entering an unhealthy and dysfunctional relationship where both partners are engaging in exhaustive behaviours that test loyalty and trust. However, perversely a victim might be unconsciously drawn to an abusive partner based on their early negative childhood or adolescent psychological experiences linking love, abuse, and mistrust together entering a relationship with an abuser who contributes to perpetuating their mistrust/abuse schema. Unfortunately, because these mistrust issues become pervasive and all-inclusive a victim afflicted with this schema believes that not a single sole can be trusted. This causes the victim to become insular and isolated, depending only on themselves, not trusting family, friends or the authorities and keeping them trapped in an abusive relationship, organisation or working environment believing that no one can help them.

Negativity/Pessimism Schema

This schema refers to one's compulsive focus on the negative aspects of life while minimising the positive aspects. These individuals are pessimistic in nature, they believe that there is no light at the end of the tunnel and obsess over negative details and potential future problems while worrying about possible deficiencies. Their outlook on life likely originated in childhood or adolescence perpetuated by parents or caregivers who worried excessively or were afflicted with the same schema. Those who possess this schema are unable to enjoy the events that are going well in their lives, repressing, suppressing, or minimising the positive emotions connected to their successes and/or emphasising the negative emotions connected to their failures.

Victims of on-going abuse may remain trapped in an abusive relationship believing that things will likely be worse if they were to leave. For example, in cases of domestic violence by a male perpetrator, the female victim adopts an attitude of "all men are the same" and so they conclude that they are better off with "the devil they know." They have an exaggerated expectation that things will ultimately go wrong no matter what choice they make, this coupled with a negative disposition makes them prone to obsessive negative thinking patterns. Long-term use of this schema may result in the manifestation of serious physical illness, substance abuse and/or addiction or eating, anxiety and behavioural disorders.

Failure Schema

This schema is driven by the belief that one is an innate failure and deficient as a result, this is combined with a pervasive feeling of inadequacy that undermines one's accomplishments. It is characterised by self-doubt, low self-esteem, anxiety, and fear of failing, feeling undeserving of one's successes, punishing oneself for perceived failures or pushing oneself to achieve unrealistic, unrelenting, or perfectionistic standards. Those afflicted with this schema believe they are not capable of performing as well as others and therefore do not take on challenges or try new skills to avoid feelings of inadequacy, failure, and shame. They may think they are inferior, stupid, inept, or untalented and therefore possess a defeatist attitude of "why bother trying" when they know they will fail anyway.

Perfectionistic endeavours or behaviours and indulging in excessive procrastination are both attempts to overcompensate for, or avoid disappointment, disapproval, rejection and the fear, anxiety and shame that accompanies failure. Victims may unconsciously be drawn to a partner (abuser) who perpetuates these feelings of inadequacy fulfilling the abusers need for superiority and/or grandiosity, while confirming the victim's fundamental belief that they are indeed a failure. Unfortunately, predator's target victims who possess this vulnerability honing in on their insecurities by aligning themselves with the victim's feelings of inadequacy and/or lulling them with a false show of empathy and understanding. Innate feelings of failure can also operate to keep a victim inured in an abusive relationship or situation believing that they are either, unworthy of and undeserving of better or they may believe that they are deserving of mistreatment and punishment.

Defence Theory – Victims

Quite often, a victim of long-term abuse is unaware that have become or are becoming a victim until they find themselves deeply inured in the abusive situation. For some, it may be the result of a combination of youthful inexperience, naïveté, underdeveloped mature defences and limited emotional and psychological capacities at the time they entered the relationship. Innocence, a trusting nature and emerging from sheltered home environments are all contributing factors that form part of the background for unsuspecting victims and are a primary attraction for predators and abusers.

Victims who enter a relationship with an abuser at a young age have not had an opportunity to gain enough necessary interpersonal relationship experience to be able to successfully anticipate potential abuse and danger and therefore are easily taken advantage of. "Innocence" is an easily discernible vulnerability that is coveted by predators, it shines like a beacon of light drawing them like a magnet to the inexperienced and naïve. However, it is important to note that, not all victims are guileless and trusting even the most intelligent, experienced, and socially aware human being can find themselves in a potentially abusive or dangerous situation or relationship.

Not all adult victims who are experiencing on-going abuse whether short or long-term will necessarily possess a background that includes a marked history of early childhood and/or teenage developmental dysfunction where they were either a witness to or had directly experienced abuse themselves. In fact, a victim may have come from a seemingly normal, nurturing, and adjusted family background where there was no overt or obvious evidence of neglect or abuse. However, whether their personal history includes notable dysfunction, some victims of on-going long-term abuse share a psychological and emotional maladaptive commonality that is referred to as an "undeveloped/enmeshed-self" schema (refer to p113). Victims with this schema believe they cannot live or enjoy life without the constant emotional support of a significant other such as a spouse/intimate partner, parent, or mentor.

The "undeveloped or enmeshed self" is a part of oneself that has not successfully evolved emotionally and psychologically from adolescence into adulthood. A victim who is afflicted with this schema has not had enough life experience to develop a sense of self that expresses their individuality or an ego-identity that reflects who they are. These individuals believe that they cannot cope with or enjoy life without the constant support of a significant other party in whom they have allotted all their trust and faith. They have not had an opportunity to develop the mature defences (refer to mature defences p44) necessary for healthy relationships and therefore possess some level of emotional and psychological naïveté that limits their understanding of people and their dark natures.

A victim with an undeveloped or enmeshed self may easily fall prey to a predator having not fully completed the individuation and social developmental processes that are necessary to embrace adulthood and reduce their vulnerability to a potential abuser. The bond that is created with the abuser is one that further inhibits a victim's individual growth, and encourages dependency and enmeshment with the perpetrator. Personal boundaries become unclear and they lose themselves, becoming a satellite figure to the abuser, whose needs must become the victim's top priority. The abuser supresses the victim's freedom of expression, discouraging independent thinking and therefore the victim does not make decisions or act contrary to that of their abuser.

For other victims, it may be a natural progression to enter an abusive adult relationship having come from a background where they were a witness to or had experienced abuse themselves, only to repeat a cycle that they have not had an opportunity to evolve from and have become psychologically and emotionally accustomed to. These victims have grown up in dysfunctional relationships and environments developing distorted misconceptions about themselves, others, and the world at large, having experienced some level of psychological and emotional arrested development. They tend to possess entrenched conscious and/or unconscious negative beliefs, seeing themselves as fundamentally flawed, who may also concurrently be afflicted with a "defectiveness and shame" schema (refer to p107). Victims with this schema experience debilitating shame who believe they are physically, emotionally and/or psychologically defective, and therefore unworthy of being loved and cared for.

Those who exist at the extreme end of the defectiveness/shame schema are victims who believe they deserve to be mistreated and/or punished. Their backgrounds may or may not include dysfunctional developmental issues; however, they may have been reared in environments that espoused prohibitive, archaic, misogynistic, and suppressive cultural and religious influences and/or beliefs that support the negative principles.

However, a victim who finds themselves in an abusive relationship who has come from a seemingly healthy enough childhood or adolescent upbringing may also find that they possess negative conscious and/or unconscious psychological and emotional beliefs about themselves, others, and the world at large. We have already established that all human beings possess defences; therefore, we can postulate that victims develop defences in much the same way as their abusive counterparts.

Defences are universal in nature and similar in context, they can have a corresponding effect for both the victim and the abuser, however they will be utilised in different ways and for different reasons. For example, the defence of dissociation for a perpetrator of violence may be used, to separate and distance themselves from an act of abuse with the purpose of minimising conscious participation to reduce their accountability and/or avoid emotions such as guilt, shame, or remorse. The defence of dissociation for a victim may be used to separate themselves from the reality of the violence/abuse being perpetrated on them by distancing themselves psychologically and emotionally to diminish or negate the impact of the abuse.

Defence mechanisms come into being as a protective measure to either manage, completely negate, or minimise unwanted and/or unacceptable thoughts, feelings, desires, and impulses which may also be viewed as a type of psychological and emotional self-deception. All victims possess particular defences that can increase their vulnerability or susceptibility to danger and may play a role in limiting or inhibiting the capacity to separate from an abuser and/or abusive situation. The need to explore the origins of the defences most used by victims of abuse, why they came into being and how they impact on a victim will give us a deeper insight and understanding of their psychological and emotional anatomy. The following list contains possible defences that a victim may possess, they may have any combination or all these defences.

Defence (Victim): Dissociation

Victims of abuse may instinctually use the defence of dissociation as a form of reducing the harmful impact of abuse. This is an innate defence which most human beings possess establishing itself in early childhood and formed out of necessity to distance and protect the developing psyche from emotional and psychological distress. It becomes activated when the mind perceives an overwhelming real or imagined threat, triggering a reaction that causes the conscious mind to separate from the reality of an event that is too traumatic to accept. There are varied levels of dissociation from mild such as, day dreaming or "losing touch" of one's awareness by being absorbed by a book or movie, through to the extreme end of the dissociative scale where one can blank-out complete events and suffer from amnesia or a dissociative identity disorder. Victims who suffer from dissociative related symptoms will likely slot the memory of the abuse into one of the following compartments in the mind to either:

- Never be opened or remembered – The effect of abuse on a victim has many variables that determine how their psyche will cope: their age at the time of the abuse, their emotional and psychological maturity, their level of cognitive function and the severity of the abuse. These are all factors that when combined can cause the mind to block out entire traumatic events.
- To be involuntarily opened and remembered (not by conscious choice) – A traumatic memory can lay dormant in a compartment of the psyche until an unexpected external situation triggers this suppressed memory (which can occur at any time after the event an hour, a day, a week, a month, or years after the event). The triggered memory of an event may be remembered in its entirety or it may be partial depicting only an aspect or aspects of the traumatic event.

- To be opened and remembered with partial dissociation – It is possible for the dissociative process to present itself in the form of "splitting" wherein a part of the mind separates from actual event whilst the victim can maintain some level of conscious awareness.

It may appear as if the mind and body have split off from each other, one part of the mind has separated from the traumatic event and is observing the event while it is occurring with detachment as if watching a scene in a movie. It can be experienced as a feeling of unreality and may seem as if time has slowed down, resulting in giving a victim an accessible memory even though it has possibly muted one or more aspects of the event possibly an emotional, psychological, or physical element of the traumatic incident.

Victims of on-going or long-term domestic and family abuse, random acts of extreme violence, sexual abuse, torture, and those who have been kidnapped and/or held hostage will more than likely have experienced some level of dissociation in order to survive their ordeals. Dissociation can provide separation from the actuality and the reality of an abusive event by either minimising, completely blanking-out or blocking aspects of the physical, emotional, and psychological distress. Some victims are left with a surreal feeling, questioning whether the abusive event actually took place this may last for hours, days, weeks, months, or years. Those who endure severe trauma whether it is a singular event or on-going abuse may dissociate through a process known as PTSD (post-traumatic stress disorder) or they may develop other serious dissociative disorders.

In adults, some of the more notable dissociative effects of long-term abuse can present as extreme physical, emotional, and psychological fatigue, confusion, forgetfulness and mild to severe memory loss. As time goes on, victims of on-going abuse will become exhausted, finding it more and more difficult to stay centred in the present (reality) where they are undergoing consistent and sometimes unrelenting abuse. This can trigger a need to retreat through dissociation wherein victims can experience a state of numbness or nothingness. They may feel the need to sleep all the time, experience impaired cognitive function becoming more susceptible to developing a disorder known as CFS (chronic fatigue syndrome) which is characterised by extreme fatigue. Conversely, dissociation can also have the opposite effect where a victim retreats into fantasy filling in blank spaces with fabrications, creating illusions, consistently daydreaming or they may experience insomnia, nightmares, and behavioural disorders such as OCD (obsessive compulsive disorder) which is characterised by unreasonable thoughts and fears (obsessions) that lead to compulsive behaviours.

Other common symptoms of dissociation are depression, substance abuse, addiction, sleeping, anxiety and eating disorders and chronic illness in the form of digestion issues, headaches, migraines, neck and back pain or hypertension. Children and adolescents present with the many of the same psychological, emotional, and physical issues as the adults mentioned above however, depending on their age behaviours may include bed wetting, an inability to stay focused at school, fatigue, irritability, learning difficulties and sleeping, eating, anxiety and behavioural disorders including acting out.

There seems to be an ever-increasing number of patients being diagnosed with "psychological disorders" that present themselves with similar diagnostic characteristics to each other, making it difficult for physicians to identify a disorder with complete accuracy. As a result, children and adolescents who suffer from PTSD (post-traumatic stress disorder) or similar associated dissociative conditions are quite often misdiagnosed. They may be thought to have a common childhood behavioural disorder known as "attention deficit hyperactivity disorder" (ADHD or ADD), which is a chronic condition with symptoms such as inattentiveness, impulsivity, and hyperactivity (which begins in childhood and can persist to adulthood), when in fact they be experiencing dissociative symptoms from bearing witness to or being the victim of neglect and abuse.

Dissociative Disorders

At the extreme end of the dissociative scale, there are victims who develop a "dissociative identity disorder" (DID or multiple personality disorder) which is the development of two or more distinct identities or "personality states". This is a result of severe and overwhelming traumatic experiences of abuse, most found in adults who have experienced sexual abuse and neglect during their childhood and/or adolescent developmental years. This defence although essential for psychological and emotional survival can become extremely detrimental to a victim's overall wellbeing when it remains on-going having never been addressed with some form of therapeutic intervention. Victims who suffer from dissociative disorders resist acknowledging overwhelming feelings of terror, anxiety, pain, humiliation, shame, guilt, or helplessness that has resulted from either a singular traumatic event or on-going acts of abuse in their life. They may have developed any of the following dissociative disorders in response to overwhelming emotional and psychological trauma:

- Post-traumatic Stress-Disorder – A victim afflicted with this disorder may experience, "flashbacks" to traumatic events and/or temporary memory loss also known as the "blanking out" of traumatic events. They experience feeling disconnected or detached from their emotions and their external world and may have a distorted or blurred sense of reality.
- Depersonalisation/Derealisation Disorder – A victim afflicted with this disorder can experience feeling a sense of general emotional detachment from the actuality of the lived experience of their life. It is as if they are watching themselves in a movie, time may feel as if it has slowed down, accompanied by a sense of unreality. They can experience difficulty concentrating and temporary memory loss or in some extreme cases, they cannot recognise themselves in the mirror.
- Dissociative Fugue – A victim afflicted with this disorder can experience a sudden and complete loss of memory of who they are, which may last hours, days weeks or months. When the victim comes out of the dissociative fugue, they will experience confusion and an inability to recollect the events that have taken place after the onset of the fugue. In some cases, they do not realise that they are experiencing a memory loss and may invent a completely new identity.
- Dissociative Amnesia – A victim afflicted with this disorder can experience various types of amnesia:
- Localised amnesia – this is short-term memory loss of a traumatic event, perhaps for a few hours or days.
- Selective amnesia – this reflects sketchy or incomplete memories of a traumatic event.
- Systemised amnesia – this is specific memory block with no recollection of a particular traumatic incident or the period associated with the trauma.
- General amnesia – this is experienced as difficulty remembering significant details of their life.

Defence (Victim): Compartmentalisation

Compartmentalisation is for the most part an unconscious psychological defence mechanism designed to resolve internal conflict (cognitive dissonance), anxiety and/or tension by isolating inconsistent or contradicting thoughts, emotions, or beliefs from each other.

By compartmentalising traumatic events, some victims receive a temporary reprieve and/or relief from the impact of psychological and emotional suffering. It can provide protection and distance from a frightening or anxiety provoking event that the mind does not have the capacity to accept. We see this quite often with victims who were involved in extreme acts of violence who have no memory of the incident or the events leading up to it. In on-going or long-term abusive scenarios, such as enslavement or domestic and family abuse, compartmentalisation is a method of intervention for those who struggle with reconciling the conflicting or opposing thoughts and emotions they may hold towards their abuser. The perpetrator whether purposeful or not creates states of confusion in the victim by possibly claiming to love and/or care for them while at the same time perpetrating horrendous acts of abuse on them.

This causes the victim to experience untenable cognitive, psychological, and emotional conflict between wanting or needing to believe that they are loved, cared for, and valued by the abuser and the opposing reality of experiencing the opposite. The need, to avoid the feelings of betrayal, extreme internal distress, dread, anxiety, panic and/or horror that accompanies the abusive acts may trigger the onset of the defence of dissociation via compartmentalisation. The victim separates the abuser's abusive acts into one compartment not to be acknowledged or addressed and only sees or accepts the "good" in the abuser. Whether it is the abuser's premeditated intention to cause the victim internal conflict or not the result is still the same with the abuser taking full advantage of the situation.

Abusers such as child sexual offenders and domestic and family abusers are experts at using psychological and emotional manipulation and coercion. They create confusion in their victim, their words of praise and affection are at odds with their actions, they intimate that they love, care for, and have the victim's best interests at heart while at the same time using and abusing them. They are known to employ a commonly used abusive tactic called "gaslighting," this is a deliberate act to manipulate the perception of the victim's reality to create an environment where they are in a constant state of emotionally charged "cognitive dissonance" (internal disharmony) and therefore pliant and compliant.

The abuser causes the victim to question their thinking, persuading them to accept an untruth as a truth, a premeditated and purposeful endeavour aimed at distorting the perception that the abuse actually took place. This causes the victim to experience a deep inner psychological and emotional conflict which can result in triggering a need to detach or separate (compartmentalise) the opposing feelings and thoughts to survive in the two disparate worlds. Unfortunately, on-going, long-term abuse eventually takes a physical, emotional, and psychological toll regardless of a victim's defence mechanisms, resulting in the manifestation of anxiety, sleeping, and eating disorders, chronic illness, depression, acting-out, personality and behavioural disorders, substance abuse, addiction, self-harm, and suicide.

Defence (Victim): Denial

Let us first establish that denial is a defence mechanism that most human beings experience, it is elemental in nature acting instinctually, a survival technique that activates automatically usually without conscious participation in response to a real or perceived threat.

Denial is one of the most used psychological defence mechanisms shared by both abusers and victims alike. Its purpose is to block the harmful emotional and psychological impact that results from unacceptable external events and circumstances or internal disturbing thoughts and emotions. Denial occurs when a victim is unable to admit, acknowledge or accept that they are being subjected to abuse or that the perpetrator of the abuse is in fact being abusive. In some cases, a victim may not possess the capacity to understand that they are being abused and are unaware they are in denial of the impact of the harmful actions being perpetrated on them. Remember some acts of abuse are covert therefore not easily detectable and may not necessarily appear to be adverse or detrimental on the surface.

Denial is a defence common among victims of child sexual abuse, domestic and family abuse, sex traffickers and organisations such as cults and sects. Many victims of on-going or long-term abuse have been groomed over time and/or indoctrinated from a very young age into a life of abuse. They are ignorant of the world at large in varying degrees due to isolation, brain washing and the subversive manipulative and coercive tactics of their abuser/s. These victims will deny and supress or repress the existence of disturbing or uncomfortable thoughts and feelings that cause apprehension, anxiety and fear, dread or despair that can arise from abuse. This powerful defence mechanism is used by children, adolescents, and adults alike however the reasons why however will differ.

Denial in children and adolescents may come into being out of the following abusive scenarios:

- A child or adolescent cannot reconcile a parent/guardian/caregiver who supposedly loves and cares for them with the same parent/guardian/caregiver who is abusing them. It is unbearable to acknowledge the reality of the abusive actions and therefore they retreat into denial.

- A child or adolescent who idealises their parent/guardian/caregiver by ignoring, minimising and/or denying their hurtful, neglectful, and abusive actions engaging in fantasising while polarising the parent/guardian/caregiver at the opposite end of scale, from victimiser to hero/heroine.

- A child or adolescent who may have experienced early trauma from the loss of a parent due to death or divorce may have developed a fear of abandonment and therefore deny the abusive actions of the current acting parent/care-giver.

- A child or adolescent who cannot accept or process the harmful impact of the reality of the physical, emotional, and psychological abuse being perpetrated on them and therefore retreats into denial.

For children and adolescents, it is too painful to see the truth about those they love and when combined with their innate instinctual need to have love and acceptance mirrored back to them will be a powerful motivator for denial of parental abuse. They cannot understand the motivations behind the abusive parent's actions or accept the reality of the abuse that they are undergoing and so they block out whole episodes of abuse, supressing or repressing the unwanted negative and painful emotions that arise as a result. In serious cases of abuse where there is severe physical and emotional neglect, psychological torment, sexual assault including incest and/or repeated violence, young victims may develop behavioural pathologies, personality disorders, illnesses and addictions that may affect them for the rest of their life particularly if there has been no therapeutic intervention.

However, as we have discussed earlier not all abuse is overt and can easily be perpetrated in a covert and subversive manner taking a subtler form with numerous possible scenarios. For example, perhaps the abuser is a parent who sets unrealistic and age-inappropriate goals for a child that the child cannot possibly attain, setting them up for feelings of failure and incompetency. Perhaps the abuser is a parent whose narcissistic needs are always placed above the needs of their child leaving the child with feelings of inadequacy, unworthiness, and self-hatred. Regardless of whether the abuse is overt or covert children and adolescents will have a difficult time accepting the truth about hurtful parents/caregivers, possibly clinging to "false hope." False hope also known as "pathological hope" is a form of denial that helps to diminish emotional anguish when one's reality becomes too overwhelming.

Denial in adults usually comes into being out of any of the following abusive scenarios:

- A victim whose intimate partner was once kind, caring, attentive and supposedly loving cannot reconcile this same intimate partner who has become the abuser and therefore retreats into denial.

- A victim whose ego-identity is linked to their "idealised relationship" wherein keeping up appearances is essential, will deny or at the very least minimise the abusive behaviour of their intimate partner to preserve the relationship and the facade.

- A victim whose early childhood is linked to a "failure schema" cannot allow themselves to experience failure or appear as if they are failing in their intimate relationship and so will deny or at the very least minimise the abusive behaviour of the intimate partner.

- A victim who is afflicted with the "defectiveness and shame schema" suffers from unconscious deep-seated feelings of inadequacy believing they are unworthy of being loved and cared for and so will deny or at the very least minimise their abuser's actions.

- A victim who is unable to accept or process the reality of the impact of the physical, emotional, and psychological abuse being perpetrated on them and therefore retreats into denial.

- A victim who is afflicted with an "enmeshment or undeveloped self, schema" who cannot contemplate life without the intimate partner or spouse, whose whole existence is dependent on their significant other (the abuser) will deny or at the very least minimise their abuser's actions.

Denial of Reality

We have established that a victim may go into denial out of the need to negate or lessen the physical, emotional, and psychological impact associated with trauma and abuse. However, there also exists those who need to deny they are a victim at all, for some accepting being a victim is admitting that they are vulnerable and even though this is true, they will never admit this to themselves. For them, being vulnerable equates to a weakness of character and a sense of failure, which is particularly acute for those who are afflicted with a "failure or defectiveness and shame schema." Admitting to themselves that they are a victim may trigger feelings of personal inadequacy or deficiency which they cannot countenance. On the surface, it seems as if all is well in their life, there is a sense of order and they appear to be in control which they achieve by denying facts (reality) and lying to themselves and others.

Unfortunately, the truth of the matter is that they live in at best, a psychologically and emotionally, dysfunctional, and unsatisfactory relationship and at worst in a physically, emotionally, and psychologically highly abusive and dangerous relationship. There are many abusers, particularly those engaging in on-going, long-term relationships who may employ a covert abusive technique called "gaslighting" which is aimed at distorting the reality and understanding of true and actual events. This form of emotional and psychological manipulation is not only employed by an individual abuser it may also be employed by a group of people sowing seeds of doubt or denying the verity of an event causing the victim/s to question their memory, judgement, or perception of that same event.

This creates an experience of highly charged cognitive dissonance (internal conflict), deep-seated self-doubt, confusion and anxiety destabilising a victim and their capacity to make decisions. In intimate relationships or any long-term abusive situations if there is constant exposure to gaslighting, a victim may develop a psychosis or an anxiety, eating, sleeping or behavioural disorder or at the very least, it can cause a loss of confidence and feelings of low self-esteem and depression. When a victim is stripped of their ability to trust in themselves, they may develop what is known as "learned helplessness" (an acceptance of personal powerlessness) which promotes an unhealthy dependence on the abuser for emotional support and validation.

Victims will often be introduced into gaslighting by their intimate partner from the onset of their relationship, particularly if they are young and naïve. They will be unaware that they are being "gaslighted," especially if the abuser is sociopathic, psychopathic, or narcissistic in nature and therefore adept at lying and lulling their victim onto a false sense of security. This type of abuser consistently denies any wrongdoing, has no qualms distorting the truth to fulfil their perverse agendas and projects shame and blame onto the victim. In intimate relationships, it is used to deny or diminish the abuser's accountability for their abusive actions and at the same time deny or diminish the victim's re-collection of actual events.

Gaslighting is commonly used by those who commit marital or relationship infidelity, they have a propensity to distort the truth with elaborate lies, their aim is to distract and confuse an intimate partner from the truth of the events. In situations where there is on-going or long-term abuse whether it is domestic and family abuse, child sexual abuse, sex trafficking or a cult, the victim undergoes an indoctrination process whereby the abuser slowly introduces the victim into becoming accustomed to allowing the abuser to re-define their sense of reality. The perpetrators aim is to take advantage of the victim's trust, possible idealisation and need for approval from them by using their manipulative skills to cause the victim to question their memory and perception of events. Gaslighting by abusers involves a combination of psychological and emotional manipulative tactics to invalidate a victim's true experience and cause them to doubt the validity of a shared experience.

They use any or all the following techniques:

- Using dismissive language and statements towards the victim such as, "you're paranoid," "don't be stupid" or "you're crazy".
- Withholding pertinent information (lying by omission to distort the truth).

- Verbally attacking (shaming and blaming) the victim – this is often used as a method to distract the victim from "actual events," a way to divert the attention from the abuser and their actions.
- Trivialising events – the abuser downplays or minimises the seriousness of the abusive event making the victim feel as if they are over-reacting and causing them to doubt their perception of the event.
- Question the victim's credibility – many abusers believe that attack is the best form of defence and so if confronted by a victim who is questioning the facts, they attack the victim's ability to be credible causing them to doubt themselves.
- Blocking or diverting the victim from receiving information from outside sources who may counteract the abuser's version of events (which may damage the abuser's controlling position).
- Outright denial of the occurrence of an event – by completely denying an event even happened can cause a victim to question their sanity.

Minimisation: A Lesser Form of Denial

Denial is a powerful form of psychological self-deception that supports a person's delusions about themselves, others, and the world at large. However, there will be situations where complete denial is not possible, specifically in the face of overwhelming evidence to the contrary therefore, a victim may employ the lesser form of denial of "minimisation." This includes discounting, downplaying, and invalidating, making light of, trivialising, underplaying, or understating the abuser's actions. Minimisation is a way to reduce the emotional and psychological impact of abuse, provide a false sense of safety and helps to preserve the victim's dignity.

Victims often take responsibility for the abuse that was perpetrated on them by blaming themselves and rationalising or justifying the abuser's behaviour. The victim may re-define abusive events to downplay their significance, an effective way to preserve a more acceptable version of events and at the same time avoid acknowledging and dealing with unwanted emotions and thoughts. Minimising the perpetrators abusive actions is a way to avoid conscious confrontation with the abuser's negative behaviour. This helps to sustain the belief that all is well and therefore the difficult decision to remove themselves and/or those they love from the abusive situation does not have to be made.

Suppression: A Lesser Form of Denial

Suppression is a psychological defence mechanism that forces information out of awareness, it is an active fight against allowing unwanted thoughts or feelings to rise to deny their existence. Victims may suppress their natural instinctual responses to abuse, denying themselves the freedom to accept that the abuse occurred or allowing an acknowledgement and/or expression of the physical, emotional, and psychological impact of the harm being perpetrated on them. This defence may have its origins rooted in a victim's early childhood or adolescent developmental years, becoming a learned automated response to their subsequent life situation.

It would have come into being from a very young age as a defensive response at a time in their life when it was not safe to show how they really felt, or where a show of emotion was actively discouraged by a parent or guardian. Suppression ultimately does not work as a strategy, if anything it makes one more susceptible to unwanted intrusive thoughts and feelings, the more you try to force them down the more their need to spring back up. Imagine a suitcase that has been over-packed brimming at the seams, then you try putting one more item in and the suitcase bursts open. Suppression is linked to be the cause of mental health issues such as post-traumatic-stress disorder (PTSD), obsessive compulsive disorder (OCD), anxiety and depression, however, it may also be the cause of physical health issues such as illness and substance abuse or addiction.

This defence can become necessary for victims of on-going or long-term abuse who have learned to suppress their feelings towards their abuser or risk further abuse. Abusers are known to be unpredictable and retaliatory and so the victim can either risk lengthening the abusive event or heightening an already volatile situation. When the abuser is in the "throws" of their angry tirade or rageful outburst, they will not tolerate a victim expressing their opinion, particularly if it is contrary to their own. This pattern of abuse has been set-up over time wherein the victim has learned very early on in the relationship that it is not safe to share their thoughts and feelings with the abuser.

The suppression eventually becomes an automated response the moment they sense or are faced with a potentially abusive event it activates instinctively as a survival technique to protect them from further abuse or to a potentially dangerous or lethal outcome. Through automatic suppression, a victim denies themselves access to the emotions and thoughts that they know they are never allowed to express before, during and after an abusive episode. Not only is it not safe, it can be experienced as being self-defeating for a victim to allow these thoughts or emotions to surface to derail an already tenuous hold on their psychological and emotional stability.

Not all thoughts and emotions that arise from an abusive situation are directed towards the abuser, the victim will also not acknowledge the emotions and thoughts that are directed inward towards themselves such as self-loathing, self-blame, unworthiness, shame, and guilt. This is an underlying issue that can be the cause of physical health issues, behavioural and psychological disorders, substance abuse and addiction.

Somatisation: A Consequence of Denial

Somatisation is a by-product of the defence of denial; it is the manifestation of somatic symptoms (physical illness) in response to psychological distress. Denying, suppressing, or repressing unwanted or untenable thoughts and feelings will eventually give rise to physical symptoms in the form of headaches, migraines, generalised pain, fatigue, digestion issues, stomach ulcers, bowel dysfunction, back and neck pain and heart conditions. Somatisation can also be perpetuated by or responsible for substance abuse or addiction (including sexual and gambling), depression, anxiety and can lead to clinical psychological disorders such as:

- Hypochondriasis – A fear that minor symptoms of illness may be due to an underlying serious disease.
- Conversion disorder – A condition where a person has symptoms which suggest serious illness, that usually develop quickly in response to a stressful situation such as, blindness, deafness, or partial paralysis.
- Body dysmorphic disorder – An obsessive pattern of thinking associated with appearance and body image.
- Pain disorder – A condition where a person has a persistent pain that cannot be attributed to a particular physical origin.

Children and adolescents may also present with behavioural disorders such as:

- Anxiety disorder – characterised by excessive fear or worry.
- Stress disorder – characterised by symptoms of intrusive thoughts, nightmares, mood swings an arousal in avoidance of traumatic events which can be either short term (ASD) or long term (PTSD).

- Obsessive-compulsive or disruptive disorders – in the form of ADHD (attention-deficit/hyperactivity disorder) – characterised by obsessive and compulsive pathologic urges.
- Conduct disorder – characterised by a recurrent, persistent pattern of behaviour that violates the rights of others.
- Oppositional defiant disorder – characterised by recurrent or persistent pattern of negative, defiant, or hostile behaviour directed at authority figures.

Somatisation can be difficult to diagnose as the symptoms are extremely diverse and can be linked to any number of medical illnesses. It is human nature to look to the medical profession for a scientific resolution for our ailments, giving us physical, psychological, and emotional relief and a sense of comfort when they diagnose our ailment and provide us with a solution or management plan. Victims of abuse who engage in denial by repression or suppression who suffer physical ailments as a result (somatisation) may seek and receive medical treatment for their physical symptoms. However, these treatments will only give them temporary relief as they have not addressed the real underlying psychological and emotional issues that are the root cause of their illness, disorders and/or addictions.

Collective Denial:
Keeping Sexual Assault Hidden

It is not only victims, witnesses and abusers who engage in denial, nearly all human beings at one time or another have needed this defence in some capacity along with various factions in societies at large. People incorrectly assume that abusers are people that are "all bad" who only commit bad deeds and therefore easily identifiable as a result of their actions. However, people who perpetrate acts of violence, domestic abuse, sexual assault, psychological manipulation, coercion, bullying and the like may otherwise be seemingly ordinary human beings, projecting positive images of themselves. You will find that conflict can arise in a community (between those who do believe and those who do not) that are rocked with the news that a much loved and lauded public figure has been exposed for criminal and/or abusive behaviour.

Particularly a person with a high profile, who is perhaps held in high esteem for their achievements, who may be altruistic or self-sacrificing and known for their generosity or contributions to sport or the arts. When this high-profile figure comes to grief because they have been caught out or accused of committing criminal and/or abusive acts. It can establish conflicting feelings (cognitive dissonance) for those who have had a positive experience of the accused such as a friendship, working relationship, are an avid fan of their body of work or their benevolent endeavours. Denial occurs on a larger scale in these high-profile cases as there are a collective many who cannot reconcile the much-loved, highly regarded persona with the persona of the abuser who can commit monstrous deeds.

In other words, it is difficult to come to terms with the high esteem and pleasant feelings that one holds for the abuser's public persona and the abhorrent accusations about their private persona particularly those that are charged with crimes of a sexually abusive nature. This helps to explain why highly regarded public figures can perpetrate their crimes over a long period of time. Refusing to accept that a favoured public figure is in fact an abusive criminal causes societal division and further "victimises" victims. It perpetuates misogynistic thinking and ideals that either the abuse did not occur, the accuser is lying or the accuser is somehow responsible, which is in fact a form of victim blaming.

Many victims of sexual assault are reluctant to come forward as they are quite often made to feel as if they must convince friends, family, co-workers, the authorities, and the community at large that they were truly sexually abused rather than the perpetrator having to convince others and the authorities that they did not do it. Denial by multiple others that is directed at a victim can cause them to become fearful and confused, second-guessing, their account of the abuse. This results in self-blame or sharing of accountability with the perpetrator, ultimately succumbing to the collective denial.

It is perhaps instinctive but more likely necessary to want to believe that the world in general is a safe place to be, counteracting our fear of uncertainty and providing us with a feeling of security so that we may go about our daily life feeling reasonably confident and safe. The need to be able to make sense of abhorrent crime combined with the need to be able to trust in our instincts and judgement can influence how we view victims of crime, particularly crimes of a sexual nature. Feelings of fear and helplessness can arise in society as a whole in response to acts of random violence, the compulsion to make sense of the crime is necessary to restore our sense of stability and safety and assure us that the world is indeed a safe place to be.

By projecting a measure of blame onto a victim, it is possible to create a reason for the abuse when there is not one. In other words, it is easier to blame a victim for the harm perpetrated on them rather than it is to accept the vulnerability that is associated with the belief that it can happen to anyone. It provides our psyche with a measure of psychological and emotional relief to question the decisions of the victim rather than accept the reality of the terror of the randomness of crime, by rationalising that an act of violence can be somewhat predictable and therefore may be avoided.

Defence (Victim): Repression

Repression is a defence mechanism that is unconsciously activated working to keep unwanted feelings, thoughts, and desires from surfacing into conscious awareness. It is triggered when an individual is faced with a traumatic event that becomes too psychologically and emotionally overwhelming to process and is ultimately blanked out. However, even though the memory is repressed it does not guarantee that the memory will remain out of consciousness forever, it is possible for parts of, or whole traumatic events to come to light when stimulated by an incidental external trigger. Repression must not be confused with either "suppression" which is a defence that is consciously activated to remove unwanted, feelings, thoughts and desires from consciousness and "denial" which is a refusal of the truth.

Forcing parts of, or entire traumatic events and the feelings associated with them into unconsciousness will most definitely result in manifesting some level of physical, emotional and/or psychological dysfunction. Victims of abuse who possess repressed memories may exhibit eating, sleeping, anxiety, behavioural and/or personality disorders, irrational fears and phobias, substance abuse and addiction and they may experience health and inter-personal relationship issues.

These victims will not be aware of the true origins or underlying cause that may be the driving force behind their illness, disorder, phobia, or addiction. An individual who suffers from repression may project a persona that suggests that they are rational, composed, confident and competent; they appear to be in control of their emotions, sometimes in the extreme where they seem unaffected or possibly unempathetic. They show a pre-occupation with meeting other people's needs, however, seem to be unsuccessful in their intimate relationships.

Quite often unexplained fears and phobias present themselves in adulthood, however, they may have their origins rooted in a childhood incident that cannot be remembered. For example, an adult who has an irrational fear of heights may have experienced a traumatic fall from a height as a child but does not remember where the fear originated from. Adolescent victims who experienced verbal, physical and sexual abuse can often exhibit repressed memory symptoms which may manifest into negative eating, sleeping, anxiety and behavioural disorders such as ADHD (attention deficit hyperactivity disorder) acting out, shop-lifting, self-harming, excessive smoking/drinking, substance abuse and addiction, depression, suicidal thoughts, and suicide.

It is not uncommon for victims of violent crime particularly those who have experienced physical brutality to have repressed the memory of the entire traumatic event, they know something has happened to them however, they cannot recall any of the circumstances or happenings. It is as if time stood still for the duration of the abuse and restarted at some time after the abusive event took place leaving the victim with a blank space in their memory bank. Unfortunately, the impact of the abuse will have had a detrimental psychological, emotional, and physical effect on them whether they consciously remember the event or not, refer to ("The body remembers" p10). Other victims can experience another form of memory loss known as PTSD (post-traumatic stress disorder) which may be responsible for blocking out whole segments of a victim's life (in the form of amnesia) for long periods of time.

Defence (Victim): Regression

Regression is an unconsciously motivated defence mechanism of reverting to childlike or immature behaviours as a coping-strategy when faced with overwhelming feelings of stress, anxiety, fear, guilt, or shame. This defence causes individuals to regress into activities that had given them comfort, relief or was an outlet for unwanted or unacceptable emotions or impulses when they were a small child. These may include bedwetting, thumb-sucking, baby talk, incessant weeping, sulking, temper tantrums, lying, blaming others, hyperactivity, sleeping issues including nightmares and/or physical illnesses including headaches, migraines, and stomach problems. This relapse into infantilism can be experienced within any age group from childhood through to old age and may be viewed as an attempt to escape the reality of an abusive or traumatic event or series of events.

Child victims of abuse may experience varied levels of emotional, physical, psychological, and cognitive arrested development determined by the severity and duration of the abuse they have undergone. There are significant signs throughout infancy, childhood and/or adolescence that they are not meeting the normal developmental milestones expected for healthy psychological, emotional, and physical growth. They are unable to evolve from infantile behaviours such as bedwetting, thumb sucking and nail biting or they may exhibit learning difficulties, speech impediments such as stuttering or an inability or unwillingness to communicate. Adult victims of abuse who revert to regressive behaviours as a defence have patterns that were likely but not exclusively established in their early childhood that they have never out-grown or addressed.

These behaviours may carry throughout adulthood and for some may even be life-long patterns of behaviour. The "regressor" can become fixated on a specific area of their arrested development becoming gripped by a singular infantile behaviour during a particular stage of their early development. Other victims may undergo regressive behaviours that can reach adverse or chronic proportions as a result of being put under extreme and/or prolonged duress (abuse) known as "hysterical puerilism" which is a temporary or intermittent form infantile behaviour.

There are some that may be afflicted with severe personality disorganisation such as chronic schizophrenia which is a regression into very early infantile behaviour in the form baby or toddler like tendencies such as needing to be fed, bathed, dressed and in some cases, there may be a need for nappies.

Defence (Victim):
Substance Abuse and Addiction

Addiction is a defence that acts as an agent against overwhelming or unwanted feelings, thoughts, or impulses. It is an avoidance technique that numbs, diverts or disguises unconscious and/or conscious physical, emotional and psychological issues, or traumatic events. It comes in many forms, however the most notable are sexual, gambling, electronic (e.g., war gaming), shopping (compulsive buying) and drug and alcohol addiction all of which are detrimental to one's well-being. For victims of abuse, these addictions likely developed as a coping mechanism in response to emotional, physical and/or psychological trauma and mask deep-seated unresolved issues either from one's childhood and/or adolescent developmental years, or as a result of a singular or series of traumatic events later in life.

Addiction can be either "compulsive" in that the addiction controls the victim at all times and every thought or action becomes about the need to fulfil the addictions request, or the addiction can be "subjective" in that the victim has a level of control over the need to fulfil the addictions request. Whether compulsive or subjective, the addiction's purpose is to deflect, suppress, repress, or deny the underlying issues that drive the addictive behaviours and avoid the depressing, anxiety provoking, frightening and possibly self-defeating thoughts and/or emotions that are associated with the original trauma. These addictive behaviours will likely be triggered when the victim enters one of two opposing states of arousal known as "hypo-arousal" or "hyper-arousal." Both of which are adverse emotional and psychological states of being that may arise as a result of overwhelming affect (heightened feeling states).

Hypo-arousal – Hypo-arousal refers to the arousal that lies at the low end of the arousal continuum, it is an under-responsiveness to stimuli and may include symptoms such as dissociation, lethargy, inattention, sleep disorders, apathy, and inability to focus, memory loss, despair, numbness, consistent tiredness, exhaustion, depression, or feelings of hopelessness. Those who present with these symptoms may be diagnosed with CFS (chronic fatigue syndrome) a disease which may in fact have its origins rooted in a possible pre-existing unacknowledged, underlying, and untreated emotional and psychological trauma. The victim suffering with hypo-arousal may gravitate towards alcohol and/or prescription (licit) or illicit drugs, seeking to either completely numb themselves or the opposite to stimulate themselves and their nervous systems, helping them to function with day-to-day responsibilities and/or making them feel alive.

Hyper-arousal – Hyperarousal occurs when a person's body kicks into high alert in response to a real or perceived threat of danger (a primary symptom of PTSD) and is related to the "fight, flight or freeze" response. The symptoms of hyperarousal include, chronic pain (muscular or skeletal), sensory overload (sounds become amplified), sleeping disorders (including nightmares and insomnia), flashbacks of traumatic events (vivid memories of abuse), difficulty concentrating, irritability, angry outbursts, constant anxiety, panic, easily alarmed or startled, have a deep sense of guilt or shame, feel omnipotent or engage in self-destructive behaviour. For some victims, the hyperarousal is intermittent or temporary and only activates with singular stimuli, however for others who suffer from PTSD or victims of on-going abuse the hyperarousal is constantly present and is closely linked with the need to be hypervigilant. A victim suffering with hyper-arousal may gravitate towards alcohol and substance abuse, gambling, gaming, sexual or shopping (compulsive buying) related addictions seeking to calm, distract or deaden their nervous system and curb disturbing, intrusive and destabilising thoughts, and emotions.

Defence (Victim):
Hypervigilance – A Defence and a Symptom

Hypervigilance is a symptom of hyper-arousal and one of the main symptoms of PTSD (post-traumatic-stress disorder); it is triggered in response to either a singular traumatic/abusive event or is a result of on-going trauma or abuse. When activated, it mobilises multiple arousal systems as if the body is in "fight or flight" readiness, on the alert for a real or perceived threat and is vigilantly scanning the environment for danger. The symptoms of hypervigilance may include, relentless, feelings of fear and panic, anxiety, persistent worrying, sleeping disorders, easily startled, or alarmed, hyper-sensitive to sound, highly strung, restlessness, apprehension, continual state of distress, excessive sweating, rapid heartbeat, or elevated blood pressure.

Hypervigilance inevitably leads to cyclic system collapses of extreme exhaustion and fatigue. It is a combination of a series of both conscious and unconscious automated defensive responses, kicking the victim into instant high alert (hyperarousal), wherein the victim immediately scans for signs of danger from both an unpredictable abuser and/or what is likely a highly volatile environment. This defence is commonly found in victims suffering from PTSD (post-traumatic stress disorder) as a result of a singular act of brutality or on-going or long-term domestic abuse or enslavement.

The need to protect themselves and/or those they love from abuse is ever-present and so life becomes elemental, in the sense that all their actions are centred on survival and minimising and/or diffusing potentially perilous scenarios. Constant hypervigilance can often lead to paranoia where normally innocuous events are amplified to an irrational level with the victim feeling as if no one can be trusted and everyone is out to get them. Unfortunately, when a victim has undergone long-term exposure to abuse their "hypervigilance" can lead to substance abuse and addiction in order to manage their hypersensitivity or help to numb feelings of helplessness, terror, guilt, shame, and anxiety.

Defence (Victim): Rationalisation

Rationalisations are a defence mechanism employed to offer rational explanations (false reasons) to justify unacceptable thoughts, beliefs, feelings, and actions and at the same time help avoid addressing the real unconscious and underlying reasons that motivate the defence in the first place (refer to p43 immature defences). We all at one time or another use rationalisations in our everyday lives helping us to avoid uncomfortable thoughts and emotions. For example, not getting that job that you applied for but really wanted, you might rationalise the disappointment away by claiming that it was too far to commute to every day and would have been inconvenient anyway, or perhaps not winning first prize in that competition you entered, you might rationalise that the competition was "rigged", rather than accept that what you produced was not good enough thus avoid feelings of failure.

As you have guessed, rationalisations can work in a self-deceptive manner to keep us from those feelings and thoughts that can undermine or derail our self-esteem, self-worth, or our perception of ourselves (ego-ideal or ego-identity). This defence is commonly formed (not exclusively) in our early childhood or adolescence and like many other defences it came into being to compensate for our perceived failures or short-comings and from our inability to cope with or process feelings of fear, anxiety, shame, guilt, or unworthiness. In 1957, renowned American Social Psychologist Leon Festinger postulated that in order to avoid the discomfort of "cognitive dissonance" (inner tension) over opposing cognitions and/or emotions, a person may invent a "comfortable illusion" also known as a rationalisation.

Many victims of family and domestic abuse or any type of enduring abuse may be impeded or blocked from seeking aid or leaving an abusive relationship or organisation as a result of being at the mercy of their maladaptive rationalisations. Consider this as a form of self-deception, wherein for example, the victim deludes themselves into believing that things are not as bad as they really are, or that the abuse perpetrated on them is not going to happen again. Victims will deny, suppress, or repress emotions or thoughts that threaten to contradict their intention to tolerate or stay in the abusive relationship.

They may rationalise their injuries (psychological, emotional, and physical) by minimising, justifying, or absolving the abuser of the culpability of their harmful actions or they may redirect blame onto themselves, others and/or the circumstances surrounding the abuse. Some victims engage in rationalising their abuser's behaviour because they cannot reconcile the duality of the parent, caregiver, relative, family friend or intimate partner whom they may revere, love, care for and trust as the same person who is abusing them. Or conversely, they may fear losing the abuser's "supposed" love, affection and/or protection and cannot imagine a life without the abuser in it. Their actions are likely based on misconceptions and dysfunctional beliefs known as "schemas" that they developed about themselves, others, and the world at large. Schemas are strongly held beliefs that underpin long-standing, enduring negative patterns of behaviour that are self-perpetuating and extremely resistant to change.

Defence (Victim): Intellectualisation

According to Sigmund Freud (founder of psychoanalysis) "Intellectualisation" is a defence mechanism that utilises intellectual reasoning to avoid undesirable feelings that are associated with distressing events. The aim of this defence is to minimise or block any emotional discomfort that is caused by stressful and/or anxiety provoking events by addressing only the facts while discarding or supressing one's natural emotional responses. It is categorised as a "neurotic defence" (refer to neurotic defences p44) acting as a short-term coping mechanism. On the surface, one may appear to be tranquil, uncaring, or indifferent in response to a distressing event, however well below the surface there may exist a cauldron of simmering emotion. Imagine a jack in the box that is continuously wound and not released, progressively increasing in tension, it will likely reach a breaking point like that of continuously blocked or repressed emotion that is slowly building up over a period of time, it can only remain locked down for so long.

The result of long-term use of "intellectualisation" can lead to substance abuse and/or addiction, depression, psychosis and eating, sleeping, anxiety and behavioural disorders such as OCD (obsessive compulsive disorder) and other possible physical health related illnesses. As the defence suggests, it involves addressing a stressful (emotional) situation in a cognitive (cerebral) manner, victims of abuse may resort to this defence to avoid feelings of fear, shame, guilt, unworthiness, anxiety, helplessness, or hopelessness. Paradoxically, victims may also use intellectualisation to counter feelings of powerlessness believing that their intellect provides them with the sense that they have total control over an emotionally challenging situation and/or their life in general.

By removing the emotion from the equation, it enables a victim to "deal and not feel," a defensive response that gives them a way in which to live with, and survive an abusive event or an adverse home, work, or social situation. It acts as a coping strategy and is often incorrectly interchanged with the defence of rationalisation. They are in fact distinctly different defences, rationalisation involves unconsciously driven, cognitive justification of one's actions to compensate for real underlying negative and debilitating emotions.

Whereas intellectualisation involves conscious awareness and cognitive participation by using logic and reason (intellect) to process a perhaps traumatic or at the very least unnerving event by actively avoiding any associated emotionally conflicting feelings. There are times when using this defence is essential especially for those individuals who are specifically trained to separate from their emotions in order to get a job done. For example, individuals who work in particularly stressful, anxiety provoking and life-threatening fields of employment such as doctors, paramedics, fire-fighters, emergency workers, policemen/women and soldiers who are deployed to front-line battle fields.

These workers are specifically trained to utilise this defence for their emotional, psychological, and physical survival to be effective when confronted with volatile or highly charged events. However, even though this is not ideal when it comes to their personal life, it is necessary for them to make calm, logical life-saving decisions in highly stressful and traumatic circumstances.

Intellectualisation also known as "isolation of affect" is a defence that may have established itself earlier in life perhaps in childhood or adolescence, at a time when it was either not permitted, not encouraged or not safe to experience appropriately expressed emotions to corresponding life events. Subsequently developing into an instinctive defensive response to emotionally and psychologically distressing events, particularly for victims who are consistently besieged with abuse it can become second nature to embrace an "all dealing and no feeling" pattern of behaviour to keep overwhelming feelings such as fear and anxiety at bay. Using intellect as defence is found to be prominent among victims who possess ordered and structured thinking patterns, particularly those with already established analytical mindsets who do not cope well with chaos. These victims may come across as having successful lives, relationships, or careers, some of whom may be holding positions of importance, prominence, or influence in society and yet behind their carefully constructed but fragile façades they are a hiding dark secret.

Defence (Victim): Displacement

Displacement is an unconscious redirection of one's own underlying, unacknowledged, and unresolved emotions such as fear, anxiety, frustration, anger, and rage from its original and largely threatening source to a less threatening recipient to reduce the impact of the unwanted feelings and restore emotional balance. Less threatening targets may be friends, family, work colleagues or random strangers, for example, someone who is experiencing job dissatisfaction who is having a particularly bad day at work, may re-direct their anger and frustration onto a stranger through "road rage" on their way home from work.

An intimate partner who is experiencing personal dissatisfaction or feelings of inadequacy and failure with themselves may displace these unwanted emotions towards their significant other via an outward expression of frustration and rage against them. Some victims of abuse turn unexpressed frustration and anger that should be directed towards their abuser, inwardly towards themselves. "Rage against self" is a redirection of "justifiable rage" that is turned inwards towards oneself instead of outward towards the abuser where it rightfully belongs. Continued use of the defence of displacement can lead to eating, sleeping, anxiety and behavioural disorders, acting-out, substance abuse and addiction and/or physical illness.

This defence is employed by victims of abuse whose emotions have been denied, suppressed, or repressed and therefore are not being consciously acknowledged, addressed, or resolved in a healthy and adaptive manner. Some victims manage to keep a tight lid on their emotions and may do so over their entire lifetime, however others are not able to successfully contain their unresolved emotions and as a result are seeking an outlet for relief and release. Many victims of abuse who suffer from denial, suppression, or repression of emotion, have learned through experience that it is not safe to express how they feel out of fear of reprisal from their abuser or they may have been taught in early childhood or adolescence that it was not acceptable or permitted to express how they felt.

When emotions are not acknowledged, adequately addressed, and processed, a victim of abuse may redirect them towards others through either covert passive aggressive behaviours or through outright overtly hostile behaviours. Some of these victims appear to others as if they possess an aggressive and antagonistic personality, who engage in bullying and abusive behaviours. This in fact is true as some victims of abuse do employ this mode of behaviour to compensate for or counteract their own unaccepted abuse and victimisation.

Understanding Victims of Abuse

We now understand how character structure, defence mechanisms and maladaptive schemas influence a victim's emotional states, decisions, interactions, and behaviours, determining their overall experience of life. However, there also exists various other negative psychological and emotional patterns of behaviour that drive a victim's thoughts, emotions, actions, and beliefs that do not come under the above defence categories. These thoughts, behaviours and impulses work in a negative manner keeping a victim trapped in a maladaptive and detrimental relationship or situation and inhibit rehabilitative processes. They include critical attachment to one's ego-ideal, self-talk also known as "self to self," fear of abandonment and loss of illusory self.

Critical attachment to the ego-ideal of oneself

Some victims have a predominant unhealthy psychological and emotional attachment to their "ego-ideal" (ego-identity) of themselves, in the sense that they believe that the image they project out to the world is who they are in their entirety. If one or more of the foundations on which this ego-ideal is built, is threatened, it can cause a fracture to, or a complete collapse of an already fragile "psyche." The need to sustain and support the "ego-ideal" is perceived by the psyche as being highly critical (life-threatening), if a danger is perceived it will immediately trigger the onset of emotional and psychological defensive action.

In other words, when a victim's only source of self-esteem and/or self-worth is attached to their ego-ideal then it will be accompanied by a desperate need to maintain the outwardly projected image they hold of themselves that perhaps portrays them as being talented, important, and successful or accomplished whatever the case may be. For some victims of on-going or long-term abuse, the projection of their "ego ideal" to all those who exist outside of their abusive relationship conveys the message that all is well in their world. They may want or need to be seen as happy, confident, accomplished, or successful in their chosen lifestyle, relationship and/or vocation.

In order to maintain this façade, many victims deny the existence of abuse or will convince themselves that things are not as bad as they really are. Some use minimisations to downplay the seriousness of abusive events by justifying the abuser's actions with excuses such as "they were over-tired," "they didn't mean it" or "they were under a lot of pressure at work today". Some victims may negate the abusive behaviour with rationalisations such as "he/she didn't hit me so it's not abuse" or they may completely exonerate the abuser with mitigations that include self-blame with statements that start with, "If only I had of" or "I should have."

Others engage in complete denial or suppression of true events defending against having to accept their reality, making upholding their desired façade and avoiding cognitive dissonance (inner conflict) easier. However, as we know long-term dis-acknowledgment of abuse can lead to the development of eating, anxiety or behavioural disorders, substance abuse, addictions and/or physical illness. To maintain their tenuous façades (ego-ideals), victims will need to expend an enormous amount of energy trying to convince themselves and others that all is well and that they are in control of their world, when in fact the opposite is true. In an effort to manage the "dissonance" (conflict) that arises between their real underlying unresolved emotional and psychological issues and their need for their much-desired façade, the victim will engage in exhaustive defensive processes which are likely to eventually take an emotional, psychological and physical toll on the victim.

Self-Talk

Self-Talk also known as "self to self" refers to the ongoing internal conversations we have with ourselves that monitors and controls how we feel and determines our every action. It is a running monologue that interprets and processes our second-to-second observations, feelings, actions, and interactions. It is influenced by our life experiences and is based on our beliefs about ourselves, others, and the world at large. Self-Talk can act in two ways; firstly, it may be observational in that it may act as if it is disconnected somewhat from the actual experience at hand, as if the mind is observing a scene while engaging in a running commentary like a news presenter might when expounding the daily news.

Secondly, the self-talk might be an all-consuming inner conversation that becomes compelling to the exclusion of all other external influences or input, which can be positive or negative in nature either lifting or lowering our physical, emotional, or psychological status. Unfortunately, it is in our nature as human beings that we are predisposed to indulge our negative self-talk as our first recourse. Negative self-talk can become a powerfully dysfunctional force as it seems to gather momentum the longer it goes on, an incessant dominant internal voice can grip the mind convincing the thinker into believing that the self-talk is true and completely valid. This type of enthrallment leads to irrational and grossly over-exaggerated adverse thoughts that are not based on reality and are damaging and counterproductive. Self-talk can become obsessive for those who suffer from depression and/or anxiety particularly those with disorders of this nature causing them to experience overwhelming emotional and psychological turmoil.

These individuals tend to catastrophise events by dramatising, distorting, or magnifying an incident or situation that does not warrant it. Negative self-talk is generated from a person's fundamental beliefs, only becoming destructive in nature if the beliefs that were formed originated out of damaging and/or abusive experiences in earlier life. For example, a child may have developed poor self-esteem during childhood through the experience of overly critical and demanding parents resulting in the developed of the belief that they will never be good enough.

This belief is then carried through to adulthood becoming an overly critical and demanding internal voice that monopolises their psyche, encouraging them to set unrealistic goals that they are likely to fail to achieve and therefore the self-talk becomes prophetic in that it solidifies the belief that they are indeed "not good enough." For victims of abuse, self-talk is not only negative but can be extremely detrimental when it is the only voice they listen to and that voice is either compulsive, manic or hysteric in nature. When inner dialogue is centred on negative, self-critical, or fearful thinking, it can limit the capacity to allow new information to enter and challenge the negative thought or belief making it difficult if not impossible to stop the downward trajectory of those thoughts. Imagine for example that your mind is a multi-stack CD player of responses with a limited capacity for five CDs, which are continuously playing on repeat.

This will automatically limit your choice of response to issues and events that occur in your life to those five CDs (responses). Many victims of abuse suffer from varied feelings of low or no self-esteem, unworthiness, self-loathing, failure, shame, guilt, anxiety and/or fear, making their self-talk a constant running dialogue that is paralysing, self-defeating and self-destructive. Self to self-conversations for example, can build fear, debilitating terror, self-doubt, and low self-esteem perhaps fanning existing deep seeded feelings of worthlessness which in turn can inhibit, confine, or incapacitate a victim preventing them from leaving an abusive relationship, situation and from seeking aid.

Victims of ongoing abuse can develop a maladaptive dependency on their self to self-conversations, particularly those who do not have someone they trust to confide in and who have no new and external input. It becomes an essential method of emotional and psychological survival which is needed to self soothe in times of fear, stress, and anxiety in order to minimise the impact of abusive events. It may also be used to rationalise the abuser's behaviour, take the blame for the abuser's actions, or justify the victim's reasons for staying or conversely to substantiate (validate) their fears and anxieties. The dysfunctional dependency on their self-talk has grown out of an environment of real fear of the abuser's retribution should they speak of their abuse to others or seek aid.

Their inner dialogue becomes a habituated pattern of behaviour to manage feelings of hopelessness, helplessness, and fear, not knowing whom they can trust, believing that no one can help them and so they have no choice but to rely on themselves. Unfortunately, self-talk ultimately isolates a victim of abuse from others, keeping them trapped in abusive situations for long periods of time, their self-talk can become repetitively negative and debilitating by escalating fears, reinforcing unworthiness, self-doubt and self-loathing, and bringing about a defeatist attitude.

Fear of Abandonment

Fear of abandonment is an issue that plagues many individuals, however when linked to a victim of abuse it can be become extremely detrimental to their emotional and psychological wellbeing. It is characterised by one person's unhealthy co-dependency on a significant other and is typically accompanied by feelings of insecurity and anxiety over possible rejection or abandonment. Those who are afflicted with this fear tend to display maladaptive thoughts, emotions, and behaviours such as hypersensitivity to criticism, be overly pleasing, clingy, unreasonably jealous and suffer from feelings of insecurity, worthlessness, and separation anxiety.

There are some, however, who may experience opposite emotions wherein they may have difficulty achieving emotional intimacy, are reluctant to fully commit in a relationship, they may attach to an unavailable partner or are quick to move on and thereby avoid getting attached. The degree to which a person is faced with this fear will determine how they live their lives and experience their relationships. Those at the extreme end of the spectrum may become phobic, displaying manic behaviours, and thought patterns that reflect abject fear and panic at the possibility of a real or perceived threat to a relationship with an individual they are dependent on. This type of behaviour is commonly found in children and adults who suffer with borderline personality disorders.

Individuals who have experienced loss early in their life of a significant other, perhaps a parent or caregiver either through divorce, death or those who have experienced abuse through neglect in early childhood or adolescence can develop varied levels of fear, insecurity and a distrust of others and the world at large. Secure attachment with others can only be achieved when parents or caretakers are consistently available and attuned to their child's needs of feeling safe, cared for, and loved. Therefore, inconsistency in relationship constancy during one's childhood or adolescence whether intentional or not can lead to attachment insecurity and the formation of the model on which all future relationships are based.

In cases of victims of intimate partner abuse (family and domestic abuse), the unhealthy maladaptive dependency on the abuser is likely shaped on the victim's experience of loss or abuse from their early developmental years. This can be one of the underlying issues that works to keep a victim attached to their abuser. In some maladaptive relationships, the abuser may display the same pattern of behaviour that the victim experienced as a child/adolescent and had become accustomed to as a result. With this type of behaviour, the abuser appears to be available, attentive, and meeting the victim's needs, and then without reason the abuser withdraws becoming unavailable, indifferent, or rejecting in the next.

This type of erratic behaviour is destabilising and causes extreme fear and anxiety, triggering long held insecurities in a victim who is already suffering from feelings of unworthiness, low self-esteem, and an under-developed sense of self, particularly those with an "abandonment/instability schema." Fear of rejection and abandonment can bind a victim to an abuser; those who live in fear of losing their intimate partner can become desperate and may assume the role of the pursuer in the relationship despite being abused to sustain the connection with the abuser no matter how malignant the connection is. Conversely, victims of abuse may be in a relationship with an abuser who possesses an "abandonment/instability" schema, which would have formed in the same way as victim, in early childhood or adolescence and for the same reasons. The abuser suffers from the same fears and insecurities as someone who has attachment issues; however, they react differently when they feel a real or imagined threat of being abandoned or rejected by becoming abusively possessive, controlling, jealous, dominating, and violent.

Loss of Illusory-Self

We all possess an ego-identity (ego-ideal) of ourselves; it is part of normal human development; you need an identity to be able to function in the world and recognise yourself as an individual. It begins to develop around two years of age, solidifies itself around the age of seven to nine years old and continues to evolve into adulthood. Your ego-identity is a mental and emotional construct influenced by your core beliefs and reflects who you think you are and how you believe you are perceived by others. An important part of maturing is to be able to separate the "ego-ideal" of yourself from your "authentic self" that part of you that represents your true needs, wants and desires reflecting your personal uniqueness.

A victim of abuse who is suffering from "critical attachment" to their ego-identity may consequently have developed fictional illusions about themselves, about their life and about their relationships. When I say "illusions," I am referring to a projected delusion which defines who one thinks they are and how they believe their life or relationship to be, that is not based on true events or reality. The need to believe in the projected illusion is so powerful that it overrides actuality, authenticity and rational thought and is driven or supported by maladaptive beliefs (schemas) and defences. Victims form a critical attachment to their "illusory self," "illusory life" and/or "illusory relationship/s" whose primary function has been to provide them with a desired self-image, a sense of self-worth, confidence, certainty, security, and purpose while underpinning what they believe to be their primary identity.

If, however, an illusion is threatened, breached, or repudiated, it can cause a disruption to, or complete upheaval of their emotional and psychological equilibrium. For some, the loss of one's illusion is akin to experiencing the death of a loved one, causing an enormous amount of grief, pain, sadness, disillusionment, and depression and/or creating feelings of extreme anxiety, fear, anger, or rage. Imagine a puzzle in the image of oneself that reflects a complete picture, then imagine this puzzle with integral pieces missing that once held that puzzle together.

When a false foundation on which an illusion is built has been exposed for its untruthfulness, it may feel as if one's world is coming apart which cannot be endured by the fragile "psyche" of the one holding the illusion. In order to protect the illusion and counter any threats, victims of abuse will engage in conscious and unconscious defensive measures to avoid the collision between what is truth and what is fallacy. For example, a victim of infidelity by a philandering partner who does not question their cheating partners half-truths and lies, rationalises the abuser's behaviours with excuses and suppresses, minimises, or denies the infidelity itself and the psychological and emotional harmful impact it is having on them in order to maintain their illusion.

Victims of abuse who have a dependent attachment to their abuser who is perhaps an intimate partner, parent/step-parent, relative or caregiver, someone they look up to, love or idolise may create a much needed or desired illusory projection onto the abuser that is contrary to their reality, but is needed for their emotional and psychological survival. The biggest hurdle is breaching the bubble of illusion that a victim has erected in place of true events, however once a victim overcomes this hurdle, they will experience possible depression and a deep sadness. This is an expression of grief over the loss of a projected illusion that never really existed and having to accept and deal with the disillusionment that the abuser is not the person they believed them to be and their life is not what they believed it to be.

Understanding the Effects of
Abuse on Victims

The negative and harmful impact that abuse can have on a victim will vary depending on the duration and severity of the abuse that the victim has undergone. Unlike physical abuse psychological, verbal, and emotional abuse is not evident visually but it is just as harmful and destructive and will without doubt create mild to severe levels of trauma in a victim. The effects of the abuse will manifest in many ways. Victims will experience any or all the following, a lowering of their self-esteem and their self-image, they will lose trust in themselves, they will lose trust in significant others and they will lose trust in the world at large leaving them feeling isolated, lonely, and depressed.

Most victims feel varying degrees of helplessness, futility, anxiety, shame, guilt, and fear and depending on the severity and longevity of the abuse may lead to PTSD (post-traumatic stress disorder), eating, sleeping, anxiety and behavioural disorders, physical illness, addiction, substance abuse, psychosis, and can also result in suicide. Please note: victims who are experiencing PTSD (post-traumatic stress dis-order) are unlikely or unable to report their abusive experience to the authorities due to the nature of the "affect" of the disorder, which inhibits or distorts an accurate account of events causing mild to severe memory loss, denial, suppression, or repression.

We are all aware of the physical signs of violence and assault on the human body as it will leave obvious visible wounds in the form of bruising, scratches, lacerations, abrasions, broken-bones, scars and so on. However, not all abuse leaves obvious signs, quite often a perpetrator may simply use physical intimidation accompanied by verbal threats to control, manipulate or coerce their victim which has the same effect as using physical violence would ensure. The perpetrator does not necessarily have to be big in size to be intimidating and controlling either, they may simply use physically threatening stances such as standing over or holding down a victim to achieve their desired goal.

Perpetrators who engage in verbal abuse to belittle, demean, humiliate, and degrade a victim have a threefold purpose. Firstly, it is used subjugate and pressure the victim to remain pliant and compliant, secondly, it will elevate the ego of the perpetrator by feeding their need to feel superior and/or grandiose and thirdly, to assert their dominance and control over the victim making the perpetrator feel powerful or omnipotent. Verbal abuse is aimed at disempowering a victim, empowering the abuser and at the same time providing an outlet for the perpetrator to vent their current frustrations and their negative unresolved emotions upon.

Abuse particularly in the form of a threat to commit violence to a victim is just as frightening, intimidating, harmful and affecting on a victim as the violence itself. In fact, the threat of intent to commit violence to a victim is the most used tool by a perpetrator to dominate, manipulate, coerce, and control a victim and/or a situation. It is just as destructive to a victim's wellbeing as physical abuse and will always result in psychological and emotional wounding, particularly for those who have undergone long-term abuse.

Constant threats of harm are geared at undermining the security and confidence of a victim, keeping them off-balance and creating an environment of uncertainty that gives the abuser leverage for manipulation. The type of abuse is a continuous psychological and emotional assault on the mind and the senses of a victim that become extremely fatiguing, draining the victim of the ability to fight, thereby ensuring their submission. It can be extremely injurious to the victim's psyche, and is as deeply harmful as if they were physically brutalised or maimed.

It is very unlikely that current statistics can accurately reflect the prevalence of domestic abuse, sexual assault and bullying that is occurring in our society today as there are a surprising amount of these types of crimes which are not being reported and for very good reason. Some victims fear being ridiculed, not believed, or blamed for the abuse being perpetrated on them. Others fear retribution from the abuser or being ostracised from the community or religious order they belong to or by their family, friends, or workplace peers. There is a lack of knowledge and understanding by some members in the community of what constitutes abusive behaviour and how victims should act causing them to judge or vilify victims they believe have contributed to their own victimhood.

Generally, violence of any kind is considered abhorrent and unacceptable behaviour by most in society however there also exists some who bear an apathetic attitude, lack empathy and are ignorant of the serious and lasting effects acts of violence and abuse can have on a victim.

Victims of Sexual Assault/Abuse

Historically societies around the world have always held their share of predators and abusers; however, with the advent of electronic technology they are now successfully using the internet to find and groom potential victims. Other predators are taking advantage of the availability of various types of legal and illegal drugs such as date rape drugs as a means to incapacitate a potential victim. The reality is that rape and other sexual acts of violence are occurring more often than is being reported to the authorities and this happens for several reasons.

Victims of sexual assault who have been incapacitated by a drug can experience going in and out of consciousness, they become dazed, confused, and disorientated and may not realise that they have been drugged and assaulted as the drug can be in their system for some time after being ingested. These victims can feel varying degrees of shock, shame, guilt, and fear when they realise what has happened to them, in which case a crucial period of time may have lapsed between the incident and the reporting of the incident to the authorities. This can make it difficult (not impossible) to successfully prosecute the perpetrator/s as there may be a loss of tangible physical evidence that would greatly aid the prosecution to gain a conviction in the trial.

There are many genuine fears held by victims of sexual assault which can result in a reluctance to report the assault to authorities as many victims are terrified of the repercussions it may have on their personal relationships with their significant other, their friends, their family, their co-workers, the religious denomination they belong to or their community at large. The victims that are members of misogynistic, fundamentalist religious orders and/or societies may be terrified of being judged, rejected, ostracised, or punished by other members within these religious orders or societies to which they belong as well as their family and friends.

In some cultures, a woman is blamed for being sexually assaulted and portrayed as the villain not the rapist, based on the belief that the woman must have enticed the rapist in some way or that she has put herself in harm's way through her own negligence. The misogyny stems from the premise that men are not wholly responsible for, or in control of their actions when it comes to sex and sexual arousal and as a result redirect blame for their actions onto the female victim. Males who possess this type of misogynistic thinking also believe that they are entitled to have sex with their partners whether their partners are willing or not and that this is not rape but their given right.

The effect of a sexual assault physically on a victim may be healed medically, however the impact that it has psychologically and emotionally is extremely overwhelming and can leave a victim with long term negative repercussions that are devastating. Their sense of trust in others and the world at large has been deeply shaken, for some this can result in substance abuse, addiction, eating, sleeping, anxiety and behavioural disorders, physical illness and may be responsible for varying degrees of a condition known as PTSD (post-traumatic stress disorder). In some cases, particularly with teenage victims of sexual assault it can lead to extreme behaviours that can put their life in danger, including indiscriminate sexual promiscuity. Victims often struggle to survive, let alone overcome the effects of sexual abuse despite having therapeutic intervention it may take months, years in some cases, regardless of the restorative action taken can still leave a victim with irreparable life-long damaging repercussions.

Why Victims of Abuse Remain Silent About Their Abuse and Trapped as a Result

A victim may be your grandparent, your parent, your sibling, your daughter, your son, your next-door neighbour, your work or sport colleague, your coach, your boss, or your best friend in other words it can be anyone and you might never know that they are a victim of abuse unless they choose to tell you. Most victims of abuse apart from those who may have obvious behavioural issues (addictions and disorders) or visible physical injuries can remain imperceptible to another person if the victim chooses, and as a result likely suffering their abuse behind a wall of silence. In order to fully understand their victimology, we must explore why many victims of sexual assault, domestic abuse and bullying remain victims of ongoing abuse rather than seek help, and why victims of isolated violence and abuse do not report the incident to authorities or tell their loved ones.

There are many victims of abuse who do not want others to know that they are being abused and there are many victims who cannot let others know they are being abused, with reasons that are varied and complex. I will remind you that because the psychological and emotional make-up of every human being is different and is unique to that human being alone, it will also stand to reason, that how a victim responds to any given abusive situation will also be different. However, the reasons why they choose to remain silent about their abuse will be universally similar. Following, you will find a list of the various types of victims and the many reasons why they remain silent about their abuse, why crimes go unreported and undetected and why family and domestic violence, bullying and sexual assault remain prevalent despite society's concerted effort to decrease the incidence.

Types of Victims

Victims Who Fear Being Persecuted, Blamed or Rejected by their Intimate Partner, Family, Friends, or their Community

Historically in many cultures, religions and societies, women were portrayed as either being good (virginal and chaste) or being bad (sirens or witches) and responsible for luring men into behaving badly. In other words, women either entice men or cast spells over men, inciting them to act irrationally, with violence and without consciousness. Suggesting that women possess some mystical power over a man's baser instincts or sexuality, and therefore casting them as the villain. These teachings support the sexist belief that circumstances beyond a male's control causes them to act in a mindless manner and therefore a male cannot be held accountable for submitting to their baser sexual and/or aggressive urges, needs or desires. Some cultures, religions and societies have evolved from these outmoded ways of thinking, others have not.

Those cultures, religions and societies that have not evolved possess a history which is steeped in archaic and misogynistic doctrine, allowing the antiquated thinking to inform and influence their current day practices and beliefs. One of the main beliefs is that a female is always at fault when it comes to crimes of a sexual nature and/or in cases of family and domestic abuse. If she is sexually harassed or assaulted by a male perpetrator or if she is a victim of family and domestic abuse, they believe that she must have provoked the perpetrator into acting in an abusive manner towards her or she may have been deemed as deserving of mistreatment from the perpetrator.

These victims are reluctant to report their abuse or remove themselves from a harmful relationship as they fear judgement, censure, persecution, punishment or being ostracised by other family members or the religious order or society to which they belong. Many of these victims who are born into and therefore indoctrinated into these cultures and religions from a young age do not expect to be supported or helped by community aid services or given the protection they need.

Perpetrators of family and domestic abuse who come from these same backgrounds will minimise, excuse, or justify their abusive behaviour, believing the victim is deserving of being punished, particularly if the victim disobeyed their rules or edicts. Victims who are afraid that they will be rejected by those they love, respect, and rely on are likely to remain silent about their abuse and not want to put their personal or familial relationships at risk.

In some cases, female victims who are bullied, harassed, or sexually assaulted by a family friend, work colleague or a stranger may keep silent about the abuse and the abuser because they fear being blamed, rejected, or punished by their intimate partner, parents, or other family members. It is not uncommon for a victim to be reluctant if not terrified, that their intimate partner or their family will not understand or accept the victim's account of the abuse. They may blame the victim suggesting that they were responsible for being assaulted by placing themselves in harm's way or they may even go so far as to say that the victim incited the perpetrator into attacking or harassing them regardless of the circumstances.

Victims Who Fear They Will Not Be Believed

There are many victims of crimes of abuse who fear that other family members, their friends, their employer, their intimate partner, or the authorities will not believe that they are or have been a victim of abuse. This occurs when the accused (perpetrator) of the abuse is well-liked, revered, important, influential, popular, or idolised either in a personal, professional and/or public capacity. These fears are genuine for victims who have to face exposing someone that other members of their family, friends, workplace peers or members of society hold in high esteem, revere, love and/or have faith and trust in. It is difficult enough for the victim to deal with the abuse itself, let alone contend with the possibility that they will not be believed. They also have to face the prospect that they may be rejected, abandoned, or ostracised by those they love or have to face public ridicule and/or censure by supporters of the accused. This can be daunting if not terrifying for victims and is a major reason why many abusers go unpunished and can continue to abuse for longer periods of time.

In recent times, we have witnessed many reports in the media of crimes of a varied sexually abusive nature, purportedly committed by an "A list" of well-known and highly regarded public figures. Some were celebrities, others were socially, politically, and religiously influential members of society. These abusers have been accused of perpetrating the most abhorrent and heinous crimes of sexual abuse including, paedophilia, sexual assault, kidnapping, sexual slavery, and human trafficking. They have flourished without consequence for great lengths of time, some even for decades during which time they harmed a great number of victims before being brought to justice. These perpetrators have used their popularity, influence, and power (financial, social, or political) to discredit a victim's credibility or to intimidate and threaten them into silence. As a result, the victim has been made to think and feel as if they will not be believed if they expose the perpetrator and report the incident/s to the authorities.

If a victim does act against the abuser, then it is highly likely that the abuser will apply pressure by threatening or coercing the victim into withdrawing the accusations made against them if allegations have been made. Victims of abuse committed by powerful and/or influential people have been either manipulated, bullied, threatened, coerced, shamed, or guilted into remaining silent about the abuse and therefore reluctant or fearful of coming forward.

Perpetrators such as these have honed their skills over time and are known to either shift the blame onto the victim by manipulating the victim into believing that they were responsible for the abuse perpetrated on them or they may use a tactic known as "gaslighting." Gaslighting is a deliberate ploy used by abusers that involves psychological and emotional manipulations to distort the truth and redefine the victim's reality of abusive events, causing the victim to experience confusion and self-doubt and questioning whether the abuse took place at all. Or conversely, the perpetrator will use their power and popularity to influence the media to manipulate an outcome and/or charm their family, friends, fans and/or the community at large. We should be asking ourselves the question how many other high-profile predators and abusers are among us operating under the belief that their status elevates them above the rules and regulations that govern the rest of society.

Victims Who Fear Retribution from the Abuser

One of the most prevailing reasons why victims of domestic abuse, sexual assault and bullying do not report the crimes committed against them is because they fear retribution from the abuser for themselves and/or their loved ones. And understandably so, as many abusers would have definitely made it clear to their victim that they will retaliate if the victim seeks aid, tells someone, or reports the incident or incidents to the authorities. The threat to kill or commit further violence and abuse to a victim or to a victim's loved ones by an abuser is an extremely effective coercion tactic used to keep victims compliant, pliant, and silent, whether the threats are applied to a singular abusive event or consistently in cases of on-going abuse. For victims of domestic and familial abuse, it is known to be the most effectively used method of domination and control as the victims are terrified of the abuser who has been bullying, intimidating, threatening, and battering the victim into submission for some time.

Perpetrators of domestic abuse believe that they are the ultimate authority in their intimate relationships and in their homes, and will not tolerate any interference from outsiders. These abusers are under the misconception that their intimate partner and their children whether from a de-facto relationship or not belong to them and are perceived as property of the abuser to do with as they please. Domestic abusers once agitated, can act out without restraint if they are threatened by an outside authority and may retaliate in the extreme by permanently maiming or even murdering the victim and/or someone the victim loves. Please note, that fear of a perpetrator, for a victim who has suffered long-term abuse can be paralysing and will more than likely prevent the victim seeking help.

It is clear why victims who are terrified of the consequences from their abusers do not seek aid, and understandable why they go to great lengths to hide their abusive situations. Statistics are always changing as our society changes however one thing is for certain the statistics reflecting violence against women and children is increasing and that domestic violence rates are higher in rural areas.

Statistics prove that on average:

- One woman a week in Australia is murdered by her current or former partner.
- One in four women experience emotional abuse by a current or former partner since the age of fifteen.

- One in five women has experienced sexual violence since the age of fifteen.
- One in three women has experienced physical violence since the age of fifteen.
- Eighty-five percent of women have been sexually harassed,
- Almost forty percent of women continued to experience violence from their partner while temporarily separated.
- Almost ten women a day are hospitalised for assault perpetrated by a spouse or domestic partner.
- One in six women has experienced stalking since the age of twenty-five.

Statistics provided by "Our Watch" a non-for-profit organisation, established by the Victorian and Commonwealth Government, includes all states and territories (Australia).

Victims Who Are Silenced by Other Family Members Who Protect an Abuser in Their Midst

Some family members will go to great lengths to ignore, rationalise, minimise, or justify the behaviour of another family member's abusive actions, and are quite likely to deny that the abuser is responsible for the abuse that they are being accused of perpetrating. Denying the existence of abuse is a response that may occur among members of a family group who cannot allow themselves to imagine that the abuser, someone they love and hold in high esteem is capable of the abuse they are being accused of. In fact, they may vehemently disbelieve the victim, responding with anger towards them and possibly engaging in retaliatory behaviour aimed at punishing the victim or intimidating the victim into a retraction of the accusation.

Some victims fear that disclosure of their abuse may result in being abandoned, rejected, or alienated by significant members of their family and so they will remain silent rather than take that risk. Conversely, there are also family members who will go as far as to suppress or prevent a victim from seeking aid or reporting abuse because they are afraid of experiencing any accompanying possible private or public shame that exposing the abuser may bring to themselves and their family regardless of who the abuser is, whether they are a family member, family friend or in some cases even a stranger.

There also exists domestic settings whose family members will either ignore or feel indifferent to another family member's (victim's) plight. They may believe that by remaining on the peripheral of the abuser's awareness and by ignoring the abuser's activities, they can avoid becoming a victim themselves. Others may ignore an abuser's activities because they are dependent on the abuser for financial support, protection and/or survival and do not want to jeopardise their own relationship with the abuser. Family members who remain "indifferent" to the abuser's actions and the victim's plight are likely to possess some type of psychological dysfunction themselves, evidenced by their apathy, lack of empathy and/or capacity to remain unaffected by the victim's suffering.

These types of family members are enablers for the perpetrator's activities, allowing the abuser to continue to mistreat a victim without consequence, contributing to the abuse by compounding the abusive behaviour with their silence. Victims may view the family's actions as sanctioning the abuser's behaviour, thereby lending support to the possible dysfunctional belief held by the victim that they are flawed, unlovable and or defective in some way and deserving of mistreatment. Victims who have grown up in an environment where they have been the consistent target of abuse, whether it was perpetrated by one or more members of the family have likely become accustomed to being the family scapegoat.

They have been forcefully acclimatised to ill-treatment and conditioned into believing that they are indeed flawed, incompetent, and powerless not only by the abusers themselves but also by the other family members who supported the abuser/s with their indifference. In some cases, there are family members who are related to victim that will blame the victim for being responsible for the abuse being perpetrated on them by the abuser, believing that the victim instigated or incited the abuser to act abusively towards them.

It is not uncommon for these family members to rationalise, minimise or justify the abuser's behaviour, protecting the abuser and blaming the victim whom they consider deserving of the abuse. Some may even go as far as supporting and/or condoning the abuser's behaviour, making them an accessory to the abuse itself and further victimising the victim.

Victims Who Possess Maladaptive Feelings of Loyalty Towards Their Abuser

Victims who possess misplaced feeling of loyalty to their abuser more than likely experienced some level of what is known as "traumatic bonding" with an abuser, either in a past relationship during their childhood or adolescence with a parent/caregiver or subsequently with a partner in an intimate relationship. Traumatic bonding is the result of on-going cycles of abuse between a victim and an abuser creating an unhealthy and powerful emotional and psychological attachment that is resistant to change and inspires unwavering devotion and loyalty from the victim to the abuser. A "trauma bond" is created when the victim develops sympathy, affection and/or love for the abuser despite their abusive actions.

The bond may develop over days, weeks, months, or years and is typified by cycles of abuse followed by remorse from the abuser and/or rationalisations by the victim that minimise or justify the abuser's actions. Children, adolescents, and intimate partner's, are found among the most common victims of "traumatic bonding" which largely stems from their innate need to be cared for, loved, and accepted by the abuser (parent, caregiver or significant other). The dysfunctional relationship is formed when the victim develops maladaptive feelings of love and loyalty towards their abuser, protecting them despite being abused, unable to accept their bad side. These victims are terrified of being, rejected, abandoned, or ostracised by those they believe they love and would rather live with their abusive caregiver/parent/intimate partner than not, and so will remain silent about their abuse. Some victims will feel a need to protect their abuser because of erroneous and misplaced feelings of loyalty towards the abuser, feelings that may have developed from a victim's previous adverse, dysfunctional experiences in life.

Misplaced feelings of loyalty to an abuser can be found in victims who have suffered some level of psychological, emotional and/or physical abuse in their early childhood or teenage developmental years whether they were a victim directly themselves or a witness to abusive behaviour. Either way they have come to believe that the abusive actions perpetrated on them or to others, to be normal and/or acceptable behaviour in relationships. If this is the case, a victim will have developed an unhealthy, co-dependant relationship with a current abuser, based on their dysfunctional past where love and abuse are fused.

There is a deep need to remain loyal to the abuser as they have perhaps done in their past, creating an unshakable faithfulness that the abuser readily encourages if not demands. Victims who have been born into, or indoctrinated into an existing abusive cult, sect, or an extreme fundamentalist religious order, have likely undergone varied levels of emotional, psychological and/or physical abuse possibly over extended periods of time. The abuser/s would have applied consistent and unrelenting manipulative, intimidating and/or coercive tactics that have induced subjugation, compliance, and a forced loyalty from the victim to the abuser/s and their cause.

Consequently, establishing a corrosive and malignant bonding between the victim and the abuser similar to that of those afflicted with "Stockholm syndrome." When organisations of this nature are recruiting, they carefully select victims that possess easily identifiable vulnerabilities such as runaways, the homeless, someone who is isolated or estranged from their loved ones, those who are experiencing grief and/or loneliness, or it may be teenagers or young adults who feel like they are outcasts. These victims are targeted because they are easier to exploit, brainwash and intimidate into being secretive and silent about the organisation's practices. Note: "Stockholm syndrome" is defined as a psychological and/or emotional tendency of a hostage to develop a bond with, identify with or sympathise with his/her captor.

Victims Afflicted with a Deep Sense of Unworthiness

There are victims who possess a deep-rooted belief about themselves that they are unworthy of being valued, loved, respected, and cared for, a result of dysfunctional and damaging life experiences. This type of negative belief about oneself was more than likely formed in early childhood or during one's adolescent developmental years and then cemented in the psyche through subsequent negative and detrimental experiences and relationships. It is possible to be consciously aware of one's own beliefs about oneself, however, it is unlikely, most of us are unaware of our deep-rooted negative beliefs about ourselves, others, and the world at large and unconscious to the impact that these negative beliefs have on our lives. A belief whether positive or negative will underpin every decision we make and every action we take, influencing the direction and quality of our personal and professional lives.

These negative emotions will also influence our geographic, economic, and environmental circumstances as well as our motivations, goals, and our relationships. The belief that one is unworthy is often accompanied by feelings of being undeserving and the thinking that one is fundamentally flawed, which is incredibly disempowering. It limits healthy emotional and psychological growth and undermines relationships, ambitions, and achievements. If a victim is afflicted with this belief, then the victim may never reach their possible full potential or attain their desired goals and may suffer from anxiety, depression, despondency, hopelessness, low self-esteem, a general sense of failure and they may also experience debilitating feelings of shame, humiliation, and self-disgust.

To compensate, they may engage in perfectionistic behaviour, setting personal and professional goals that are likely unattainable and when they fail to reach these unrealistic goals, have fulfilled their self-prophesied belief that they are indeed unworthy and undeserving. This will also be reflected in their social, family, and intimate partner relationships, wherein they engage in maladaptive and dysfunctional personal relationships that continue to perpetuate the belief that they are not worthy or deserving of better.

In intimate partner relationships, a victim with this affliction is psychologically and emotionally more vulnerable to becoming prey to an abuser. This happens because they believe they are "less than" or "unequal" to their intimate counterpart and may consciously and/or unconsciously subjugate themselves to an intimate partner.

However, let us remember that abusers in intimate partner relationships are drawn to, and actively seek partners that they know they can dominate and control and so they are drawn to someone who displays signs of possessing, low self-esteem, insecurity, and self-doubt. In the early stages of a relationship, the abuser will disarm and charm the intended victim in order to search for vulnerabilities that they may later exploit to their advantage. Victims who believe they are unworthy are a target for the psychopathic, narcissistic, sociopathic, or sadistic predator who will exploit the perceived vulnerability to gain power over a victim by colluding with the victim's feelings of unworthiness. The abuser can then take advantage of the victims "Achilles-heel" while simultaneously having their own need to feel superior, exalted and in control satiated.

Quite often, victims who harbour fundamental feelings of unworthiness will on some level feel as if they are deserving of the abuse that is being perpetrated on them, or if not, the abuser will encourage them to think and feel as if they are deserving of the mistreatment being perpetrated on them. The need to experience on-going self-castigation or penance for real or perceived failures and/or shortcomings is a potential by-product of the belief that one is essentially worthless. The need to punish oneself or be punished is rooted in the victim's early childhood or past relationship experiences of abuse wherein the then abuser had led the victim to believe that they are indeed deficient or flawed in some way and thereby justifying the current abuser's maltreatment in the present.

Some victims with this belief system will remain silent about their abuse because they are not consciously aware of the underlying negative belief, they hold of themselves and thereby unintentionally becoming a co-conspirator with the abuser by unconsciously aligning themselves with the abuser's negative beliefs about them. Other victims remain silent about their abuse because they are afflicted with deep feelings of shame and self-disgust and as a result feel deserving of the abuse perpetrated on them. The victims that are not aware that they are being abused may have been born into or were indoctrinated into abusive environments from their birth or an early and markedly impressionable age, whose mistreatment they were forced to adapt to and accept as their "normal" way of life.

The harmful, dysfunctional aspects of their abuse eventually becoming an innate part of their psyche and the driving force behind their maladaptive beliefs about themselves, others, and the world at large. They have been subjected to consistent and unrelenting psychological, emotional and/or physical abuse including brainwashing and isolation tactics. These victims may have been born, adopted, or fostered into abusive family environments or they may have endured abuse as a member of a cult, fundamentalist religious order or child trafficking ring. All these victims possess the unconscious and/or conscious belief they are insignificant or secondary.

There are, however, other negative influencing factors that may contribute to and support the psychological belief that one is fundamentally valueless and undeserving of better which may have developed from experiences of emotional, psychological and/or physical abuse (including sexual abuse). A belief that may have developed during and possibly throughout early childhood and/or adolescence either at home, school or in one's social environment. The child/adolescent may have been subjected to either neglectful, poor, or non-existent parenting or poverty while growing up.

They may have experienced adverse, damaging incidents of abuse perpetrated by their peers at school and/or socially (being shunned or bullied). They may have had negative experiences with an educational institution with negligent or bulling teachers and/or schooling authorities. They may have possessed an undiagnosed and untreated learning difficulty or suffered from a physical or intellectual learning disability, or they may have been marginalised by peers, teachers and/or society at large because of their appearance, sexual orientation, culture, religion or race. Regardless of the origin that caused the onset of the belief that one is unworthy of being treated with care, respect, affection and love it remains a major contributing factor to a victim's inability to release themselves from a current abusive relationship or environment.

Victims Afflicted with a Deep Sense of Shame and/or Guilt

It is common for victims both male and female, whether they are a child, adolescent, or adult to remain silent about their abuse because of deeply felt shame and/or guilt. This is particularly true of victims of abuse of a sexual nature whether it is sexual harassment, unwanted touching, or sexual assault (including rape). In some cases of sexual assault, the victim's body may have responded sexually to the abuse being perpetrated on them, leading the victim to believe that on some level they "wanted the abuse to happen" and were therefore complicit in the abusive event. In fact, both female and male victims can experience some sort of sexual arousal or even orgasm during a sexual act of abuse.

This is because our sexual organs are designed to respond to physical stimulation whether there is conscious participation or not. The body by itself cannot discern if the touch is wanted or unwanted, it simply responds to stimuli as it was designed to do. However, this does not in any way mean that the abuse is wanted by the victim, but that the body has responded despite the abuser's touch being unwanted, adding to the false sense of guilt and shame that victims of sexual abuse carry.

Human beings are born with an innate need to be loved, valued, and cared for, from birth onwards we are unconsciously seeking these needs to be fulfilled by those people responsible for our wellbeing and protection, our guardians/parents and/or caregivers. When a child or adolescent is abused by "those" they believe love them, they are assailed with overwhelming confusion, not able to understand why someone they love and trust and who they assume loves and cares for them in return is harming them.

The confusion triggers the onset of varied levels of internal conflict, resulting in high levels of stress and anxiety attempting to make sense of the conflicting messages they are receiving from their guardian/parent/caregiver. In order to cope, the child or adolescent develops coping strategies in the form of defences such as denial, suppression, repression, regression, dissociation, somatisation (physical illness), psychosis and eating, sleeping and behavioural disorders frequently concluding that they must in some way be at fault. They may come to believe that they are either innately inadequate, thinking themselves unworthy, flawed, or defective in some way or that they have done something wrong and deserve the abuse they are receiving.

Either way, many abused children and adolescents are likely to develop deep-rooted feelings of shame and/or guilt, blaming themselves for the abuse perpetrated on them. Some victims of sexual assault blame themselves for the abuse being perpetrated on them perhaps thinking that they may have been able to prevent the abuse, believing that they "should have" been able to defend themselves or that they have in some way contributed to their abuse, having somehow put themselves in harm's way.

This stems from the assumption that we as human beings have total control over what happens to us "at all times" provided we adhere to all warnings about danger and take appropriate safety precautions, deluding ourselves into believing that the probability of something bad happening to us is unlikely. The reality is that despite all our safeguards we are still at risk of random or calculated acts of violence and abuse from someone we know or an absolute stranger. Unfortunately, despite this truth victims of abuse are still likely to undergo deep levels of shame and/or guilt, blaming themselves, especially those who have undergone any type of sexual violation particularly sexual assault, keeping them from seeking aid or speaking out.

Some victims of abuse experience debilitating levels of shame and/or guilt as a result of the strict religious and/or cultural beliefs that they have been raised with and are expected to adhere to. Their beliefs are based on archaic tenets that have unrelenting standards and are misogynistic and/or punitive in nature. The out-dated beliefs of the culture or religion further victimise a victim, in which they are made to think and feel as if they are responsible for and/or deserving of the abuse being perpetrated on them, causing them to suffer with profound levels of personal shame and/or guilt.

Other victims may have their whole identity based on, and linked to whom they portray to their friends, workplace associates or peers, other family members or society at large, particularly for those who are publicly celebrated or renowned for their achievements. These victims are not likely disclose their abuse to anyone for fear of exposing their shame publicly or becoming the target of ridicule or censure from their peers or the public. The need to maintain the projected image that nothing is wrong is of principal importance to them especially those who hold a "critical attachment" to the "ego-ideal." (Refer to critical attachment – p142).

These victims will find it emotionally and psychologically catastrophic to admit that their lives are anything less than perfect. They will remain silent about their abuse, hiding their feelings of shame and/or guilt behind deliberately crafted façades of success, happiness, and contentment, overly fixated on what other people may think of them and unable to detach from their projected persona. Sadly, we live in a society that perpetuates the need to portray "perfectionism" in all things, and equates success and happiness with physical beauty, social status, material accruement and financial standing leaving little room for acceptance of the ordinary or different and perceiving failure to achieve as inadequacy.

Victims Trapped by the Influence a High Profile or Authority Figure has in the Community

We are all aware that abuse occurs in every society, in every shape and form ranging from the mild end of the spectrum to the severe, perpetrated by criminal types that we are familiar with. However, it is substantially more distressing when the abuse is committed by someone who possesses influence and authority in our society such as a judge, police officer, council member or a high-profile figure-head such as a business mogul or a political/religious leader. This is simply because we hold them in high regard, expecting more from them, having placed our trust and faith in them to serve and protect, expecting them to be ethical, principled and to act honourably. Unfortunately, this is not the case, perpetrators of crimes of bullying, violence, sexual harassment, sexual assault, and paedophilia can also be found among members of our society that we would like to believe are above such behaviour. Perpetrators of abuse who have attained some level of authority and influence in our community, may use and abuse their power to sway public opinion, manipulate rules and regulations to their advantage or intimidate and coerce their victim into retracting their accusation or into maintaining their silence. This makes reporting incidents of abuse daunting if not frightening for a victim and will likely prevent them from seeking aid. Some victims are extremely reluctant to come forward about their abuse because they are afraid of further mistreatment or retribution from the abuser or that they will not be believed by others.

Quite often, victims are persecuted for coming forward about their abuse by their friends and/or the community at large who hold the perpetrator of the abuse in high esteem for their presumed good character and their accomplishments, finding it hard to believe that the person accused of the abuse is capable of committing the crime/s of which they are accused.

Victims Afraid of Having Their Reputations Maligned, Discredited or Ridiculed

Whether a victim is male or female they may be reluctant to expose that they have been, or are currently a victim of abuse due to being afraid of having their reputations privately and/or publicly vilified by their school, social or workplace peers and/or the wider community. These victims are terrified of public exposure, experiencing high levels of distress, anxiety and apprehension believing that their abuse will become news via public forums such as the internet, opening their abuse up to public scrutiny and/or the "stigma" connected to sexual assault.

This is particularly distressing for victims who have suffered abuse of a sexual nature who are already struggling with dealing the effects of the traumatic event. This type of vilification is commonly perpetrated by adolescents in school yards, members of college or university campuses, adults in any social or workplace environment and the wider community. Females may be labelled "whores or sluts" and made the target of disparaging, debasing and demoralising remarks, gestures, and campaigns. Males who are bullied and or sexually assaulted are labelled as being "weak" and seen as "inadequate." They are emasculated and fall victim to the same denigrating attacks as female victims, maybe even more so as our male culture is based the belief that men should be strong enough to defend themselves.

Victims Trapped by Their Religious Beliefs and/or Moral and Cultural Strictures

In some religions and cultures, it is considered a taboo or a sin to leave one's partner and divorce is deeply frowned upon and/or prohibited. A member of such an extreme religion who chooses to leave their partner may fear being alienated by their friends and family or being shunned and/or excommunicated from the religious order and/or the community they have grown up with.

This can be emotionally, psychologically, and spiritually challenging for a victim who has grown up with a religion that has been a big influence throughout their life and formed a part of their identity. In some religions and cultures, it can be terrifying for a victim to leave their abusive relationship knowing that it may lead to violent retribution from their abusive intimate partner and/or the abusive partner's family. A victim may also fear retribution from their own birth family as leaving a marriage can be considered an act of defiance and/or disobedience that will shame their family. Some families from strict religious orders will not tolerate being shamed among their peers or in the eyes of their community and therefore the family will feel a need to punish their own progeny to restore respect. These victims have very good reason to have grave fears for their safety if they choose to leave their partner, as their lives are threatened by the abusive partner, the abusive partner's family and/or their own birth family.

In some countries, religions are the main influence on the culture of the society in which they flourish and as is typical of a fundamentalist religion that is steeped in archaic and misogynistically based beliefs, the male is considered the ruler of his domain and therefore holds absolute authority over his wife and children. These combined factors will make it very difficult if not impossible for a victim of domestic abuse to leave their abusive partner. The abuser is permitted to punish his wife or children however and to whatever degree he chooses and can and will often do this physically, as he will not tolerate any kind of behaviour, he deems to be disobedient or challenging to his authority. His actions are condoned by the religion and culture that he belongs to as their beliefs align, giving him permission to act as violently as he chooses within his family perimeters. He may make a marriage alliance for his children without their consent to someone of his choosing, there are girls barely out of puberty who are victims of this practice who are forced to marry someone against their will or risk being punished by their parents.

These punishments are physical beatings, which can and have resulted in serious bodily injury including maiming and in some cases death, they act as a deterrent that keep victims trapped in untenable situations. **Please note:** not all males that are members of these religions and cultures are domineering, controlling, violent and abusive in their nature or with their loved ones.

Victims Trapped by the Religious Belief That They Are Deserving of Their Abuse

Some victims are trapped by the religious and/or spiritual belief that they are deserving of their abuse as a form of punishment for a real or perceived wrongful action they believe they have performed or a "sin" they have committed. Others who may possess a progressive spiritual predilection, believe that they are paying penance in this lifetime, for a past life transgression. They are convinced that something they did in a past life-time is "karmically" influencing or possibly directing, the quality of their present life and that they are responsible for personal atonement and therefore may endure an abusive relationship or situation as a result.

Victims Trapped by a Language Barrier

There are victims of abuse particularly domestic violence, sexual assault, and work-related abuses such as sexual harassment, bullying and "sweat-shop" related conditions, who due to their language barrier keep silent about their abuse. Unfortunately, having a language barrier puts a person in a higher risk category for exploitation, making them more vulnerable to potential predators.

When it comes to workplace related abuse, immigrants and refugees who have not had an opportunity to learn to speak the primary local language of the country they have immigrated to, are likely to have limited employment opportunities becoming easy targets for workplace exploitation. Because of the language barrier, they may remain in ignorance of their human and legal rights leaving them vulnerable to unscrupulous employers. These employers are known to exploit a victim for personal and/or financial gain by not providing adequate healthy and safe environmental conditions, underpaying, over working, being verbally abusive, sexually harassing and even raping female victims under their employ.

They are known for using intimidating, coercive, and threatening behaviours to manipulate their employees into being compliant and silent about their working conditions and their employer's demands. The victims are always under the threat of being dismissed by their employer, which is extremely distressing for those employees who are dependent on their job for either, residency related issues or because this is their only source of income on which they and possibly their family rely.

When it comes to domestic and family abuse, women are at the highest risk of becoming a victim of random acts of violence and family and domestic abuse. However, women who have a language barrier are likely to be trapped in abusive relationships for longer periods of time and unlikely to seek aid. Their inability to understand, speak, read, or write English, can act to isolate them from the rest of the community and prevent them from being able to communicate with the authorities, seek legal aid, obtain protection orders, learn about their civil rights, receive appropriate medical or psychological care, or access their local community resources (i.e., women's shelters and policing bodies). Their language barrier makes them a more vulnerable and appealing target to predators who are looking to exploit this vulnerability to their advantage and it ensures that "the victim" is unlikely to seek aid or report abuse.

Victims of Isolation

According to the Australian Institute of Family Studies, the rates of Domestic and Family violence are higher in regional, rural, and remote areas than in highly populated urban areas due to the geographical and social structures in these communities. This is evidenced by several government studies that have brought to light how prevalent it is even though they have not ascertained exact figures. However just as it is in urban Australia, women are the most targeted victims followed by children, who because of their isolation are even less likely to take action or formally report their abuse to the authorities. There are two main categories of victims that come from these communities the "Involuntary" and the "Voluntary."

Involuntary

These are victims who have been intentionally physically isolated via psychological, emotional and/or physical manipulation or forced to reside in a rural or remote location by their abuser. Living in remote areas is a common tool used by perpetrators to keep prying eyes at a distance, it ensures that their abusive behaviour remains undetected and protects them from interference by external forces and therefore helps them to maintain control over their victim. As a result of this isolation our victim is unable to easily access a policing body or an aid centre and may not even know that they exist, or they are too terrified of their perpetrator to ask for help.

They have been purposely isolated to keep them socially ignorant of mainstream society and its dictates and some are permitted only limited or no academic education. Often, the abuser will further isolate a victim by regulating or even completely cutting off any interaction the victim may have with the outside world, including the victim's friends and family if they have any. The isolation protects the abuser and makes it difficult for the authorities to intervene in a timely manner due to the distance from the local community.

Voluntary

The victims of abuse who live in regional, rural, or remote communities by choice, are perhaps members of our indigenous, agricultural, and farming communities or grew up in a country town and remained in that same or another similar community. Geographical isolation is easily exploited by perpetrators of domestic and family violence, they are more easily able to exercise their controlling and dominating needs over their victim. They may veto the victim's access to phones, transport, other family members, friends, and their local community, using force in the form of threats (verbal, physical or with a weapon) or outright violence. The isolation acts as a barrier to accessing immediate support and deterring victims from reporting abuse as they are not likely to have readily available or prompt responsive action from policing or medical bodies should they need it.

There is a commonly shared prevailing view in rural communities that "family problems" are not talked about outside of the family unit acting as a deterrent to avoid public censure or becoming fodder for local community gossip. Victims are discouraged from disclosing their abuse out of fear of being shamed, vilified, or having a stigma attached to themselves. According to research (Carrington, Mcintosh, Hogg & Scott's – 2013) they concluded that rural communities tend to be predisposed to struggling with "hypermasculinity" and misogyny in their male population due to a destabilisation of traditional rural masculine roles and may be considered one of the main contributing factors for the violence which includes bullying, homophobia, sexual assault and family and domestic violence.

Hypermasculinity is defined as a psychological term for the exaggeration of male stereotypical behaviour that is based on strength, aggression, and sexuality.

Victims Trapped by Financial Dependence on Their Employer

Some victims may fear reporting being abused by their employer as it may jeopardise losing their employment, their career, and a vital income on which they and their family are financially dependent. A victim who is singularly dependent on their employment for their financial survival may become vulnerable to a deceitful, manipulative, or coercive supervisor, manager, or employer, who has no qualms taking advantage of the victim's dependence on their income. The abuser's intentions may be sexually motivated (including sexual harassment, unwanted touching, and assault) or they may abuse the victim by over-working them, asking them to perform jobs that are not in their job description, or they may use the victim as their scapegoat when things go wrong. Some victims are in a field of employment where limited career opportunities exist who are afraid of not being able to progress in their chosen profession if they lose their current position, which an exploitative senior controller or employer will take advantage of. Some victims fear being shunned by others in their profession for reporting their abusive but popular employer to the authorities or may fear being ostracised from their profession by other employers, which would significantly narrow their choice should they seek employment elsewhere, either way they put their income at risk.

Victims Trapped by Financial Dependence on a Significant Other

Controlling, manipulative and abusive intimate partners will purposefully limit their victim's access to what should be shared funds, they are likely to be selfish and miserly, however, the main reason is to exercise or maintain control over their partner (victim) and the assets. The abuser will do everything in their power to manipulate or coerce a victim into becoming financially dependent on them. Some abusers secure shared assets and trust funds, tying them up in complex financial arrangements which they do not disclose to the victim, this is just another attempt to control the victim by keeping them in the dark. There are victims who have foregone embracing a career or sustaining an existing career or business in order to raise children and manage the domestic responsibilities that caring for a family usually demands.

This may be through mutual choice between a couple or it may be the result of a coercive and controlling partner, either way it paves the way for one partner to become the main income-earner in the household. For an abuser, this becomes an opportunity to exploit what may have become a necessary circumstance for child rearing, by taking full advantage of their partner's financial dependence on them. Quite often, a victim has placed themselves in a financially vulnerable position to an abuser without realising it, trusting in their significant other to look out for the families' collective best interests.

Please note however, that this victim pool is not exclusive to intimate partners, it may also include other family or caretaking scenarios which may include children, adolescents and/or handicapped, disabled or elderly dependants. Regardless of the relationship, the abuser will exercise tight control over the family finances allowing minimal or no direct access by the victim, they will make all decisions about social outings and gifts bought and closely monitor household and investment expenditure including how and on what the victim spends their food and grocery allowance. Some abusers even go so far as to accompany the victim when they shop to ensure the money is spent in a manner they approve of. Their aim is to keep their victim ignorant of financial matters and financially dependent on them so that they can threaten a victim's economic security to maintain control or to intimidate them into being pliant, compliant, and silent about their abuser's abusive behaviour.

The Witness

Witnesses to violence and abuse whether it is to a single random act, or on-going acts of abuse are in fact victims themselves. The repercussions of abuse can be just as psychologically and emotionally traumatising to a witness as they are to a victim.

Introduction

Bearing witness to violence and abuse in any capacity whether it is a single random act or ongoing acts of abuse can have the same profound psychological and emotional harmful impact on a witness as it does on a victim. Whether the witness is consciously aware of it or not, they are likely to experience varying degrees of the same or similar "affect" (emotional and/or psychological trauma) as the victim themselves is experiencing as a direct result of their abuse, such as fear, anxiety, terror, anger, rage, shame, guilt, powerlessness, and hopelessness.

In fact, a witness must also be a victim albeit in an indirect way, they may respond to the abuser and the abusive action taken in the same way as that of the victim themselves, reacting to their experience by activating the onset of psychological, emotional and behavioural defences and schemas. The witness may develop any of the defences and schemas listed under "victim's defences" (refer to victim defences p118–p139). Some of the most common being dissociation, rationalisation, repression, suppression, denial, somatisation (physical illness), depression, substance abuse and addiction or eating, sleeping and anxiety behavioural disorders and in the more serious cases PTSD (post-traumatic stress disorder).

There are two possible sub-categories that a witness may fit into, the first is known as a "direct and present witness" and the second is known as a "third party witness." A "direct or present witness" is someone who has through any circumstance accidental or otherwise become a direct witness to a singular or random act of abuse or on-going acts of abuse. A "third party witness" is someone in whom the actual victim or a "direct and present witness" has confided the abuse to, in other words, the "third party witness" was not present when the abusive incident took place but was apprised of the abuse later. A "third party witness" may also be someone who has witnessed the abused victim's injuries despite not being present when the abuse took place, even though the victim has not confided in them.

The harmful impact of witnessing violence and abuse and how a witness responds to it at the time it occurred will be determined by several defining factors and influences.

- The witnesses' emotional, psychological, and cognitive level of development and maturity.
- Were they at any time a victim of abuse themselves?
- Their living conditions i.e., war, poverty, or political suppression.
- Their economic circumstances.
- Their religious, political, and cultural beliefs.
- Their upbringing i.e., in what manner they were reared and how has it shaped them.

All these factors contribute to determining the conscious and unconscious emotional, psychological, and behavioural responses that may occur as a consequence of the violence/abuse they have witnessed. There are sets of recurring but distinct circumstances that occur that help us to place witnesses into specific categories in order to analyse how they are affected and why they respond the way in which they do. Following, you will find a list of these categories, explaining the differing types of witnesses that exist along with an outline of the specific conditions and influences factors that surround each unique circumstance.

Types of Witnesses

The Witness Who Keeps Silent out of Fear

There are many witnesses in domestic and family abuse situations who are under threat from the abuser, fearing retribution for themselves should they speak about what they are witnessing, or they may be economically dependent on the abuser and may fear losing their financial support or being ejected from their home. Some witnesses whose character structures are primarily anxious, timid, withdrawn, or introverted are naturally fearful of intimidating people and environments. They are likely to remain silent about what they are witnessing hoping that they will not be noticed by the abuser and draw unwanted attention to themselves fearful of becoming the abusers next target. Witnesses may experience the same or similar feelings of helplessness, powerlessness, and fear as that of the victim, they do so because the abuser may have power or authority over both the victim and the witness and as a result, they may fall into any of the following categories:

In the workplace:

- The witness and victim may share the same employer (who is the victim's abuser) and are reluctant to report the employer to authorities or help the victim because they are afraid of losing their employment (on which they and their family may be financially dependent).
- The witness is from a foreign country and may have been sponsored by their employer (abuser) and are afraid losing their job or being deported.
- The witness may feel intimidated by their employer or other co-workers because they are struggling with a language barrier.
- The witness who is struggling with a language barrier is not aware of what is and is not acceptable behaviour in the workplace.

- The witness fears that the people in charge will support the perpetrator, especially if the perpetrator is well-known, popular, and important to the reputation and success of the organisation to which they both belong.

In the witnesses personal or social arena:

- The witness is a related to the abuser and cannot speak out as they are under the abuser's authority and/or legal guardianship.
- The witness is related to the abuser and is afraid of retribution from the abuser.
- The witness is afraid of being shunned or ostracised from their social group, religious order, or community if they speak out.
- The witness fears they will not be believed because the perpetrator is an influential and/or authority figure in society such as a judge, politician, or religious leader or because the perpetrator is a high profile, famous, much loved and adored public figure such as a movie/television star, a highly acclaimed musician or a sporting icon.

Some witnesses maintain a strict silence about an abuser's abusive activities by pretending ignorance of the abuser's activities; this is because they fear that if the abuser is exposed, they will open themselves or their family up to experience personal and/or public shame, censure, and/or ridicule. They may fear being ostracised and/or scrutinised by other family members, co-workers, and friends or on a larger scale the community to which they belong because of their association to the abuser.

The Angry and/or Frustrated Witness

A witness may have a direct and personal relationship with the victim and therefore feel a deep desire to help them. They may share a relationship in their place of employment, social circle or on a more intimate level with a family member. This witness has the victim's best intentions in mind when trying to help them, and may possibly go to great lengths to render aid, offer moral and emotional support, and encourage the victim to seek aid. However, when the victim shows a reluctance to accept the aid being offered and it appears that they are not going to help themselves get free of the abusive relationship/situation, or report the abuser, the witness may find themselves feeling extremely disappointed, frustrated, and angry with the victim. It is not uncommon for a victim not to act on the advice offered by others no matter how well intentioned the advice is, unfortunately it may even have an opposite and adverse effect on the relationship between the witness and the victim.

The relationship may undergo a radical change, where at one time the witness held feelings of compassion, understanding and empathy towards the victim; those feelings have subsequently evolved into frustration and anger towards the victim. After a period of time, some witnesses anger and frustration may possibly advance developing into feelings of apathy (indifference) or antipathy (animosity) towards the victim's plight perhaps "washing their hands" so to speak, of the victim and their situation with an attitude of "I've done all I can" or thinking that "they deserve what they get" if they (victim) won't do anything about it. Conversely, victims who have displayed signs that they are not ready to change their abusive situation or report an abusive incident may also reject the witnesses well-intentioned offer of support or aid and may even distance themselves or completely cut themselves of from the relationship they once shared with the witness.

The Witness Who Protects the Abuser out of Misplaced Loyalty.

There can also arise a scenario wherein a witness who is closely associated to the abuser becomes conflicted as a result of a misplaced sense of loyalty towards the abuser. They may be connected to the abuser through friendship, perhaps they are a close long-term friend or they may be directly related to the abuser through marriage or family, such as an intimate partner, grandparent, aunt, uncle, sibling, cousin, or they are the son or daughter of the abuser. In this case, the witness may be someone who adores, admires, or loves the abuser who cannot accept that the person they love is capable of, or responsible for perpetrating abuse.

The inability to reconcile the abuser's abusive actions may lead to psychological defensive action being taken by the witness in the form of denial, minimisation, rationalisation, suppression, or repression in an attempt to avoid any emotional and psychological cognitive dissonance (inner conflict) that they might be experiencing. Witnesses in this situation may go to great lengths to protect the abuser, convincing themselves and others that the person they hold in high esteem is the person they believe them to be. In some cases, witnesses resolve their conflicting emotions by blaming the victim for the abusive event/s in order to deflect from, minimise or exonerate the abuser's actions and may turn any adverse feelings disappointment, frustration, and anger about the situation from the abuser onto the victim.

The Witness Who has Experienced Abuse in Their Past.

We have already established that a witness to violence and abuse regardless of the degree of seriousness of the abuse (mild or severe), may not have realised that as a witness they have been affected psychologically and emotionally to some degree, whether they are consciously aware of it or not. A witness may be unaware that they carry unresolved issues from an experience in their past until they are confronted with a current adverse experience. For some, witnessing abuse in a present circumstance, can act as a stimulus, trigging a latent or unacknowledged memory or memories from the witness's earlier life when they had a direct experience of abuse themselves or they were a witness to abuse at that earlier time.

If the issues surrounding the earlier experiences were addressed at the time they occurred in an adequate manner, then remembering the earlier adverse experience will not affect them in a negative way or paralyse them as happens in some cases. In fact, they are likely to respond to their current situation using their past experience as a catalyst to act in a positive and/or supportive manner towards the victim, eager to help them in any way they can, motivated by a deep sense of genuine, heartfelt empathy and understanding. However, this is not always the case, some witnesses who have been a "witness to" or a victim themselves in their past may respond to a current situation in the opposite way, not wanting to, or being able to support or help the victim or themselves.

This usually occurs because the issues and emotions surrounding the past injurious experience such as anxiety, fear, powerlessness, impotence, shame and/or guilt were supressed, ignored, or denied and consequently were not addressed or resolved at the time they occurred. The lack of therapeutic intervention causing the witness to develop maladaptive coping mechanisms (defences) and leaving them with some level of repressed traumatic affect. For some, the unresolved issues and emotions associated with the earlier traumatic memory have been lying dormant in the recesses of the witness's psyche, only coming to the forefront as a result of being brought on by the present-day abusive scenario. The witness may be assailed with overwhelming, conflicting emotions, responding by both aligning with the victim with feelings of empathy and understanding towards them, and at the same time colluding with the victim's feelings of powerlessness and fear.

However, the fear and powerlessness are the prevailing overwhelming emotions, causing the witness extreme distress, creating a kind of emotional and psychological paralysis through crisis, immobilising the witness, and impeding them from helping or supporting the victim in the current situation. Some witnesses who possess a history that had some level of abuse in it, may react to a current situation with an insensitive or apathetic attitude towards the victim, by completely ignoring the current situation that they are witnessing, appearing uncaring and unempathetic towards the victim. This is because the witness may disassociate from the present incident to protect themselves from re-experiencing a painful and frightening past event and as a result will not allow themselves to feel the emotions associated with victimhood which at one time in their past made them feel powerless, fearful, and vulnerable.

The Involuntary or Accidental Witness

An involuntary and/or accidental witness may be anyone who has not anticipated being, or has unwillingly become either a direct or third-party witness to a singular or multiple acts of violence and abuse. However, because of circumstances beyond their control and/or because of their relationship with either the abuser or the victim, have now become unintentionally connected to an unwanted and conceivably adverse situation. It is not possible to know when a person will encounter random acts of violence and abuse because as the word suggests they can occur at any time, in any place and for reasons you are unaware of, so if you become a witness to a random act of violence you have automatically become an "accidental and involuntary witness" having had no control over the situation in which you found yourself.

Children and adolescents are regrettably but frequently found to be in both the "victim" and the "involuntary witness" pool, invariably becoming involuntary witnesses to family and domestic abuse. These children and adolescents have had no choice in the environment in which they have been born, fostered, adopted, or married (step children) into. For a child or adolescent whether they are a witness to a random act of abuse or ongoing acts of abuse, the impact on their physical, emotional, and psychological growth can be extremely detrimental as they have not yet had the opportunity to develop mature coping mechanisms.

Consequently, witnessing abuse at a young age will without doubt be inhibitive to their natural and healthy developmental progression, causing harmful and possibly long-lasting injury to their young and fragile emerging psyches. It will likely result in triggering the onset of maladaptive coping mechanisms (refer to defence theory p118–139) as a compensatory measure much like the victim themselves. Many adult abusers are blind to the presence of their offspring when they are caught up in the thrall of their abusive activity. This occurs regardless of whom the abuser has targeted, whether it is a random stranger, an intimate partner, a relative, a friend or another of the witness's siblings. If, however the abuser is alcohol or drug affected, their abusive behaviours are heightened and their peripheral and cognitive awareness lowered and as a result they may not be able to retain a partial or whole recollection of the abusive events that took place and therefore were unaware that there were witnesses present.

There also exists the type of ignorant abuser who believes that children are indeed "deaf and dumb" so to speak. This abuser labours under the misconception that children are too young to understand what they are witnessing, believing children are either incapable of comprehending abusive behaviour or unlikely to remember. Other abusers may be of the school of thought that a child or adolescent witness is not affected by what they witnessed because it was not them the abuse was directed at. Sociopathic, psychopathic, and sadistic abusers by their very nature simply do not care who is present when they are abusing another, they are too absorbed in their abusive activities and intentions. These types of abusers are lacking in empathy and concern for other human beings in general and can perform acts of abuse from a place of impulsivity and thoughtlessness engaging in abusive actions regardless of who is present to witness their activities.

Witnesses Can Help Without Risk

Please note: There are times when a victim can and has to help themselves and there are times when a victim is unable to help themselves and it is those times when the relation, the friend, the work colleague, the employer, or the neighbour, as the witness can seek aid on their behalf. This does not mean that you approach the perpetrator or get involved directly in the situation putting yourself and the victim at risk but it does mean that you can investigate the many and varied safe avenues that are available to help a victim. You can easily access help lines and advice that will be specific to any situation such as workplace abuse, family and domestic abuse, sex crimes and bullying. However, if you think you or someone you know is in any kind of danger, do not hesitate to call the police immediately; you may be saving someone from serious or even fatal injury.

Epilogue

Every human being deserves to live in an environment in which they feel safe, cared for, hopefully loved and in which they can thrive and flourish. In order to create the safest possible environments, reduce the incidence of violence and protect our most vulnerable we would need to address some of the major issues that are preventing us from achieving this end. Regardless of our race, religion, political beliefs, sexual orientation, or lifestyle we all want the same thing for ourselves and our children, we want to be respected and protected by the society we live in. By joining together, we can have a more powerful impact on our government and or judicial system, making the kind of statement that will get heard which is, that we need a society that will not accept any type of violence or abuse in any shape or form. As a collective voice, we can apply the necessary pressure to make the changes we need to ensure our safety and just as importantly set up a safer environment for future generations. We must make the safety and wellbeing of all human beings our greatest priority and set it above all other things.

- An attitude of zero tolerance must be adopted by all in order to effect the necessary changes that are essential for society to respond in a more significant and impacting way to resolve all the issues that surround violent and abusive behaviour. We can make a more meaningful impact through harsher punishments for all perpetrators of violent and abusive crimes sending the message that we will not tolerate this behaviour in any shape or form and will not allow this insidious behaviour to continue without harsh consequences. It is crucial that the appropriate governing bodies, authorities, and society as a whole clearly understand the lasting effects that crimes of abuse have on a victim.

- Re-evaluate our priorities in our current Criminal Justice System to address penal loopholes and how we can better empower and support our law making and policing bodies to act more effectively when dealing with violent crime and the perpetrators of those violent crimes, where the word "repeat offender" becomes a rare and uncommon term.

- Make a statement with our corrective intentions that makes an impact on criminal behaviour by implementing harsher punishments for all violent crime, particularly crimes of a sexual nature, paedophilia, and family and domestic abuse.

- Prioritise research and funding into the causation and prevention of criminal behaviour and how to more completely and more effectively protect and support victims. Numerous victims particularly those of sex crimes and family and domestic abuse are reluctant or afraid to come forward to report their abuse or seek aid for fear that they will not be adequately protected from retribution from their abuser.

- Re-educate society as whole in relation to dispelling judgement against victims. There are some members of society who through ignorance or prejudice further victimise victims by implying that they could have prevented or avoided becoming a victim of violence and have therefore contributed to their own victimhood. They tend to disbelieve victims of crimes perpetrated by high profile figures, accusing them of exaggerating, lying or as someone who is seeking attention consequently shifting the blame onto the victim.

- Address the issues concerning those members of our society of which there are a significant enough number, who hold existing, long standing, prejudicial and archaic, social, religious, or cultural beliefs towards women and the LGBTQIA plus community in a more targeted and significant way. It is through their ignorance that they continue to victimise a victim and minimise if not absolve some offenders from crimes of a sexual nature and family and domestic abuse. Their outdated beliefs are based on stereotypical male and female images and roles that are suffused in a history of inequality between men and women, in a time when women were regarded as lesser than their male counter-parts and were not afforded their basic human rights. Today this is reflected by transphobes, misogynists and homophobes who possess an underdeveloped social and emotional awareness and intelligence.

- Create awareness through knowledge; it must be a priority to educate our society on the many different aspects that contribute to bullying, domestic abuse and violent crime including early prevention, early detection, and early intervention.

It is therefore essential that we invest the necessary time and resources to educate society across all cultures, religions, age groups, genders, and occupations. Through educating the general public, we are taking a major step towards winning the battle against violence and the predators and abusers who are committing these violent acts. We can start by introducing specific age-appropriate tailored workshops that address the issues surrounding violence and abuse. Using educational institutions to target our young especially our teens as they emerge into adulthood.

The second area of focus needs to be all major adult sporting clubs and associations, social clubs, universities, colleges, workplaces private and public. Creating workshops geared towards understanding what constitutes violence, bullying, verbal, physical emotional and psychological abuse, and the impact it has on a victim, how to get help if you are a victim, how to protect yourself from becoming a victim, how to set boundaries with perpetrators and most importantly how to recognise predators, abusers, and bullies and how they operate.

Crimes of violence and abuse exist in varying degrees across the planet, in every country regardless of the culture or religion. In order to create a safer environment in which we can all flourish, significant change is essential. It will however require that all members of society unite to force the changes that are needed to protect ourselves, our children, and future generations. Our current statistical figures fail to reflect the reality of the prevalence of family and domestic abuse, sexual assault, forced pregnancy, enslavement and human trafficking that is being perpetrated. Victims are not only terrified of reporting crimes committed against them to authorities for fear of retribution from the perpetrator/s but are also unable to report these crimes because of their enforced captivity, therefore it stands to reason that the extent and severity of this type of crime has not been appropriately acknowledged or adequately addressed.

How to Minimise Your Vulnerability to Potentially Abusive Relationships and Predators

It would be ideal to live in a society where our most vulnerable could travel to any destination and at any time (day or night), without fear of being accosted, assaulted, harassed, raped, or kidnapped and where children can safely play in the front garden or ride their bikes down the street without constant supervision and still feel safe. However, unfortunately, we do not live in that utopia, and even though that is what we should be working towards as a society, our reality is a far different one. It is not only essential that we educate ourselves about predators and abusers and how they operate, we also need to take action to minimise our vulnerability to danger and become proactive in protecting ourselves as well as others. Whether you are simply socialising, dating, or entering a relationship, take some time to consider the following safety measures to reduce your vulnerability to a predator:

Educate yourself

There is an abundance of information easily accessible on the internet or in your local library covering many relevant subjects such as, healthy, and unhealthy relationships, what constitutes abusive behaviour, how to help yourself if you are a victim, where to get help and how to help others. The more you know the better equipped you will be to protect yourself and your loved ones.

Use your Intuition

One of the most underused and underrated protective devices that we as human beings already possess and are born with is our "innate intuition." When we are faced with a potential danger, our intuition will automatically activate, presenting itself in various physical ways, most commonly but not exclusively as a prickling sensation at the nape of our neck, a shiver, a slight tingling sensation on the surface of our skin or in our fingertips or a sinking feeling such as a slight pang that hits low in our abdomen.

If you find yourself in a situation where you are interacting with another person/s and something does not feel right or does not ring true, then it is quite possible that your intuition has kicked in to let you know that something is indeed wrong. We are not unlike our animal counterparts who all possess various kinds of distinct innate warning systems that informs them of possible danger, human beings are no different, and our bodies perceive danger before our mind has registered a warning. However, unfortunately throughout history and as part of our human evolutionary processes, man has strongly supported science-based teachings that have focused on cerebral pursuits principally (Intellectual and analytical) minimising or discounting any other schools of thought. So, it will come as no surprise that for a very long-time human beings have been encouraged to stay centred in their minds, using reason and logic in all situations hence the saying "level headed" resulting in less importance being placed in our own natural inclinations and instincts.

It takes practice to train yourself to listen to and trust your intuition, but the reward will be worth the effort. It may save your life or the life of someone you love and care about one day, I am sure if you think back over your previous life experiences you will recall a time when you experienced a positive outcome from listening to your intuition. Learn to trust your Intuition or "gut instinct" it never lies and it has your best interest at heart, whenever your intuition sends you a warning signal this is the time to ask yourself how does this circumstance make me feel. If you are ever feeling uneasy or uncomfortable with someone or a situation, this is your body telling you that something is not right and this is the time to reassess your safety and if need be, remove yourself and/or those you love.

Look beneath the surface

Never assume that you are adept at spotting a potential predator/abuser think of them as "imageless," they have no specific physical visual image that separates them from ourselves. There are many who have an agenda that is well hidden and a practiced façade that they have cultivated through trial and error over time. This fake persona has worked for them in the past giving them a measure of success giving them confidence, remember their chosen environment will be wherever their specific victim pool exists.

Do not be deluded by a projected façade, you must take the time to look beneath the surface; this will require that you "not" take a person you have just met at face value. Do not engage in risky behaviour, sexual or otherwise with a stranger or someone you do not know well enough to be vulnerable with. It is also important to remember that with every interaction you have with someone new in your life whether it is via telephone, an internet-dating site or in person ask yourself the following questions. What are their actions telling me, do their actions equal their words, what is their body language telling me and most importantly what is my intuition telling me?

Check the facts –

Remember "If you have nothing to hide, you hide nothing"

We have established that abusers have no qualms lying, in fact they pride themselves on their ability to manage situations and relationships with lies. They are adept at twisting facts, fabricating elaborate untruths, and manipulating reality, so when entering a relationship, you will need to look deeper to check the validity of the "supposed" facts. You can and should re-visit the "facts" with the person you are dating as often as you need to but, particularly if you harbour even the smallest doubt about the information supplied to you. If someone is in a committed relationship with pure intentions, then their aim should be to cultivate an environment based on honesty and trust, and so there would be no reason to keep electronic devices such as a phone or computer in lock mode, barring complete access from their partner.

This behaviour is definitely a red flag and should be investigated, there are many predators/abusers who have secrets and lies that they are afraid of exposing, which becomes evident if they strongly oppose and resist allowing a partner to share innocently intended access. They may defend their actions with more lies insisting that it is a breach of their privacy or that they are waiting for an important call etc. For abusers, lying is a major part of their identity, they do it so often that it becomes instinctive. However, this can also be responsible for their downfall particularly if they forget "who they told what to" and get caught out. If you have caught your partner lying about something you consider significant in your relationship, then you must ask the question what else are they lying about, remember if you have nothing to hide, you hide nothing.

When dating or socialising

By taking a proactive role towards your own wellbeing when socialising, you can minimise your vulnerability to dangerous situations and to predators, there are many precautions you can take to improve your level of safety.

- After a night out, if possible, travel home accompanied by a trusted friend especially if catching a taxi/uber or taking some form of public transport home.
- If you intend to travel home on your own after a social event or a night out, make sure that you have enough money to pay for your transport home before you leave.
- If you are alone and taking a taxi/uber or public transport to go home, make sure that you are not drug or alcohol affected to a degree that leaves you vulnerable to a predator.
- Take responsibility for your drinking and/or drug taking when you are socialising, this may mean that you need to inform a trusted friend of your intention to drink (over the limit) or take drugs so that if the need arises this trusted friend is going to be there for you to ensure your safety and wellbeing.
- Assess your level of danger clearly before drinking and/or drug taking when you are socialising, if you do not have a trusted friend with you, remember friends of friends can be predators.
- Take note of and responsibility for your personal drinking and/or drug taking pattern when you are out socialising, as even trusted friends can get tired of looking after someone who makes it a habit of depending on them to look after you at the expense of having a good time themselves and may not be there for you when you need them.
- Every time you travel to and from any destination, take precautions to ensure your own safety, let someone know where you are going to or coming from.

Every time you socialise you need to adequately assess your risk factors, taking into consideration the following:

- When meeting someone new for a first date, let someone who you trust and who cares about your wellbeing know where you are going to meet this "new someone" and how long you will be (perhaps activate a tracking app).
- If you are going somewhere alone and find yourself with friends or associates that you do not know very well and cannot entirely trust, you will need to keep your wits about you by reducing your alcohol intake and not taking a mind-altering drug.
- Do not accept a ride home from someone you just met and barely know even though you have been introduced to them by a friend.
- Do not accept a ride home from someone who has a public profile such as sporting, radio, music, or television personality with the assumption that you are safe, remember despite their high profile they are still a stranger to you.
- Under no circumstances do you leave where you are and relative safety with someone you just met to go to their place or another venue under the assumption that you are safe.
- Do not accept free drinks offered to you if you have not witnessed that drink being poured by a bartender yourself. Be aware that "date rape" drugs are resource for predators.
- Always let someone you trust such as a family member, roommate or partner know where you are going and what time to expect you home.

The Character Trait Checklist for Identifying an Existing or Potential Abuser

Check the following list for any combination of behavioural character traits that may signal a warning of the existence of a potential predator/abuser/bully.

Predators, abusers, and bullies are known to be charming, manipulative, narcissistic, sociopathic, sadistic and/or psychopathic and they may possess any combination or all the following associated character traits:

- Lack real empathy – they can mimic empathy when needed but not for a convincing period of time.
- Are manipulative – using their charm to exploit, delude and deceive.
- Are narcissistic – self-absorbed, self-centred, and selfish.
- Exhibit controlling behaviours.
- Can be possessive, envious and/or jealous.
- Are consummate and consistent liars – mixing half-truths with elaborate lies.
- Can display sadistic behaviours – emotionally, physically, and psychologically cruel and remorseless.
- Are secretive about their life, past and/or present.
- Are adept at "gaslighting" – by distorting the truth (reality) in order to create confusion for personal gain.
- Can be passive aggressive or physically violent – using coercion and bullying tactics to intimidate and control.
- Can exhibit manic and/or violent behaviours as a result of alcohol and substance abuse.
- Can exhibit manic and/or violent behaviours due to inability to control their anger/rage.

- Are likely to use psychological and emotional manipulations – often in the form of verbal insults used to undermine a victim's confidence and/or they belittle, demean, and humiliate with the intention to intimidate and control.
- Can use financial manipulations to control a victim.
- Are likely to separate and/or isolate a victim from those closest to them.
- Can be sexually promiscuous – having more than one or multiple partners simultaneously.
- Tend to commit adultery, they find fidelity difficult.
- They are unable to achieve real emotional intimacy with another human being and only engage in physical intimacy for the purpose of sexual activity. They find all other physical intimacies such as kissing, hugging and handholding to be a means to end (sex and sexual gratification) and is otherwise avoided or kept to a minimum.

If your intimate partner, co-worker, employer, friend, or family member is exhibiting a combination of most or all the above characteristics, then he or she is someone to be concerned about. However, before you make any decisions about how you are going to respond to this information it is important that you seek further clarification and advice from an "expert resource," particularly if you are unsure or confused. You can contact by phone or on line a professional therapist or a local or national hotline of which there are many and speak to a trained psychologist or psychotherapist in this specific field, they will respect your need for anonymity if required. Do not accuse or confront an abuser directly as they may retaliate if they feel threatened however, if you believe that you or someone close to you is in immediate danger, then call the authorities (police) who are trained to deal with abusive and violent offenders who will decide what action needs to be taken.

A Guide for Victims

How can I help myself? – What can I do?

It requires courage to take responsibility for yourself, to move forward and live fully in the present, however the rewards are magnificent. You will gain freedom from an oppressive situation, remove feelings of constant anxiety and fear, re-discover yourself, develop new goals, be at liberty to make choices for yourself, feel safe and secure, be yourself without fear of retribution and most importantly be an example for your children, family, and other victims of abuse.

Consider the following steps as a guideline:

1. First and foremost, you must make the decision to want to help yourself and your co-dependants if you have any, this is by no means an easy decision to make and understandably so. However, once you have wrapped your mind around the fact that you need save yourself and those you love, you will have taken one of the most integral steps towards gaining freedom.

2. If you decide you want out of this relationship, then you must be very certain, because it requires a committed fortitude. Unfortunately, it will always feel like you are taking two steps forward, one step back, and so perseverance, determination and doggedness are required and remember to stay focused on your goals.

3. If you find yourself feeling overwhelmed, start by taking small steps, perhaps initially just committing yourself to doing some research (it is surprising at how such a small action can empower you).

4. If you have a partner (abuser) who is monitoring or checking your phone and internet usage, then you will need to become resourceful. If it is possible use a trusted friend's phone or internet connection or perhaps you can use the internet at the library, your place of employment or an internet café when making enquires.

5. You need to devise a plan of action for your exit strategy, actually you may need several plans of action and they need to be flexible, in other words if you have to change your plans to another day, destination or time of departure, then do so (assessing your level of danger at all times). Remember never underestimate your abuser, a situation can escalate to dangerous levels very quickly if the abuser is not coping and becomes angry or enraged.

6. Prepare your family and/or close friends if you think they may be unsafe when you exit. It is a well-known fact that many domestic abusers make threats towards the family and friends of a victim.

7. Let someone you trust know of your plans, should the situation become worrisome or dangerous and in case you need help. However, be very careful who you include in this list as they must without doubt be loyal to you and trustworthy (remember you may be trusting them with both you and your loved ones' lives) or alternately you could advise the authorities or a counsellor of your intentions.

8. If there are children involved who need to exit with you and they are at an age where they have some understanding of the situation at hand, then it may be best to prepare them just prior to exiting. For some, it may be just before exiting for others it may require days, weeks, or months of preparation.

9. Do your homework:
   - Find out where the nearest refuge or shelter (safe house) is located, they will take women and children in danger of domestic violence. Make sure you research their procedures and protocols for entry ahead of time.
   - Find out where the nearest police station is situated in case it is needed as a destination for your emergency exit (check their opening hours to ensure it is always manned).
   - Find out who can help you and who best suits you, there are many help lines on the internet and in the yellow pages with highly skilled and attuned psychologists, psychotherapists, counsellors, and advice services.

   Please note: These organisations are aware of your need for privacy, they understand the need to be discrete, sensitive to your situation and will respect your need for anonymity if requested.

10. Hide a spare key or keys in a strategic place where you can get to it quickly, making certain that it is in a place your abuser will never think to look. It may include keys such as a dead lock house key and it must hold a spare car key (if you have a car).

11. If possible, hide some cash (at least enough for a taxi ride and/or a public phone) or a spare ATM or credit card, with the spare keys.

12. Arm yourself with knowledge – read, investigate, and seek advice, the more cognitive, emotional, and psychological understanding you gain of yourself and your abuser the more informed your decisions and choices will be. Research there are plenty of free services on line that can provide vital information including those regarding your legal rights (this is a great way to regain your power).

    * Custody laws – If children are involved.
    * Criminal law – Restraining or protection orders.
    * Property law
    * Divorce law

13. This next step is the most difficult of all the steps that you are going to need to undertake to move towards your freedom, however this step will also prove to be the most vital and the most rewarding. It involves taking a journey inward to explore your own personal emotional and psychological landscape, you will need to know more about yourself and your inner workings in order to create a new and more stable life in the future. Moving forward will require that you seek some type of psychological and emotional aid and/or treatment in the form of a psychotherapist, psychologist, or counsellor.

    These trained professionals will help you along your journey giving you a safe place to explore your present situation, your options and help you with your decision-making process while offering advice and providing you with emotional support without judgment. You do not have to do this on your own when there are a myriad of trained professionals and organisations that offer assistance while providing privacy. However, if you cannot afford private sessions there exists many diverse free community aid services and help lines for victims of abuse (look online or in the yellow pages).

14. To move forward, you need to be "present fully in the now" so you can make rational decisions regarding your actions from moment to moment, be alert to possible danger and to be tactically elastic (able to change your stance instantly if needed). Being "present" simply put, means that a person is cognitively and emotionally attuned to what is occurring in their immediate present experience. Victims of abuse for obvious reasons can struggle to be "present fully in the now" because they are suffering from symptoms of PTSD (post-traumatic stress disorder), fear and exhaustion or defences such as dissociation (splitting off) or denial. Your psychologist, psychotherapist or counsellor can help you to recognise and deal with these symptoms, remember, you cannot work on your abuser nor can your therapist, you can only work on yourself. Understanding yourself is an important key not only to finding your way out of a destructive relationship but also to gain the strength of conviction needed to take positive action towards attaining freedom, reclaiming yourself and your power and ensuring that you do not find yourself in another abusive relationship in the future. Taking a journey, inwards through self-discovery by exploring and opening yourself to your past and how it shaped you whether it is with a therapist, through acquiring knowledge (research though reading) or both, will be life-changing. It will help you to heal old wounds, change dysfunctional patterns of behaviour and challenge beliefs that no longer serve you.

- Start by taking a closer look at how you were parented, go back to your early childhood and teenage years, is there any experience that stands out.
- Examine your core beliefs about love, family, relationships, intimacy, sex, and sexuality, money, and religion. Where and when did these beliefs originate, and do they serve you well now or have they become burdensome or obsolete.
- Explore your family history, are there any family secrets, are there any similarities between your life and those of your predecessors, what does it tell you, and how does that influence who you are today.
- Explore your defences with a therapist using the categories mentioned i.n defence theory; do they influence your life in a positive or negative way?

Six Golden Rules

1. Never, ever take the blame for someone else's abusive actions towards you.

2. Never refer to yourself in a negative light or call yourself derogatory names such as I am stupid, dumb, ugly etc., nothing is gained from this self-defeating behaviour.

3. Never ever say to yourself "I should have known better," no one wants bad things to happen to them, circumstances beyond your control took that choice from you. By saying "I should have known better" is the same as accepting some level of responsibility for your abuser's actions.

4. Never accept accountability for another's abusive actions towards you, however there will be times when you must accept responsibility for your choices, because without accepting responsibility for your choices, you will never be able to learn from your experiences. Remember taking responsibility for your choices does not in any way absolve your abuser/s from their actions, but allows you to be open to make the changes you need to secure a safer and happier future for yourself and your loved ones.

5. Do not let your past trauma define your future life, get help, there is plenty on offer. If it does not work out with a particular organisation, therapist, or type of therapy, keep searching until you find what feels right for you.

6. Remember, you are not alone, there are others suffering just like yourself, but more importantly there are others truly willing and able to help you.

Glossary

The following is a glossary of the most used terms:

1. **Predator/abuser/bully** is someone who intentionally causes emotional, psychological and/or physical harm to another whether it is a single random act or short or long-term abuse. They are anyone who falls into the following categories, sociopaths and sociopathic liars, psychopaths, sexual offenders, kidnappers, killers, paedophiles, human traffickers, stalkers, adulterers and serial adulterers, domestic abusers, home, social and workplace bullies and internet and social media bullies and predators.

2. **A victim** is someone at the receiving end of any intentional behaviour deemed harmful to their emotional, psychological, and physical wellbeing whether it be a singular random incident or short or long-term abuse.

3. **A Witness** is any person who may through no fault of their own find themselves bearing witness to an act or acts of abuse.

4. **Emotional and psychological abuse** is defined as any intentional treatment towards another that may diminish their sense of identity, self-worth, self-esteem, and their dignity.

5. **Physical abuse** is defined as any intentional treatment towards another which causes bodily injury.

6. **Child abuse** refers to any psychological, emotional, sexual, or physical mistreatment or neglect by an adult towards someone who is under the age of 18 years.

7. **Family and Domestic abuse** is an action taken or a pattern of actions that include, controlling and coercive, threatening, degrading and violent behaviour. This includes, psychological, emotional, physical, and sexual abuse, financial or economic abuse and harassment, bullying and stalking (including online or telephone).

8. **The Criminal Justice System** consists of three main parts, Law enforcement agencies (police), Courts and Corrections for detaining and supervising offenders (prison and probation agencies). The five main goals of the Criminal Justice System are Retribution, Incapacitation, rehabilitation, Deterrence and Restoration.

9. **Psychopath/Sociopath** – A psychopath/sociopath is someone who displays signs of possessing an "antisocial personality disorder" and who engages in violent, abusive, and criminal behaviour without remorse for their actions or empathy towards others. The term "psychopath" was initially introduced in 1900, succeeded by the term "sociopath", the reference to "sociopath" was introduced in the 1930s to emphasise the damage they inflicted on society. They both have the same meaning and are therefore interchangeable however, some clinicians prefer to use the term "psychopath" to define the more seriously affected by the disorder and more dangerous than the sociopath.

References/Resources

Early Childhood and Adolescent Development and Trauma
Author: Eric Erikson – Childhood and Society.
Author: D. W. Winnicot – Deprivation and Delinquency.
Author: Babette Rothschild – The Body Remembers.
Author: Alice Miller – The Body Never Lies.

Behavioural Theories
Author: Albert Bandura – Social Learning Theory
Author: Eric Erikson – Identity, Youth and Crisis

Cognitive Dissonance
Author: Leon Festinger – The Theory of Cognitive dissonance.

Character Structure.
Author: Alexander Lowen – The language of the Body.
Author: Wilhelm Reich – Character analysis.
Author: C. G. Jung – Psychological Types.
Author: Dan Kiley – "The Peter Pan Syndrome" – men who never grew up.
                    (Includes the "Wendy Dilemma").

Schema Theory
Author: Jean Piaget and Barbel Inhelder – The Psychology of the Child.

Defence Theory
Author: Paul Klein – Psychology and Freudian Theory.
Author: Anna Freud – The Ego and the Mechanisms of Defence.

Sexual Abuse

Author: Matt Atkinson – Resurrection After Rape.

Author: Dr Jessica Taylor – Why Women are Blamed for Everything.

Author: Lydia Cacho – Slavery Inc.: The Untold Story of International Sex Trafficking.

Author: Jennifer Temkin and Barbara Krahe – Sexual Assault and the Justice Gap: A question of attitude.

Bullying and Sexual Harassment

Author: Susan Strauss – Sexual Harassment and Bullying: A Guide to Keeping Kids Safe and Holding Schools Accountable.

IPV – Intimate Partner Violence

Author: Casey T. Taft, Christopher M. Murphy, and Suzannah K. Creech – Trauma-Informed Treatment and Prevention of IPV.